PRINCIPLES
OF
STATISTICAL
DATA
HANDLING

For Robin

PRINCIPLES OF STATISTICAL DATA HANDLING

FRED DAVIDSON

SAGE Publications
International Educational and Professional Publisher
Thousand Oaks   London   New Delhi

For information address:

SAGE Publications, Inc.
2455 Teller Road
Thousand Oaks, California 91320
E-mail: order@sagepub.com

SAGE Publications Ltd.
6 Bonhill Street
London EC2A 4PU
United Kingdom

SAGE Publications India Pvt. Ltd.
M-32 Market
Greater Kailash I
New Delhi 110 048 India

Printed in the United States of America

Library of Congress Cataloging-in-Publication Data

Davidson, Fred.
    Principles of statistical data handling / author, Fred Davidson.
      p.   cm.
    Includes bibliographical references and index.
    ISBN 0-7619-0102-7 (cloth: alk. paper). — ISBN 0-7619-0103-5
(pbk.: alk. paper)
     1. Social sciences—Statistical methods—Data processing.
    2. Educational statistics—Data processing. I. Title.
HA32.D385 1996
300'.1'5195—dc20   95-41821

96 97 98 99 10 9 8 7 6 5 4 3 2 1

This book is printed on acid-free paper.

Sage Production Editor: Diana E. Axelsen
Sage Typesetter: Janelle LeMaster

Contents

Preface

For over a decade, I have found myself frequently placed into the role of consultant on the analysis of statistical data on computers. I serve in this role for a number of people; students, fellow teachers, and administrators of educational institutions are included in the group. In addition, a common thread running through my own work in that period has been the handling of statistical data on computers. I wrote this text because of a need for a book that illustrates the fundamental, practical principles of getting data ready for statistical analysis on computers. Many books seem to deal with programming for particular statistical analyses, but few detail the painful experience of going from a stack of disorganized hard copy to on-line data that are trustworthy. The latter need is the domain of this book.

In particular, for whom might such a book be handy?

- The administrator of an educational program or institution who maintains a database of student entry and advancement information would benefit from advice on data handling. Furthermore, students in that program would benefit by being better represented; a central theme to better data handling is removal of error in data and expansion of data types to include information not previously thought possible.
- Graduate and undergraduate students in education (in particular) and social science programs (more generally) are becoming more and more data literate. *Data literacy* is not only knowledge of the growing use of computers in all aspects of academia but also the motivation for using those computers: the data they contain. No education or social science training course does its students justice without some exposure to organized, broad-based computer data collection.
- The novice researcher in education and social science can benefit from constructive advice on the input, debugging, and manipulation of data—data on which his or her research and career depend.

Realistically, however, a book on data handling would most probably be used by two groups: (a) graduate students and novice researchers who want to expand their knowledge of the research use of computers in the social sciences, including education, and (b) educators who want to improve data gathering in their teaching institutions.

I believe that this book should serve well as a companion text to existing books on statistics and research design. It is not necessary to write another book on doing statistics and research design in the social sciences. Several excellent books of that genre already exist, including longer volumes such as Minium, King, and Bear (1993) and the superb volume by the late Fred Kerlinger (1986); and shorter general introductions (e.g., Lewis-Beck, 1995). In addition, books have been written on specific statistical procedures —for example, Lewis-Beck (1980), Schroeder, Sjoquist, and Stephan (1986), and Iversen and Norpoth (1987). As a trainer of graduate students entering educational research, I find that these existing books on statistical methods serve quite well in teaching statistical principles and procedures. And it is not necessary to write a book about particular statistical procedures on computers; Cody and

Smith (1991), for example, have done a nice job at that with regard to SAS (a statistical software package formerly known as the Statistical Analysis System). But their book is intended mainly to teach people how to perform particular statistical routines. Although they deal with data handling, they (of necessity) do not dwell on it much.

There seems to be a gap. The gap concerns the process of input, manipulation, and debugging statistical data—the process of getting data ready for analysis. That is the gap this book tries to fill.

I contend that a book on that topic must be principled, rather than a simple collection of tips and tricks of the trade. I describe the structure of the book and justify a principled approach in Chapter 1, but in a nutshell the idea is this: Data handling has certain universal concepts that apply no matter what the data-gathering context or the computer software. These universals can be stated as principles—brief claims of general truth that also state (or imply) direct advice. Those general universals—those principles—are what these chapters explore. And those principles are the most important product of what follows.

I would like to acknowledge many people who have influenced or helped in the creation of this book:

Principle 4.2 is named after Professor Leigh Burstein of UCLA, from whom I took an excellent course in statistical regression. His advice on data magnitude in that class is the direct genesis of Principle 4.2. Professor Burstein died at an early age in 1994, and so that principle is also included here in his memory. For more on Burstein and his work, see the memoria in *Educational Measurement: Issues and Practices* (Vol. 13, No. 4, 1994), *American Educational Research Journal* (Vol. 23, No. 3, 1995), and *Educational Evaluation and Policy Analysis* (Vol. 17, No. 3, 1995).

I would also like to recognize backing and support from many other people. First, I acknowledge Evelyn Hatch and Anne Lazaraton for help in the early stages of what became this book. I also thank my students in several seminars and tutorials at the University of Illinois who read earlier drafts and provided useful comments. Kathy Ryan deserves special thanks for linking me up with Sage Publications, Inc. At Sage, I owe deep gratitude to C. Deborah Laughton, Esther Papegaay, Linda Poderski, Diana

Axelsen, Janelle LeMaster, and Dianne Woo. Reviewers John Creswell, University of Nebraska; George Engelhard, Emory University; Carl Huberty, University of Georgia; and Paul Vogt, SUNY, Albany, all gave me extremely useful feedback. Last, I thank Robin Dodson for her abiding trust and support during all these donkey's years and for reading the whole blasted thing . . . several times.

Introduction
A Principled Approach

Overview/Outline

1.1. GETTING STARTED

Data are everywhere. As a mental exercise and to convince yourself of that platitude, think about those little plastic ATM cards our society is using with increasing frequency. *ATM* stands for "automated teller machine." The card to which I refer is what lets you withdraw cash 24 hours a day from such a machine. My mental exercise is simple: Envision an encounter with an ATM in which you get cash, and then imagine what must be behind that encounter. When you put a card into an ATM and punch in your secret code (*PIN*, or "personal identification number"), many complex things happen. The ATM must determine

1. Is the card valid?
2. Is the PIN valid?
3. Is the home bank of the card owner registered with this ATM?
4. Does the home bank report sufficient funds to cover the withdrawal?
5. Does the ATM have sufficient cash to cover the withdrawal?
6. Can the ATM print a receipt?

These questions are but a sample of what must go on. I'd like to dwell on question 4. What is implied as the ATM queries your home bank to determine whether your withdrawal can be covered? The ATM must be able to obtain information—data—from the magnetic strip on the back of your ATM card. It must be able to compare secret information, the PIN—also data—to an internal encrypted password file to determine whether they match. It must also compare your card to your home bank, and for that it must determine and contact your home bank, and for that it must consult a data record of all home banks at its disposal. Then, on contacting the home bank, the ATM must request information—also data— from the record of your home bank account. Data, data, data. Nested, related, linked, verified, secure, and all accessed very quickly. Dwell for a moment on what happens when you use an ATM card, and you will sense data at work.

This book is not about banking. It is about the use of data in education and social science research. You can convince yourself of the prevalence of data in that setting by a similar mental exercise. Imagine a language teaching institution—call it EAI for English Associates, Inc. (We use this hypothetical institution throughout the book, and I describe it more fully in Chapter 2.) It has several hundred English schools in many countries. EAI is making a lot of money from the teaching of English as a foreign language (EFL).

Consider, for a moment, just the monetary aspect of this enterprise. How does EAI keep track of its profits worldwide or country by country? Answer: data. How does EAI ensure that it has sufficient funds to pay teachers, buy materials, install the latest computer labs, and so forth? Answer: data. How does EAI know that students are improving their English—how does EAI map progress? Answer: EAI must handle data. It must input them with care, manipulate and revise them as needed, and remove errors—all before they are analyzed.

EAI is by no means unique. My example could be any school—profit oriented or publicly supported. I could have suggested a high school, a multisection university chemistry course, or a for-profit driver education school. Likewise, I could have suggested any form of organized data gathering for behavioral sciences—for example, a psychological experiment or a large grant-funded survey project. I selected EAI primarily because it is a data context with which I am very familiar. EAI's data can be generalized to other settings, and I encourage you to do so as you read this book.

In either example—the ATM card or EAI—the data must be "handled." Either on paper or in a computer, human beings must get the data ready before they analyze it substantively. *Substantive analysis* answers questions of interest to the data's user. For example, looking at an educational database to see how many students separate along some characteristic (e.g., gender) is substantive if that information is to be used for some later systemic decision, report, or dialogue. If you are trying to determine whether your data contain errors (e.g., if you are determining whether you have only two values for gender in the data), however, then you are performing *data handling*, and not substantive analysis. In this book, I do not treat substantive analysis very much. I am primarily concerned with the "getting ready" part of statistical analysis.[1]

This book is an attempt to unify the data-handling process, regardless of its setting, via a number of principles. A *principle* is a contention of general truth, and as most principles in this book are phrased, it is either overt or implied advice. The principles in this book can be at various levels of generality: Some are quite short and direct; others are rather long, possibly containing several propositions. But they all share one thing in common: They coalesce a solution to a certain data-handling problem (or set of problems) into a relatively brief statement. The principles are the themes of this book; they are what you should take away from your reading.

That said, let's begin the principled exploration of statistical data handling with a few definitions.

1.2. WHAT ARE DATA? AND WHAT ARE STATISTICAL DATA?

The questions in the title of this section are difficult. Before we can go further, we need some sort of working definition, some operationalization, some semantic ballpark in which we can play.

Let's define *data* as any form of organized information that has been gathered about a topic or topics of interest. Let me break apart that definition.

First, data are organized. The data analyst has some rubric or template around which the data are arranged. Typically, the organization reflects a structure about examining human beings; that is, I am presuming that the most common type of statistical data we use in our profession is data about people. It does not have to be, however; it could be data about teaching materials, about schools, about countries, or about other units of analysis. Whatever we want to analyze—people, materials, schools—those are the units of our data observation, and those are what we structure and organize.

Second, data are information. That seems like a pedestrian reminder, but it is really rather critical. I claim it is critical because I believe that data should not only be information but also be informative. It should be information that has relevance, currency, and depth. It should not be a waste of time.

Third, data are gathered. Data can be gathered in many ways, but there is always some sort of transformative process in which a data handler converts observations about the world into some encoded form for later analysis. Sometimes data are collected in an experiment. Sometimes they are collected in available extant databases. An example of the former is a controlled investigation in an instructional lab where the researcher wants to measure student attitude about the lab equipment while that equipment is in use. An example of the latter is data gathered as part of the normal operation of a school, such as our sample school, EAI. The principles I espouse in this book should apply equally well to both cases: empirical research and the nonresearch administrative database. The principles should also apply to a marriage of the two cases. For example, an administrative database could be subjected to research enquiry; sometimes managers of such databases use available data in a manner very similar to a more controlled experiment. Regardless of the source of the data, if they are ultimately subjected to some sort of statistical analysis or if they are amenable to such analysis as I define *amenable* below, then they are within the province of this book, and the principles of this book should apply.

Fourth, data are concerned with a topic or topics of interest. This concept overlaps with the idea of informativeness above, but it also suggests the concept of focus: The data gatherer has certain questions or suspicions about the data, or possibly she or he has some particular worries about people represented in a data set, and whenever we interact with data, we are usually driven by some focused need. We want to know, for example, whether the students like that instructional lab. We want to know the average age of students at our language school. Whatever we want to know, we want to know it—and that "it" is crucial. I contend that we live with data in a purposive way. Data are not a backdrop or an ambient field. They are a repository designed to satisfy focused human enquiry.

In this book, I treat statistical data. Generally, I define *statistical data* as any data form that is *amenable* to numerical calculations or that is useful in numerical calculations. For example, data on the performance of students on a test are amenable to mathematics: We can compute an average performance. It could be that the learners are in several groups—for example, EFL learners at EAI from different native languages (NLs): Arabic, Italian, Spanish, and so on. Those NL groups are not numerical. It would not make sense to talk of "computing an average NL." But we might want to compute an average test performance on an EFL test by the Spanish speakers, the Italian speakers, and the Arabic speakers. Hence, data on NL would be "statistical"—as would be that test score—and both the test score and the NL information would be within the domain of this book. Furthermore, forms of statistical analysis can be used strictly with such non-numerical data (e.g., NL). It is possible, for example, to have a research project that examines only categories and to still derive a statistic that is interpreted similarly to statistics that require numerical data. (The chi-square test is a good example of such analysis.)

In short, the definition of a *statistical* data set is derived from part of my definition of data, above. It relates to the focus or topic(s) of interest. If that focus implies recourse to any statistics at all, even simple display tables, then I consider that data set to be statistical.

This book does not cover one important form of data: text data. I do not discuss the input, manipulation, and debugging of corpora or discourse transcriptions (e.g., court transcripts). Those are data, and by my definition above, they could be organized and structured, and they could certainly be used to investigate topic(s) of interest. But analysis of those data is typically not done with statistics, unless one runs (for example) a word frequency count. In that case, the frequency counts themselves form statistical data, albeit data that originate from a nonstatistical source.

1.3. "ATOMS AND MOLECULES": YOU CAN ONLY CONCLUDE ABOUT WHAT YOU MEASURE

The above definitional discussion is rather abstract. Definitions often are abstract, and I acknowledge that. I hope and trust that the rest of this book will help flesh out the definitions above.

One more potentially abstract issue in any data gathering is universal and critical: measuring what you intend to measure. I discuss it here, and in so doing, I motivate the first two principles of this book. Hence, the following discussion is the first example of the inductive pattern that follows in the next chapters, in which I pose a need or dilemma and resolve it with a discussion leading to a short principle.

Suppose you are a chemist. You are concerned with the behavior of matter under certain conditions. Matter is organized into molecules, which themselves are comprised of atoms, and atoms are comprised of even smaller subatomic particles. For the sake of simplicity, let's keep our analogy to molecules and atoms and avoid any metaphorical quarks.

As a chemist, you want to know how two molecules interact. You perhaps want to subject them to heat and see whether they bond or break apart. Or perhaps you want to subject them to cold and see whether they bond or break apart. So you design an experiment in which—and this next bit is critical—you manipulate the molecules and find out what happens. If that is the way you do it, then when you write up your experimental report, you can announce a finding about the molecules.

But suppose you are interested in the atoms and not the molecules. Suppose you suspect that a certain bonding involves certain atoms of the molecules and does not involve other atoms. If you want to announce a finding about the atoms, then you must figure out how to measure both the atoms *and* the molecules. You cannot claim any result about the atoms if you measure only the molecules (or their action). But if you observe or can infer about the atoms (or their action), you can then claim results about both the atoms and the molecules because you know which atoms make up the molecules.

Data are like atoms and molecules. Data have the same observational problem. For example, assume we have an educational test comprised of 75 questions. Each question is scored right/wrong, such that the students receive 1 point or mark for each right answer and zero points for each wrong answer. The sum of the "rights" is the total score. Assume the test measures language ability and is arranged in three subtests: reading, vocabulary, and grammar. If you record the following information about each person, you are at the level of the molecule:

Molecular Data Level

Total score for the test
Subtotal score for the reading section
Subtotal score for the vocabulary section
Subtotal score for the grammar section

But if you record information at the following level, you are at the level of the atom:

Atomic Data Level

Score for item 1: right or wrong?
Score for item 2: right or wrong?
Score for item 3: right or wrong?
:
:   (etc.)
:
Score for item 75: right or wrong?

You can always reclaim the "molecules" (the score for each subtest) by simply adding up the number of "right" items for that test. If, for example, the reading test is items 1 to 25, then the number of right items for each person within items 1 to 25 (only) is that person's reading subtotal: It is a molecule. The analogy continues because the total score is either (a) the sum of the three subtotals or (b) the sum of the right answers out of all 75 items.

If your need—your topic(s) of interest—is the items themselves, then you must record information for each person on each item. If you want to know whether a given item is difficult or easy, you have to record the right or wrong for each person on each item. If, however, your interest is at the level of the subscores or total score, you might not need to do so. But if you record only the subtotal and the total scores for each person, you cannot go backward and reclaim the item-level information. It is wise to be able to envision where your atoms and molecules lie, and that can be encapsulated in Principle 1.1.

Principle 1.1: The Atomicity Principle

You cannot analyze below the data level that you observe. (You cannot analyze atoms if all you measure are molecules.)

What makes this principle tricky is that sometimes it is not easy to determine what the atoms really are because you do not know precisely what use might be made of the data in the future. That is why I prefer the general trend-like term *atomicity.*[2]

Atomicity is something of a problem in all data gathering: trying to draw conclusions about data that are more specific than the data gathered. What is also interesting is that sometimes a correct level of atomicity has been gathered but, for some reason, the researcher has ignored it. Consider the following example.

Researcher A is interested in the effect of age on second/foreign language acquisition. He collects the date of first exposure to the target language (TL) to be learned of each subject in his experiment. On the basis of his reading of literature in this topic, he "polychotomizes" the data into age bands: 0 to 2 years when first exposed to the TL, 2 to 4 years, 4 to 6 years, and so forth. Suppose he reads further in the literature and finds that some researchers treat age as a continuum. These other analysts contend there is too much variability in human development to set up fixed bands. Is Researcher A out of luck? No—he has the atoms; he recorded age of exposure. He formed the molecules from the age atoms, presumably by subtracting that date from the date of the experiment.

Suppose, however, Researcher A had asked his subjects: "When did you start learning the TL? Choose one: (a) when I was between 0 and 2 years of age, (b) when I was between 2 and 4 years of age . . ." and so forth. If that is how he gathered his data, *then he cannot go backward unless he remeasures his subjects.* He does not have the atoms. He has the molecules.

Suppose, however, the literature provides no support for treating age as a continuum. Suppose countless arguments and experiments show that human development, though continuous, is reasonably polychotomous as well and that such developmental age bands are substantive and real. In that case, the bands are the atoms and the continuum would be misleading "subatomic" information. To return to the analogy of the chemist, it is not necessary for the chemist to know subatomic structure if all that is needed (to explain bonding) is knowledge of the atoms. The atomicity of the chemist's study is the atom itself; the atomicity of the above age/language learning scenario could be the band or the continuous age values, depending on his understanding of the research question and the literature.

A related principle deserves notice:

Principle 1.2: The Appropriate Data Principle

You cannot analyze what you do not measure.

In fact, Principle 1.2 may not be a principle at all. It could be something like a corollary to Principle 1.1, for if we wish to analyze atoms, we should not measure only molecules. Alternatively, Principle 1.2 may be seen to subsume Principle 1.1. I separate them here for a pragmatic reason. In my years of data analysis and service as a statistical consultant and teacher, I have found that Principles 1.2 and 1.1 are different in the impact they have on data analysts. Principle 1.2 is a reminder that says simply: So you want to draw conclusions about X? Well, you have to measure X, and not Y. That is pretty obvious on the surface, but it can plague researchers who simply forget to include some measure of interest in their study or discover later that some crucial variable was not examined—a variable that could have explained everything.

Principle 1.1, however, is somewhat more technical and fundamental. It is, I believe, the beginning of the decision we make about what data are and what they can tell us. I believe it is easier to decide what to measure than to decide what its atoms really are. The researcher above probably clearly understood, from early in his interest in the topic, that age was a critical variable in his project. But not until later in the investigation does he hit on the subtlety of atomicity. For example, perhaps he gets odd results when treating age as categorical bands. On looking back at his raw data, he sees that he did not record age as a continuous variable: He asked subjects to report bands in a questionnaire. He's sunk. He cannot go backward unless he remeasures his subjects. Had he thought of Principle 1.1 from the start, however, he might have designed his questionnaire differently and been able to rescue the study. For that reason, I made Principle 1.1 the first one in the book. As you first encounter data of interest to you, ask yourself, What are its atoms? Or more specifically, What are the atoms in which I am interested? Encountering that question early in data acquisition will help immensely later on.

If you use Principles 1.1 and 1.2 as I advise here, then you are using them properly. You are thinking of the principles before you collect and store your data, and by so doing, you are avoiding problems later on; this is how to use all the principles in this book. You are anticipating, for example, a need to study each item in your classroom test and not only the total scores. You are anticipating, for example, that age might be best treated as a continuous measure rather than in bands. In either case, you can later return to the molecule (subtotals or age bands) if you have the atoms (items or continuous age values).

1.4. SOCIAL CONTEXT OF DATA

One benefit of Principles 1.1 and 1.2 is that they require us to think about the impact of our data. Are we getting the right kind of information? Are we missing something important? This concern is particularly critical when (as is often the case) social and behavioral data pertain to people and will lead to important decisions about people's lives: Failing or passing an instructional course, receiving life insurance benefits, justifying some new personnel policy—all these are social decisions that are often supported by data. Hence, one more principle should be highlighted in this chapter; it is a ground rule that will apply at various points throughout the book:

Principle 1.3: The Social Consequences Principle

Data about people are about people. Data can have social consequences.

Data can guide decision making such that important social issues are effectively ignored. The data can generate de facto policy. Imagine that a school has three full scholarships to award each term. To qualify for the scholarship, a student must apply, and his or her application information must be entered into a computer database. Suppose that database program has a simple command to control the production of mailing labels: to include or not include postal codes, such as the ZIP code in the United States. Suppose further that the default is to include postal codes and that if the postal code entry is missing for a given student, then that student is omitted from mailings. Now suppose that a student submits an application and forgets to write down the postal code. The administrative staff key the information into the database, but when they go to print a pro forma note ("We have received your application and are processing it . . ."), that student gets nothing because the postal code is missing. The student is lost in the application process and therefore loses any chance for the scholarship even though she or he might have been qualified. Potentially, a candidate for the scholarship is in danger of missing a critical learning opportunity because his or her record lacks a small, pedestrian, but frustratingly crucial piece of information.

The social effects of data can affect many people. Imagine a major urban U.S. school district that oversees hundreds of schools: elementary, middle, and secondary levels. For some years, this district has run several special programs for its schools (e.g., special education, bilingual education, and gifted student programs). The district management is worried about equality of entry and exit standards for these programs across its schools, and it therefore asks a statistician at the central district office to look into the matter. The statistician consults the master school database and determines that some rudimentary data are available for each student about this question, particularly some twice-a-year test score data on the citywide achievement tests and a yes or no answer to whether the student is enrolled in each special program. The statistician runs some simple statistical tests and determines no real entry benefit based on school building; that is, a student is just as likely to have been admitted to a special program in School Y as in School Z. The district management, on hearing these results, decides that no further investigation into special programs is necessary and that the programs can continue at their current level of funding for the foreseeable future.

Students in those special programs are receiving certain instructional delivery keyed to their particular needs. It would be interesting, for example, to know whether various models of bilingual program design (and there are many such models) have a differential impact on yearly citywide achievement testing. But the database is not set up to record that information; there is no information on the particular instructional model used in these special programs. All management knows is whether or not a student is in a particular program, not how that program is structured; no differential funding decisions can be made on the basis of success or failure of certain program models. The district management cannot examine instructional method as a variable in its funding formula because it has not recorded the proper information to allow it to do so (Principle 1.2, as well as 1.3, applies here). Instruction may suffer or benefit differentially, and so too might children, on the basis of this lack of data. Whether it is proper to base school funding on success of program design is not at issue; what is at issue is that management cannot even address that question because it does not know which model each special program follows.

That example is a particular instance of Principle 1.3. The data kept by the central district office might be much more useful if additional information about program design were also recorded. The database structures have an inherent limitation—one that might have social consequences. The district collects the kinds of data with which it is most accustomed; it walks down a "worn data path," harvesting only that information it is used to. I return to the problem of a "worn path" in Chapter 5.

Let's consider further how Principle 1.3 might relate to Principles 1.1 and 1.2. There is an old expression in data handling and analysis: Garbage in, garbage out. If you record information you want, then you get answers you need. By the same token, if you record information you do not want or if you record desired information inaccurately, then you get information you do not need: garbage. That is another way of looking at the school district above. It recorded a piece of information—whether or not the student was served in a special program, and if so, what program. But that information proved to be relatively valueless: Garbage in, garbage out.

Now suppose that the district management did record information on program success variables but that, by some accident or administrative mixup, it was recorded inaccurately; suppose, for example, it recorded that School A had 90 children in bilingual education and 290 in special education, when in fact the situation was the reverse: 290 bilingual students and 90 special education students. Later analyses (even if the district has information about program success) are valueless because the initial data were wrong: Garbage in, garbage out. This latter problem—inaccurately reported data—can be solved by debugging, a topic I turn to in Chapter 4. Principles 1.1, 1.2, and 1.3 could conspire to produce a particularly difficult dilemma: information at the wrong level (1.1 and 1.2) or information recorded inaccurately (see Chapter 4, especially Principle 4.3), all of which has particularly dire effects because it leads to decisions about people (Principle 1.3). Garbage in, garbage out, and maybe people are hurt as a result.

As if that conspiracy were not enough, one more dilemma can arise: a disaster. Maybe our sample school district management recorded accurate information about its children. Maybe the data are at the right level of atomicity, and maybe the district is ready to use the data in a reasoned manner to make wise social decisions about its charges.

Maybe everything is OK.

Then, some disaster strikes: A member of the district staff accidentally erases a computer hard disk; a power outage wrecks several computers; a natural disaster destroys the district offices; some other unpredictable event happens. Principle 1.3 still is at play: There are decisions to be made about people, and even though the information *was* there, it is no longer *still* there. I now turn to that topic, which fortunately has a simple solution—a solution that should apply to all data handling, regardless of its degree of social relevance.

1.5. TWO LAWS OF COMPUTING

This book is about principles of data handling. *Principles* are general assertions and advisories about good practice, but they are not by any means enforceable laws. Certain principles, to my mind, seem more important than others: Principle 1.1 seems more critical than 1.2, and 2.1 (in the next chapter) may be the most important one in the book.

It seems to me, however, that two true laws of computing transcend the principles. I did not invent these laws; they originate somewhere in my experience, and so I attribute them to that well-known unknown author:

> Law 1: Back it up.
> Law 2: Do it now.

> —Anonymous

I have noticed that nobody seems to learn to back up data until he or she has a serious disaster with data that are personally quite important. Please prove me wrong and abide by these two laws as early in your data career as possible. There is an entire literature on backup procedures, but at its core, the process of backup is just common sense. If you do something wrong and wreck your data or programs, your backup is a spare copy—preferably one of several spares at several locations. The backup can save you from pain, hassle, and maybe loss of your job. You might enjoy looking ahead to discussion question 1 in Chapter 6; professionals treat backup very seriously indeed.

Principles 1.1 through 1.4 and the two laws of computing are the groundwork for the real nuts and bolts of data handling. If you record data at the right level (1.1 and 1.2), remember that the data might be about people (1.3), and make backups (the two laws), then the rest of this book is now at your disposal. With the possible exception of Principle 2.1, which is also foundational (but more related to Chapter 2), the principles and laws in this chapter are an appropriate starting point in a principled approach to data handling.

1.6. STRUCTURE OF THIS BOOK

All the chapters of this book are similar. The purpose of each chapter is to discuss a number of principles, which are given in each chapter and repeated in Appendix A. Generally, though not always, the discussion of each principle is inductive. I set a situation or problem, suggest how it might be resolved, and in so doing motivate and resolve the matter with a principle. Each problem or situation and the principle that answers it are related to the theme of the chapter as stated in the chapter's title. As you study this book, think about the principles closely. Your objective, as you read this book, should be to constantly ask yourself: *How does this particular principle apply to me?*

What is the justification for a principled approach to data handling? First and foremost, I contend that such principles do, in fact, exist and that to effect better use of computer data in education and broader social science, one must know what those principles are and practice them. Much as I try to guide the reader into the principles in the book, I have also found myself guided to them in my own work. This book is very much the product of my life with the nuts and bolts of data.

Second, by using data-handling principles as a guiding force to the book, you should be able to apply the book's advice to a wide variety of situations. This book is not married to a particular educational or social science data-gathering context. Of necessity, however, the examples here come from the area in which I work: foreign language education. It is easier for me to illustrate data-handling principles by using a context with which I am quite familiar. I realize that context might be unfamiliar to many readers, so I amplify it as we go along, and at times I offer analogies to other data settings.

Third, I do include discussion of statistical data analysis in Chapter 5. One cannot abstract data handling away from the ultimate data analyses; in the real world they are in a cyclical relationship. It is useful to see how to set up data for actual substantive analyses, and that is what Chapter 5 is intended to do. *Data handling* concerns the input, manipulation, and debugging of statistical data, and any other work with it up to but excluding actual substantive analyses. It also includes procedures of data and program management to make substantive analysis easier, and if output of a substantive program is used as data (as input to a later substantive analysis), then that also is the domain of data handling. But as I noted earlier in this chapter, I do not deal much with the actual substance of findings.

Fourth and finally, faulty data can lead to faulty conclusions, and because data often pertain to people (as noted by Principle 1.3), that can mean faulty conclusions about people. We need greater focus on the veracity of our conclusions, and I contend that if our principles of data structuring are sound, then that will help in making sound decisions about people. In education, faulty data can mean faulty decisions about students. With respect to research, the choice of data to analyze and their layout is itself an act of theoretical preference (as noted by McLaughlin, 1987, p. 80). Mine is not a book on the epistemology of data structures in education. By focusing on data to the degree that it does, however, it paves the way for further discussions on intentional and unintentional theoretical bias based on data organization.

Although this is a book about principles, it is nonetheless wise for me to provide some pragmatic guidance. I cannot treat only the level of principle; ultimately, that is too abstract. I must show you the principles in operation with actual software and actual data. I must anchor a book like this in the pragmatic needs of day-to-day data handling, or else the book runs the risk of being just more vapid scholarly advice. Thus, I include the implementation sections below. If you do happen to have access to the software which

I demonstrate, then you can get double the benefit: The book is both a general discussion of principles and an application of principles to a particular data platform: the Statistical Analysis System (SAS; SAS Institute, 1995) or the Statistical Package for the Social Sciences (SPSS; SPSS Inc., 1994). I ran my sample programs in Release 6.10 of SAS and Release 6.1 of SPSS, although they should run in other installations as well—either on desktop microcomputers or larger shared mainframes.

I must warn you: This book is not a full SAS or SPSS manual. I cannot replace all the wonderful resources available to learn such software. For instance, because this is a book on data structure and data handling, Chapter 5 does not cover all the ins and outs of statistical analysis in SAS and SPSS. I do not discuss such SAS and SPSS topics as checking statistical assumptions, selecting the correct error term in ANOVA, or when to use the Mantel-Haenszel versus likelihood chi-square values. Hence, I advise you to consult other sources to learn more about SAS and SPSS, for example:

— Manuals, of three types:
  Those produced by the SAS Institute or SPSS Inc. I do not cite any particular SAS or SPSS manuals in this book (aside from one instance in Chapter 5 in which I borrow a sample data set from SAS) because each company has many manuals. Before you purchase any of them, I advise you to visit a computer center or library and see which ones you prefer.
  Those produced by third-party writers (e.g., Cody & Smith, 1991)
  Those produced by local experts (e.g., if you work at a university, perhaps your computer center has authored some SAS or SPSS reference brochures)
— Consultants (see discussion questions 6 and 7 in Chapter 3).
— online tutorials (e.g., learning modules distributed with the SAS or SPSS software)
— Short courses on SAS or SPSS (e.g., those the software companies offer [which are rather expensive] or those offered by professional associations, universities, and similar agencies)
— Instruction on SAS and SPSS as part of other courses (e.g., homework assignments using these packages in a college statistics course)

I recommend that you read all of each "Implementation" section of each chapter. If you happen to use and prefer SAS, read and study the SPSS code too, and vice versa. Each software package allows me to describe data features and analytical considerations in a different manner, and you will come to have a better principled understanding of each package by studying both. In addition (see discussion question 5 in Chapter 5), by learning a bit of each package and if both are available to you, you can make a better—a more principled—decision about which one to use.

The SAS and SPSS sample programs in each chapter are written in batch style. *Batch programming* refers to a set of program command language that is submitted to the computer for processing. Following the commands, the program inputs data, acts on it, and produces results. An alternative to batch programming is *interactive programming:* The processing is done in stages in which the programmer interrupts the flow of things and makes changes. (The necessity of both the run; and the quit; commands in SAS is due to interactive programming; see p. 180.)

Recently, major statistical packages such as SAS and SPSS have also included application generators in the software. (In SAS, the application generator is called the ASSIST module. In SPSS, it has no special name; it is merely part of the default software screen.) An *application generator* is some sort of menu-driven access or dialogue query system in which the user is asked a series of pointed questions, such as: What is the name of the data file? How many people are represented by it? What sorts of statistics do you want to do? Application generators can be used interactively to produce analyses. As you answer those pointed questions, the application generator "generates" the appropriate software commands to get the results you want. And as those commands are generated, they are usually saved to some default screen window or file, which you can later examine, edit, rerun, and save permanently.

I illustrate SAS and SPSS at the level of command language. I show you the actual commands necessary to get done whatever you want to do—commands that should run on a wide variety of operating systems that run SAS or SPSS. I do not show application generators. I do not show the various menu paths and dialogue boxes by which you can have SAS or SPSS generate the commands for you. Ultimately, you will be most efficient in your programming if you do not use application generators; instead, I recommend that you come to know your software's command language.

I fully realize, however, that application generators are a boon to statistical data handling and analysis. Many people prefer them to command languages. For that reason, I include Appendix D, in which I show examples of the application generator interfaces in SAS and SPSS running under the Windows operating system for IBM/compatible microcomputers. That appendix is illustrative only, to allow you to think about two things: (a) what an application generator looks like and (b) if you have not decided whether to use a command language or a generator, which approach you might prefer.

To conclude, I advise you to "wear two hats" while you read this book. First, read and understand the principles and attempt to apply them to your setting. Second, read and understand the implementation of the principles as they appear in the command languages of two widely used programs: SAS and SPSS. Even if you do not have access to those software packages, I hope you find that both hats fit comfortably.

1.7. DISCUSSION QUESTIONS: CHAPTER 1

1. This is an exercise to convince you that data are indeed pervasive. First, write a record of every daily event in which you encounter data or in which data are probably involved (e.g., the ATM, consulting a student record file, asking a colleague a question that sends him or her to a grade book. A tip: Do this kind of log only for a few days because it can get long quite quickly!). Second, write a record of everything you do with your own data. Think about your own situation and the data you must handle: teaching, research, administration. Note everything that happens for a particular data set of keen interest to you. (This log can also become long easily.)

2. Consider a data set of importance to you. What is its ultimate purpose, and how does that purpose suggest its atoms and

molecules? Then speculate about future users of the data: Suppose, for example, the data were to be saved on disk or on a computer network and made available to persons similar to you for the next 5 years. Have you anticipated the atoms they might want to analyze? Have you, instead, left them with molecules? Likewise, what if you want to return and reanalyze the data later on; can you predict what else you might want to do with it?

3. Do you have a data story similar to those in this chapter (e.g., the ZIP code story), perhaps a story of missing data, inaccurate data, or some other data-based problem that has affected you personally? What could the designers or data handlers who created those data have done to resolve the situation? Does your situation reflect Principle 1.3?

4. In anticipation of the "Implementation" sections of each chapter, do some detective work at your setting: Determine whether SAS and/or SPSS are available to you. Obtain some local guidance on how to access each package. Visit a consultant or somebody else who uses each regularly and observe how to enter the software, perform certain basic functions (e.g., recall files, execute programs, save files), and how to exit. Determine whether you have the clearances necessary to use the software (e.g., if you work on a large shared mainframe computer, is your computer account authorized to access SAS or SPSS?).

NOTES

1. There is another conception for the "end" of data handling. Once data processing becomes second nature, you have really stopped data handling. This might not happen until your substantive analyses are themselves routine and comfortable, and in that spirit I include Chapter 6, "The 'End' of Data Handling," in which I offer advice, not about getting ready for substantive analysis, but rather about making substantive data management routine and easy.

The topics of Chapter 6 (e.g., organized data archival) might help you at the very beginning of your work on some data set or project. You might benefit from skimming that chapter before you begin to work and then reading it in order with the rest of the book. I have found that data organization—a topic of Chapter 6—tends to evolve after I have worked on a data set for some time. I find it quite difficult to predict all the organizational needs I am going to have until I have conducted some substantive analyses.

2. An alternative to *atomicity* is the phrase "unit of analysis"; that, however, is not strictly what concerns me here; but see the discussion of Principles 5.4 and 5.5 in Chapter 5. Atomicity is a property of the data independent of the analyses to which they will be subjected, but one that can affect those analyses. Sometimes the atomicity problem does not surface in time to be resolved. Suppose, for example, you want to obtain responses on individual test questions (as above) from an existing database but that whoever set up the database did not record student responses on each test item. Your need—your substantive analysis—is in jeopardy because the designers of the database did not think of something you might want to do. And yet, how could they? Perhaps they did not even know you when they set up the data. The principle involved (1.1) is more general than just thinking of the unit of analysis; it concerns far-reaching decisions made at the time the data are initially collected and entered into a computer.

That is the level at which I have written this book. A principle in this book should imply more issues than it first appears to imply. For example, Principle 1.1 suggests that a research team that sets up a database might think of their own present needs, of their own future needs, and of the needs of users of that database who are not presently team members.

2 Data Input

2.1. BACKGROUND AND DEFINITIONS

Before discussing how statistical data get into a computer, it is necessary to define some terms pertaining to data files, terms that will be useful throughout the rest of this book. Perhaps the most fundamental unit of data observation in handling data is a *case* (also often called a *record*). A case/record is a collection of information about one observation in the data set. Another related term

23

one often finds in computer data analysis is *line*. (SAS, one of the software packages described in this book, prefers *observation*, rather than *case* or *record*.) Most often, a case/record is about a person, although it need not be. We could conceive of a data set in which we collect information about each of 100 students in a particular school, and in that instance a case/record would correspond to a human being. Alternatively, we could conceive of a data set in which we have information on 100 schools, and in that instance the case/record would be each school. Furthermore, the two examples above could be linked together. Perhaps we have cases/records of people in each of 100 schools such that the many students at each school are linked into the single record describing that particular school. That is the fundamental nature of a *relational* database, a topic to which we return below. Before we can explore the difference between case/record = human and case/record = institution, I must introduce two other new definitions.

Let's suppose we collect information on people and the case/record corresponds to a person. And let's also suppose we are dealing with an institute where languages are taught. What type of information might we have? Perhaps we know sex: male or female. Perhaps we know for how many terms an individual has been in the language institute: one, two, or three (let's assume that's all that is possible). Perhaps we know further information, such as various demographic and background information for each person in the institute. Also, perhaps, we have information on each person's progress in the material being studied: perhaps an entry test score and some progress scores such as class quizzes or final exams. Finally, let's assume we have some self- reported information on each person, that we interviewed each person at some point during his or her time in the institute and found out how able each person felt in the material being studied; information like this is often in the form of a self-report scale (see Davidson & Henning, 1985; Oscarson, 1989).

Each *type* of different information we have about the people is known as a *variable* or *field*. The particular information on each variable for each person is a *value* or *entry*. This seems pretty abstract, so it is best to have a concrete, contextualized example to understand terms like *value* and *entry*.

I use the sample setting throughout this book of a company called English Associates, Inc., or EAI. This is a hypothetical, multinational, English-teaching corporation, although recently it has begun offering other languages as well (e.g., Spanish to native English speakers in the United States). Presumably, EAI has several hundred English as a foreign language (EFL) schools in many countries, and their staffs teach tens of thousands of students. Admittedly, the selection of the EAI sample setting reflects my own knowledge base (I am by training an applied linguistics researcher and an EFL teacher), but it also serves another important function: It enables me to contextualize the sample data in this book in a comprehensible manner.[1]

Let's consider an EAI school here in the United States where EFL is being taught. Perhaps a student, named Juan, has been studying there for two academic terms. Juan is a male, from Mexico, and his native language is Spanish. Let's assume we work at that EAI branch school; we have various test scores about Juan and have conducted an interview to determine his self-perceived ability.

Perhaps we have another person, called Anna, who is from northern Italy and who speaks Italian (as the native language) and German (as a near native). She has been at the institute for a single term. We also have scores and self-report data on her.

Conceptually, what we have is this:

```
           Name:  JUAN
 Native Country:  Mexico
Native Language:  Spanish
            Sex:  Male
Time at Institute:  2 terms
 Term 1, Quiz 1:  29
 Term 1, Quiz 2:  32
 Term 1, Quiz 3:  44
Term 1, Final Exam:  101
 Term 2, Quiz 1:  20
 Term 2, Quiz 2:  29
 Term 2, Quiz 3:  37
Term 2, Final Exam:  99
```

We discuss the self-report below. And for Anna, we have

```
            Name:  ANNA
  Native Country:  Italy
 Native Language:  Italian
             Sex:  Female
Time at Institute:  1 term
  Term 1, Quiz 1:  28
  Term 1, Quiz 3:  35
Term 1, Final Exam:  90
```

The entire block of information for Juan or Anna is known as a *case* or *record;* that is, two records are shown immediately above. The words that are the same for each record (e.g., *Native Country*) are the *variables/fields*. The information that changes for each variable is the *value/entry* (e.g., Mexico, Italy). The following sentence illustrates the use of the terms *case/record, variable/field,* and *value/entry:* "For Juan's case/record, the value/entry on the variable/field 'Native Country' is 'Mexico'."

You can immediately see some problems. Aside from the fact that the self-report data are not in the records yet, there are more variables for Juan than for Anna. Notice also that because neither person has been in the institute for three terms, neither person has Term 3 information. We might conceive of a fuller record such as that for a third person, called Ahmed:

```
            Name:  AHMED
  Native Country:  Egypt
 Native Language:  Arabic
             Sex:  Male
Time at Institute:  3 terms
  Term 1, Quiz 1:  23
  Term 1, Quiz 2:  23
  Term 1, Quiz 3:  39
Term 1, Final Exam:  97
  Term 2, Quiz 1:  28
  Term 2, Quiz 2:  29
  Term 2, Quiz 3:  36
Term 2, Final Exam:  99
```

```
       Term 3, Quiz 1:  18
       Term 3, Quiz 2:  21
       Term 3, Quiz 3:  40
   Term 3, Final Exam:  103
```

Therefore, conceptually, the records for Juan and Anna actually
should look like this:

```
                 Name:  JUAN
       Native Country:  Mexico
      Native Language:  Spanish
                  Sex:  Male
    Time at Institute:  2 terms
       Term 1, Quiz 1:  29
       Term 1, Quiz 2:  32
       Term 1, Quiz 3:  44
   Term 1, Final Exam:  101
       Term 2, Quiz 1:  20
       Term 2, Quiz 2:  29
       Term 2, Quiz 3:  37
   Term 2, Final Exam:  99
       Term 3, Quiz 1:  [not applicable / missing]
       Term 3, Quiz 2:  [not applicable / missing]
       Term 3, Quiz 3:  [not applicable / missing]
   Term 3, Final Exam:  [not applicable / missing]

                 Name:  ANNA
       Native Country:  Italy
      Native Language:  Italian
                  Sex:  Female
    Time at Institute:  1 term
       Term 1, Quiz 1:  34
       Term 1, Quiz 2:  28
       Term 1, Quiz 3:  35
   Term 1, Final Exam:  90
       Term 2, Quiz 1:  [not applicable / missing]
       Term 2, Quiz 2:  [not applicable / missing]
       Term 2, Quiz 3:  [not applicable / missing]
   Term 2, Final Exam:  [not applicable / missing]
```

```
        Term 3, Quiz 1:  [not applicable / missing]
        Term 3, Quiz 2:  [not applicable / missing]
        Term 3, Quiz 3:  [not applicable / missing]
   Term 3, Final Exam:  [not applicable / missing]
```

It is really easier to display these three cases/records as a *flat file*, meaning that the variables can be arranged as a set of rows and columns laid out "flat" on a table as follows. I prefer the term *row-by-column* (RBC) to *flat file*. Other common names include *multivariate data set* because it contains information on many variables, and *Nxp array* for *N* rows of cases by *p* columns of variables. In the present example, our RBC data set file is conceptually laid out as follows:

```
          C
          O            T
          U            I
    N     N       M  T  T  T    T  T  T  T    T  T  T  T    T
    A     T     S E  1  1  1    1  2  2  2    2  3  3  3    3
    M     R   L E I  Q  Q  Q    F  Q  Q  Q    F  Q  Q  Q    F
    E     Y   1 X N  1  2  3    E  1  2  3    E  1  2  3    E
[LOG]     1    1 2    2  3     3  4     4   5     5   6     6
----5----0----5----0----5----0----5----0----5----0----5----0----5
JUAN  Mexico Spanish M 2 29 32 44 101 20 29 37  99  .   .   .   .
ANNA  Italy  Italian F 1 34 28 35  90  .  .  .   .  .   .   .   .
AHMED Egypt  Arabic  M 3 23 23 39  97 28 29 36  99 18  21  40 103
```

Notice that a dot (.), above, is shorthand for not applicable / missing; I treat this in more detail below, as well as in Chapter 3. Notice also that I have now put in a *column log*, which are special lines showing the columns that each variable occupies. Such a log is also helpful in later telling computer software where information is located. We can prepare for that by constructing a data definition codebook, which might look like the following (in comparing this codebook to the data above, notice that the variable names above are printed vertically, whereas below they are printed horizontally):

```
                                                        START-STOP
VARIABLE NAME    TYPE    DESCRIPTION                      COLUMNS
-----------------------------------------------------------------
NAME             Char    Student's name                    01-05
COUNTRY          Char    Student's home country            08-12
L1               Char    Student's first language          14-20
SEX              Char    Student's sex                        22
TIMEIN           Num     Student's time in institute          24

                         Student's grades:

T1Q1             Num     Term 1, Quiz 1                    26-27
T1Q2             Num     Term 1, Quiz 2                    29-30
T1Q3             Num     Term 1, Quiz 3                    32-33
T1FE             Num     Term 1, Final Exam                35-37
T2Q1             Num     Term 2, Quiz 1                    39-40
T2Q2             Num     Term 2, Quiz 2                    42-43
T2Q3             Num     Term 2, Quiz 3                    45-46
T2FE             Num     Term 2, Final Exam                48-50
T3Q1             Num     Term 3, Quiz 1                    52-53
T3Q2             Num     Term 3, Quiz 2                    55-56
T3Q3             Num     Term 3, Quiz 3                    58-59
T3FE             Num     Term 3, Final Exam                61-63
-----------------------------------------------------------------
```

Note to Reader

See Note 2 at the end of this chapter.

Let's examine the codebook above in detail. First, notice that the columns that contain the data are called "start-stop" columns. The value of a given variable starts in one column and stops in another. Notice, for example, that T1FE starts in column 35 and stops in column 37 and that this is true even if a student scored a value on that exam that has only two digits: Notice that Anna's value of 90 for T1FE has a space in column 35 (in our data set, not the codebook). Knowledge of start-stop columns in RBC flat-file data sets is essential to get a computer to read the data accurately.

Notice also that I described all the test scores as a group. A header in the codebook says, simply: Student's grades, and everything in the codebook after that header is a grade. This works if you have thought ahead and planned to have all the grade data grouped together on each data row. The codebook would have to be somewhat more complex if we had laid out the data like this:

```
          C
          O       T
          U       I
  N       N     M T T T     T T T T   T T T T   T
  A       T     E 1 1 1 S   1 2 2 2   2 3 3 3   3
  M       R   L I Q Q Q E   F Q Q Q   F Q Q Q   F
  E       Y   1 N 1 2 3 X   E 1 2 3   E 1 2 3   E

[LOG]    1    1    2    2    3    3    4    4    5    5    6    6
----5----0----5----0----5----0----5----0----5----0----5----0----5

JUAN  Mexico  Spanish  2 29 32 44 M 101 20 29 37  99  .  .  .   .
ANNA  Italy   Italian  1 34 28 35 F  90  .  .  .   .  .  .  .   .
AHMED Egypt   Arabic   3 23 23 39 M  97 28 29 36  99 18 21 40 103
```

It would not be logical to lay out the data with a variable such as SEX embedded in a group of test score variables; we could not group the variables together in the codebook as conveniently as in the previous example. If you sense a principle coming, you are quite right, but I need to discuss a few other things first.

Notice also that the codebook has a column called TYPE. The entries in that column are Char or Num, which stand for *char*acter or *num*eric variables. (Character variables are also known as *alphanumeric*.) The distinction between char and num variables is quite fundamental in data processing, and I expand on it here.

A *numeric variable* is one on which you will or could ultimately do mathematics. A *character variable* is one on which you cannot or would not ever do mathematics. You cannot do mathematics (e.g., compute an average) of a variable such as NAME because its entries do not contain numbers. You could do math on a variable such as SEX if you entered it as 1 and 2 instead of M and F, but that would not make much sense. You would get something like the average value for SEX, which is not very sensible.[3]

Let's remind ourselves of the difference between a number and a numeral. The former is a concept; the latter is a symbol for that concept. 1 could be a number; it could be a score on a test—if a student scored a 1. It could also be a code for MALE. In both instances, it is technically a numeral, but in the latter it is not also a number; even though a 1 and 2 for SEX would admit to mathematics, such calculations would be absurd. In neither case would a code of M for MALE be admissible to mathematics, so perhaps the best thing is to code character variables as actual characters.[4]

This distinction between character and numeric variables is important in computer analysis of RBC data. Often, you will want to ask the computer to print out a set of averages and standard deviations for all the variables in your data set that can admit to mathematics. In the above data set, T1Q1 through T3FE inclusive and TIMEIN fall into that category. In virtually all modern statistical packages, you can tell the system which variables are character and which are numeric. You can then run broad statistical routines on the whole data set and look only at the numeric variables; and because you did not declare SEX as numeric, you will not, accidentally and absurdly, get an "average" value for SEX.

There is one other common variable type, although in my experience this next distinction is not critical in modern statistical packages. Some computer programs consider a character variable as a variable for which the values can be only a single character in length. SEX, above, is a character variable in that definition of character. A *string variable* is a set of more than one character. NAME, above, would be a string variable. This distinction is necessary in some true programming languages such as PASCAL, in which you need to treat the single-length characters differently from those of more than one character in length. In statistical software packages, however, this is somewhat blurred because the software takes care of the complexity of handling characters and strings. The notion of "string" does come into play, for example, in SAS in that you can perform certain operations or functions on characters. SAS calls these *string functions*. We will see a few of these in the next chapter.

Character versus *string* is but one of many terminological distinctions you may encounter in handling language-related RBC data on a computer. We have already seen some others: For example, the persons above might be called *cases* or *records*. The variables might be known in some software as *fields*, and the values might be called *entries*. Recall that we could have coded SEX as 1 or 2. Hence, *alpha(betic)numeric* is a good term to describe a variable that could be a numeral or a letter, and indeed, SPSS calls character variables *alphanumeric*.

Finally, the verb *to code* in the sense it is used here refers to the conscious decision by you, the analyst, of what possible values a variable might take. You must know what possible values a variable might have and how wide those values might be (to do the start-stop columns). You are in control of the data coding; in fact, you are in control of the entire data input, manipulation, and debugging process. You should become acquainted with terminological variation that software imposes on your data handling (e.g., the fact that SAS uses *observation* to mean a case/record). And that motivates the first principle of this chapter:

Principle 2.1: The Data Control Principle

Take control of the structure and flow of your data.

This seemingly simple principle implies many things. We have explored several aspects of control above, most of which relate to the general idea of having a codebook that defines your data. First, you should take charge of the layout of a data record: Locate similar variables adjacent to each other on a data record. Second, you should control the start-stop columns for variables: be consistent; that helps with production of the codebook. Third, you should take control of assignment of character and numeric data typing; your analysis will benefit later on. Other data structure control features are reflected in our example here. Notice, above, that missing values are designated by a placeholder in the data set—in this case, a dot. The placeholder is located consistently; you will need this later on when you read data into the computer. If you do not include some sort of placeholder, the computer may read the data inaccurately (see Chapter 3 for further discussion of the types of data disasters that can arise from inconsistent missing value policy). Notice also, above, how the data are laid out in a fashion that is easy to read. A space has been left between each value in our data set for each case; that is a luxury we have here because we can easily fit the information onto one short line. These points are but a few examples of taking control of the data.

Taking control of your data transcends the simple need to write a codebook. In many ways, Principle 2.1 is the most important in the whole book. All other principles seem to flow from it. For instance, compare it with the principles in Chapter 1. How can you decide your atomicity (Principle 1.1) unless you control your data structure? How can you know the social consequences of your data (Principle 1.3) unless you are in control of its collection? Principle 2.1 also seems to relate to many principles yet to come; a good example to foreshadow here is Principle 3.4, which reminds you to know what happens to missing data in your software by default. Maybe it is what you want to happen; maybe it is not. But unless you are in control—unless you know what happens— something could go wrong. You should exercise this control at all stages of data handling: as you first enter data into the computer and in subsequent debugging, manipulation, setup for analysis, and archival.

Data control begins with data input, and in the next section of this chapter, I discuss various methods of getting the data into the computer. Before proceeding, however, I hope you have also detected one other problem in the above sample data. Notice that the dot indicates a missing value. What if a student missed a test? What if, for example, Juan had not been present for T1Q2? A dot would also appear there. But that dot would mean a different thing than the dot for Juan on T3Q1, for instance. The T3Q2 dot would mean he was attending but did not take that exam. The T3Q1 dot means he has not yet reached his third term in the institute. It seems we need two types of missing value designators: truly missing, and missing because the student has not yet reached that term. This is a sample of the kind of problem I address in Chapter 3.

2.2. FROM HARD COPY TO ONLINE COPY

We are envisioning a data set structured like the one above, in which each row of the data is also a case/record representing a human. The columns represent variables/fields, and the cells in the RBC table represent values/entries.

Note to Reader

> The doubled variable names are probably getting awkward by now—*variable/field, case/record,* and so on—so I standardize from here on by using the terms I first learned: *case* and *variable,* but I use *entry* for *value* (I first learned *value*) because *entry* denotes the verb *to enter,* which is relevant to this part of the chapter. So from here on, it is *case, variable,* and *entry.*

So far, our data set is from one EFL institute. (We encounter, shortly, data from several institutes.) This begs the question: How did the data get into this computer file?

RBC data often begin as hard copy. *Hard copy* refers to the physical paper records containing the original information about a case; however, it could also refer to more direct data sources, such as interview ratings. In the above data set, the variables T1Q1 through T1Q3 would have originated as hard copy from one or several of the following sources: a teacher record book, actual test forms, or possibly student folders in a central file cabinet someplace in the institute. For variables such as NAME and SEX, those probably come from a central record, although we do come to know our students and probably do not need to seek a physical record to determine SEX (one's name is *sometimes* also helpful in that regard).

The classic scenario is this: You, the analyst, stack up a huge pile of hard copy next to a computer and painstakingly key in the information you need in an RBC file. That works, and sometimes it is the most efficient method. You can make your job a bit easier, however, by using an optically scanned sheet or, if that is not available, a data key-in template. I now describe each, in turn.

2.3. OPTICAL SCANNING VERSUS
DATA KEY-IN TEMPLATES

One useful method of getting data into a computer is through the use of optical scan sheets. These sheets are a series of small circles arranged so that possible values for given variables can be filled in by pencil. Figures 2.1 through 2.3 are samples of an optical scan sheet (henceforth, I use the term *opscan sheet*).

Notice that opscan sheets can read in more than just simple multiple-choice information. Figures 2.1 and 2.2 clearly show some items (e.g., 1 to 90 on the front) for which students will mark in their responses to actual multiple-choice questions. Notice also that a section of the sheet is used for reading in the student's name.

Opscan sheets can also be used by people marking the responses of a student, as in Figure 2.3. In Figure 2.3, professional evaluators rate the interviews with students and mark in the scores they want to award. This type of sheet has been around for some time and has the potential of automating a great deal of formerly painstaking human rating of language performance. Conceptually, the type of opscan sheet in Figure 2.3 could also be used for research purposes. You could use such a sheet to record research data yourself (as a researcher).

Regardless of which type of sheet is used, the general flow of events is the same: The marks are made on the opscan sheet, the sheet is placed into a scanner connected to a computer, a program is run, and the data are read into, most typically, an RBC file. The scanner may vary in size. Professional educational testing corporations often have very large scanners capable of reading many hundreds of sheets per minute. Smaller needs require smaller devices, and scanners closer in size to a desktop computer printer are also available.

At times, however, opscan is not feasible. Perhaps the data are so complex as to forbid optical scanning; for example, perhaps the data include actual field notes by a researcher. More typically, however, opscan sheets are not feasible because no optical scanner is available, most often because of cost. In that case, a data key-in template is often a good solution.

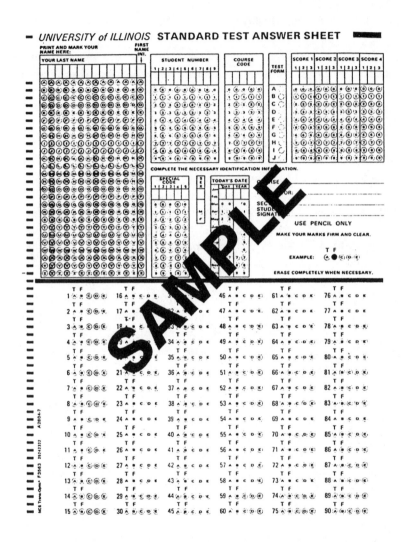

Figure 2.1. Sample Opscan Sheet: Multiple-Choice Test: Front
SOURCE: University of Illinois Standard Test Answer Sheet. Copyright 1995, University of Illinois at Urbana-Champaign. Used with permission.

Computer programs such as SAS and SPSS can be set up to form a screen key-in template or can read data from a flat file that you prepare in your preferred word processor (and save as unformatted

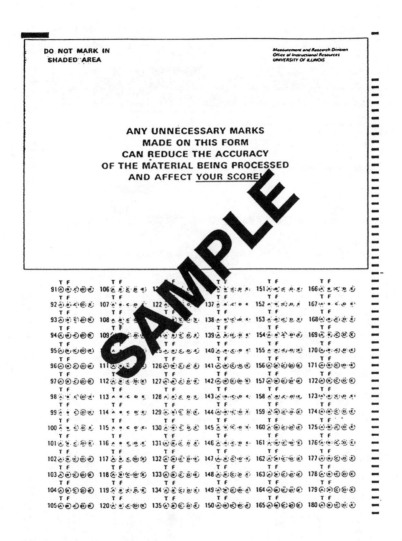

Figure 2.2. Sample Opscan Sheet: Multiple-Choice Test: Back
SOURCE: University of Illinois Standard Test Answer Sheet. Copyright 1995, University of Illinois at Urbana-Champaign. Used with permission.

text). Let's return to Juan, Anna, and Ahmed. Assume now that, from the start, we wanted to get into the data described above but also to enter the data from an interview on self-reported profi-

Paper 1

Candidate Mark Sheet   **Specimen Copy Only**

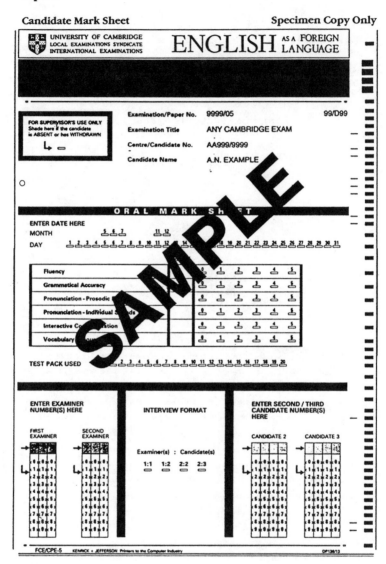

Figure 2.3. Sample Optical Scan Sheet: Rater Score Awards
SOURCE: Copyright © 1995, University of Cambridge, Local Examinations Syndicate, Cambridge, UK. Used with permission.

ciency in the target language. Perhaps we could use opscan to feed in some of the data above, but let's assume we have no budget for an optical scanner. We might use a computer program, such as SAS or SPSS, to set up a key-in template that looks precisely like the record above:

```
-------------------(Begin Screen)--------------------
    Screen 1, Record 1
                    Name:
          Native Country:
         Native Language:
                     Sex:
      Time at Institute:
          Term 1, Quiz 1:
          Term 1, Quiz 2:
          Term 1, Quiz 3:
      Term 1, Final Exam:
          Term 2, Quiz 1:
          Term 2, Quiz 2:
          Term 2, Quiz 3:
      Term 2, Final Exam:
          Term 3, Quiz 1:
          Term 3, Quiz 2:
          Term 3, Quiz 3:
      Term 3, Final Exam:
-------------------(End Screen)--------------------

-------------------(Begin Screen)--------------------
    Screen 2, Record 1
            Self/Reading:
          Self/Listening:
            Self/Writing:
           Self/Speaking:
-------------------(End Screen)--------------------
```

We could then use hard copy to key in data (e.g., test score booklets, notes on interviews, audio- or videotapes)—whatever real sources are used to produce the data. We could type the entries onto the screen, and for Juan, this might produce:

```
-------------------(Begin Screen)--------------------
   Screen 1, Record 1
                    Name:  JUAN
         Native Country:  Mexico
        Native Language:  Spanish
                     Sex:  Male
      Time at Institute:  2 terms
          Term 1, Quiz 1:  29
          Term 1, Quiz 2:  32
          Term 1, Quiz 3:  44
      Term 1, Final Exam:  101
          Term 2, Quiz 1:  20
          Term 2, Quiz 2:  29
          Term 2, Quiz 3:  37
      Term 2, Final Exam:  99
          Term 3, Quiz 1:  [not applicable / missing]
          Term 3, Quiz 2:  [not applicable / missing]
          Term 3, Quiz 3:  [not applicable / missing]
      Term 3, Final Exam:  [not applicable / missing]
--------------------(End Screen)---------------------
```

```
-------------------(Begin Screen)--------------------
   Screen 2, Record 1
          Self/Reading:  Likes to read magazines,
                          especially about sports.
         Self/Listening:  Complains that he cannot
                          follow the high-speed
                          comments of sportscasters.
                          Wants more practice with
                          TV and radio.
          Self/Writing:  Did not comment very much.
                          Note: Maybe we could get
                          him to write more if we
                          ask him to write about
                          sports!
         Self/Speaking:  Said he speaks English
                          frequently at his part-time
                          job (a music store). Said
                          he is not afraid to speak
                          English.
--------------------(End Screen)---------------------
```

The data set now contains actual comments by the interviewer. This is a bit unlike the self-report data discussed by Davidson and Henning (1985) or Oscarson (1989), who report on use of self-rating scales. Yet, there is no reason not to conceive of a data set as something broader and more flexible.

Notice in particular that the interviewer included a written comment on the self-report, to the effect that the interviewer thought Juan perhaps could be motivated to write more if he were given topics on sports. This kind of insight is precisely why data sets need to include information like the interview commentary. Although such commentary may not be analyzable by statistics, it is definitely helpful to the goals of an institution like EAI. In a way, we still have a conceptual RBC data set above, albeit one in which some entries contain more extensive textual "data." This is an example of Principles 1.3 and 5.1, in that the structure of the database attempts to reflect a larger worldview than simple rows and columns of numbers.

If you key data in by using a template, you then need to learn how to get it into a form that a computer software package (e.g., SAS, SPSS) can read. There are several options. First, some major statistical packages (e.g., SAS) have their own data template modules that allow direct entry of data in a form that SAS can subsequently analyze. Second, if you save the above data entry template as unformatted text (also known as *ASCII text*), you can program either SAS or SPSS to read the data; you simply tell the software that you have several physical lines per case. Third, other software use data key-in templates and can produce file formats that SAS, SPSS, and other software can read. Discussion question 5 relates to this topic.

Getting data into a computer can be a time-consuming process. It is quite important to make a judgment about the most efficient means for getting your data into your computer file, and I elevate that advice to the level of a principle:

Principle 2.2: The Data Input Efficiency Principle

Be efficient in getting your data into a computer file, but not at the cost of losing crucial information.

Notice the qualifying phrase in the principle above. It is critical that keying in data does not sacrifice information that may prove important later on. Let's say we did use an opscan system for the above data set. Perhaps our progress and final exams are multiple-choice; this means the final exam and progress test totals can be calculated by the computer (more on this in the next chapter). Perhaps we successfully get all the data into the computer without using a key-in template; opscan seems to have done the job, except that the self-report is missing. If EAI follows Oscarson's (1989) argument that self-reported language assessment is critical to modern learner-centered language teaching and if we believe that student assessment should benefit instruction ("backwash"—see Hughes, 1989, chap. 6, or discussions of *consequent validity* in Messick, 1989), then we also need to know that Juan likes sports and that one of our interviewers thinks sports topics may be a way to get him to write more. If we do not also capture that information about Juan, I maintain, the efficiency of opscan has been more damaging than helpful. Our drive for efficiency led us to use opscan, but at the expense of not including some key information about the learner.

At this point, ask yourself, Where does data input efficiency end and loss of information begin? Ask yourself whether, in your research/ teaching situation, you are sacrificing potentially useful information for the sake of quick data entry and prompt processing turnaround.

2.4. RECODING, COMPUTING, AND DEBUGGING: A PREVIEW

I now return to the problem posed at the beginning of the chapter: What if we have data from several language institutes? Perhaps our RBC data set might look like this:

Person Dataset:

```
 I
 N
 S          C
 T          O          T
 I          U          I
 T    N     N          M  T  T  T    T  T  T  T    T  T  T  T    T
 U    A     T     S    E  1  1  1    1  2  2  2    2  3  3  3    3
 T    M     R     L  E I  Q  Q  Q    F  Q  Q  Q    F  Q  Q  Q    F
 E    E     Y     1  X N  1  2  3    E  1  2  3    E  1  2  3    E

[LOG]     1    1     2     2     3     3     4     4     5     5     6     6
----5----0----5----0----5----0----5----0----5----0----5----0----5----0----5--
01   JUAN Mexico Spanish M 2 29 32 44 101 20 29 37 99  .    .    .    .
01   ANNA Italy  Italian F 1 34 28 35  90  .    .    .    .    .    .    .
01 AHMED Egypt  Arabic  M 3 23 23 39  97 28 29 36 99 18 21 40 103
:
:
:
02   JOSE Mexico Spanish M 3 39 32 42 102 19 29 30 90 14 15 22  88
02 MARIA Italy  Italian F 1 45 21 35  88  .    .    .    .    .    .    .
02 DAVID German German  M 3 23 23 39  97 12 13 50 98 17 27 41 100
:
:
:
03
03   (etc. for other institutes and students)
03
```

Of course, this assumes that several language institutes have the same number of terms, progress tests, final exams, and so on; this may be a weak assumption. What I want to illustrate here, however, is that we now have a two-level data set as shown in Figure 2.4. This is really no longer simple RBC data. The data are grouped, or blocked, on the variable INSTITUTE, which tells us which language school the student attended. Figure 2.4 better represents what is happening. Now let's assume we have data about each language institute. Perhaps we know the number of teachers, the location, the number of years the institute has been operating, and so on.

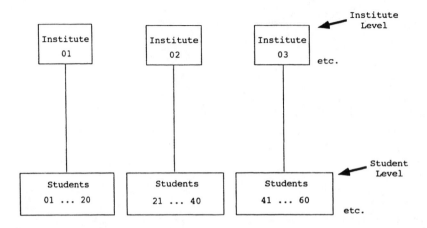

Figure 2.4. A Two-Level Hierarchical Data Set

```
Institute Data Set:

I
N        L      N
S        O      U
T        C      M
I        A  Y   T
T        T  E   C                                           N
U        I  A   H                                           A
T        O  R   R                                           M
E        N  S   S                                           E

[LOG]    1    1    2    2    3    3    4    4    5    5    6    6
----5----0----5----0----5----0----5----0----5----0----5----0----5

01 CHICAGO 40 24 ENGLISH ASSOCIATES INCORPORATED: CHICAGO BRANCH
02  LONDON 20 32 ENGLISH ASSOCIATES INCORPORATED: LONDON BRANCH
03  SYDNEY 22 30 ENGLISH ASSOCIATES INCORPORATED: SYDNEY BRANCH
(etc.)
```

We know that if a student is at institute 01, then the name of that institute is ENGLISH ASSOCIATES INCORPORATED: CHICAGO BRANCH, which has been in operation 40 years and employs 24 teachers. We have similar information about other institutes. The information in the above institute database is, in effect, inherited by each student in our original database simply by knowing the entry of the variable INSTITUTE. We do not need to key in the information from the institute database into the person database. That would be overkill. The computer can do that for us if we set up a relational operation between the information in the institute data set and the person data set. We would have, then, a database. The word *database*, to me, has always connoted something larger and more complicated. In fact, what we have here is a *relational database*, which uses a relational, hierarchical file structure to link information at two or more levels of generality. Technically, our simple RBC original person data set for Institute 01 is also a database; it is a flat-file database.

Now imagine you are keying in the data for these three institutes (or for any three related data acquisition projects, perhaps three phases of your research). So long as you have a simple code number on the person data, you can easily link it with a higher-level general data set. But to do so, you must make yourself a note that such changes or modification will be needed.

In fact, our evolving data set here will require several changes, so far. Let's list them. First are two changes we have discovered already:

1. The institute information will have to be related to the person information to form a relational database.
2. The missing value placeholder will have to be clarified: There is a difference between missing/not relevant and just plain missing. We would not want to confuse a student who had missed a test with one who had not taken a test because he or she had not yet reached that term in one of the institutes.

There are others, however:

3. The written designations for native country and first language are helpful, but what about David from Institute 02? His native language is German, and within the space available for the data layout, his native country is also German. As we are keying in the data, we are discovering that we have not left enough columns for a particular entry.

4. Also with respect to the Language variable, we must remember that Anna's first language is Italian but that, being from northern Italy, she speaks German nearly like a native. If that is important to our database, we may need to add a variable to note that Anna has fluency in two languages other than the one being studied—English.

5. Let's not forget the self-report data. We need to be able to study it and link it with the student performance data (the test scores and so on).

A principle is warranted:

Principle 2.3: The Change Awareness Principle

Data entry is an iterative process. Keep a list of the changes you will have to make (computations), the values you will have to change (recoding), and the problems you will have to solve (debugging), but try to use the computer to do as much computing and debugging as possible.

This is a rather long principle because it must accommodate several points. Data input does not stop with the key in of the last keystroke of the last entry of the last record. As you key in data, you will discover things you want to change. Inevitably, you will be 95% through a data set of 200 people and come across the name of a country that is too wide for the column width you are specifying. Inevitably, you will accidentally hit 3 for SEX or 98 for AGE; the former is implausible, and the latter is plausible but unlikely in a data set about language teaching. Inevitably, as you key it in, you will think of enhancements you can make to the data set, and you will realize that the raw material for the enhancements exists in what you already have; you will think of a new, computed variable you are going to need.

Data entry is an iterative process. As the next two chapters progress, we see that decisions made about our ongoing data set need to be reevaluated. In some cases, that reevaluation will imply a return to the hard copy and maybe (though one hopes not) more keypunching. In some cases, we will be able to get the computer to do what we want without too much extra effort.

I cannot proceed into Chapter 3 without a sincere warning, one that needs to be repeated many times throughout this book. This warning is treated in some detail in Chapter 3. Give your data as much structure as you can (Principle 2.1), and in so doing, try to develop a coherent missing-value policy. In our evolving data set, we have seen that we will need two types of missing value designators: truly missing and missing but not relevant. This we can fortunately accommodate by programming, and we do so in Chapter 3.

Frankly, in my experience at handling statistical data sets during the past decade or more, I have been tripped up more seriously by missing data than by any other type of raw data problem.

With one possible exception—forgetting to back up!

2.5. IMPLEMENTATION

In this, the first set of sample SAS and SPSS programs, I show you some data and commands necessary to input them and print them back. I comment on each SAS and SPSS command, as well as on the general structure of SAS and SPSS programs.

Suppose you have a simple RBC data set of three variables for eight students at EAI:

```
 JUAN 3 4 4
 ANNA 1 4 5
AHMED 2 3 4
JAIME 1 1 4
MARIA 3 5 1
 IMAN 3 3 3
JOSEF 1 3 4
TOMAS 1 3 4
```

The codebook for this data set might be:

```
VARIABLE
  NAME       TYPE       DESCRIPTION       COLUMNS
--------------------------------------------------
  NAME    Character   Student name         1-5
  X1       Numeric    Data on test X1       7
  X2       Numeric    Data on test X2       9
  X3       Numeric    Data on test X3      11
```

In SAS, this data set could be read as follows:

```
data ch2;
    input name $ x1 x2 x3;
cards;
JUAN  3 4 4
ANNA  1 4 5
AHMED 2 3 4
JAIME 1 1 4
MARIA 3 5 1
IMAN  3 3 3
JOSEF 1 3 4
TOMAS 1 3 4
;
run;
```

The first line (data ch2;) defines a temporary SAS data set called ch2 (for Chapter 2). This data set will exist only as long as the program runs. It is always a good idea to name your data sets as you input them to software (a practice I discuss in some detail in "Implementation" in Chapter 6) because that helps you control the flow of your data—Principle 2.1. The next line (input . . .) states four variables: NAME, X1, X2, and X3. NAME is declared as a character variable by use of the dollar sign. The other three variables are read as numeric, which is the SAS default. cards; and the single semicolon on a line by itself are something like boundary markers showing the beginning and end of the data, and run; executes the whole data input process (it tells SAS to go ahead and execute everything preceding it back to the data ch2; line). We are fortunate because our data set is arranged in neat vertical rows with no missing values. Therefore, we can use *free-field* input: We do not have to tell SAS the start-stop columns of each value even though that information did appear in our codebook.

If you want to see that the data were read correctly, you could then add these SAS command lines:

```
proc print data=ch2;
    title1 'Illustrate data set CH2 - SAS';
run;
```

proc print data=ch2; calls the SAS printout routine and applies it to our data set. We then have a title, which is a descriptive statement that will print out on the results. The run; appears again, this time to execute everything from proc print onward.

The SAS *output* (results) produced by reading the above data and printing them back would look like the following, which illustrates that the data input was accurate (compare the table below with what appears between cards; and the single semicolon above):

Illustrate data set CH2 - SAS

OBS	NAME	X1	X2	X3
1	JUAN	3	4	4
2	ANNA	1	4	5
3	AHMED	2	3	4
4	JAIME	1	1	4
5	MARIA	3	5	1
6	IMAN	3	3	3
7	JOSEF	1	3	4
8	TOMAS	1	3	4

To read these data in SPSS, you could use the following commands:

```
data list list
   / name (a5) x1 x2 x3.
begin data
JUAN   3 4 4
ANNA   1 4 5
AHMED  2 3 4
JAIME  1 1 4
MARIA  3 5 1
IMAN   3 3 3
JOSEF  1 3 4
TOMAS  1 3 4
end data.
   save outfile=ch2.
execute.
```

SPSS RBC data input is similar to that for SAS. data list list is both a command and an option: The words data list are the command, and the second list is the option, which in this case requests freefield data input. If your data are freefield, you must inform SPSS of that fact, whereas in SAS, that is not necessary. The line / name (a5) x1 x2 x3 is analogous to the input line in SAS; it names the variables we read. (a5) is the SPSS designator for a character variable: The a portion stands for "alphanumeric," and the 5 is the maximum width in number of characters we want to read in. As with SAS, numeric input is the default, so only the NAME variable must be designated by its type. begin data and end data. serve as boundary markers for the data set itself, much as cards; and the single semicolon do in SAS.

File handling is somewhat different in SPSS. You need to manually save a temporary file; save outfile=ch2 saves a temporary copy of your data set. It will be permanently saved on your computer's hard disk unless you use the erase command, as I describe in Chapter 3. Finally, the SPSS execute command is like run; in SAS: It tells SPSS to go ahead and execute everything that precedes it. What actually happens in SAS and SPSS is that run; and execute cause the software to execute all commands back to but excluding the most previous run; or execute. This is how you can form program blocks, as I describe below.

You could print the data back with these SPSS commands:

```
get file=ch2.
    title 'Illustrate data set CH2 - SPSS'.
    list.
execute.
```

Again, the above SPSS code is similar to that in SAS, but it differs in one key respect: You use a command to get the file and then list (print) it. Outside that, the title and execute commands work in a manner similar to that in SAS. The above SPSS code would yield an SPSS "listing" (results) that looks like this:

Illustrate data set CH2 - SPSS

NAME	X1	X2	X3
JUAN	3.00	4.00	4.00
ANNA	1.00	4.00	5.00
AHMED	2.00	3.00	4.00
JAIME	1.00	1.00	4.00
MARIA	3.00	5.00	1.00
IMAN	3.00	3.00	3.00
JOSEF	1.00	3.00	4.00
TOMAS	1.00	3.00	4.00

Number of cases read: 8   Number of cases listed: 8

Illustrate data set CH2 - SPSS

In the code and results of both programs, some interesting comparisons emerge. First, each software package has a different default *command terminator,* which is the punctuation symbol that ends a command. In SAS, it is a semicolon; in SPSS, it is a period. In both packages, these defaults can be changed. (An SPSS programmer could set the software to use the ubiquitous SAS semicolon if desired.) One useful similarity is that a command can wrap over two lines in both SAS and SPSS—for example, the SPSS data list command for which the line beginning / name is actually an option even though it appears on a new physical line.

It is interesting to see some defaults in the style of the printouts. SAS prints out an internal variable called *OBS,* which is the row number of the input RBC data set, but SPSS does not do this. Additionally, the level of precision (number of decimal places) also differs. SAS prints single-digit integers because that is what we read in from our RBC data. The SPSS default, however, is to print to two decimal places, and so its results are padded with zeros. The OBS and precision issues illustrate the need to understand the default settings of your software, a topic I take up as Principle 3.4.

In both programs, I use titling to describe the program functions. In SAS, you can have up to nine titles (e.g., `title1, title2`) in the input code that will echo back on the output. In SPSS, you can have two (`title` and `subtitle`). Generally, you should place titles just before or just after the command to which they apply (e.g., the location of the SPSS `title` right before the `list` command). On the results, SAS titling is always printed above the particular output to which it applies, whereas in SPSS, this is variable—sometimes printed above, sometimes below, and sometimes in both positions as in the example I show here.

The implementation examples above illustrate reading in an easy RBC data set in SAS and SPSS. As this book progresses, you will see repeated SAS and SPSS examples of RBC input. Sometimes I read in data in a manner similar to that shown here—freefield. Sometimes I specify start-stop columns, as we do in the codebook above. I advise that as you study the "Implementation" sections of later chapters, return and review the samples given in this chapter.

In addition, in later chapters, I have additional titling, and you will see more of my programming style—such as extensive use of indentation and blank lines. I also show you how to insert *comments* into the programs: lines with remarks that are not treated as commands at all. In addition, I make extensive use of command line wrapping, especially when reading in non-freefield data. Another important convention is the *program block*, which is a collection of related commands (e.g., from `data` or `proc` to `run;` in SAS or from most commands to `execute` in SPSS). Program blocks are not strictly necessary, but they are permitted by each software package. All these conventions clarify what a program is doing and enhance its readability. I use a programming style that illustrates an important principle in this book, 2.1: "Take control of the structure and flow of your data." If I cannot look at one of my programs and read it and understand what it is doing—quickly and easily—then I feel a loss of control.

2.6. DISCUSSION QUESTIONS: CHAPTER 2

1. In your research and/or teaching setting, identify some hard copy data. These might be survey forms, test answer sheets, and student compositions with component scores for grammar and content. Using SAS or SPSS (if available) or other software of your choice, put the data into a computer file.

   Track this process. Keep a log of what happens and when and record problems and how they are solved. How might the process be made more efficient? If possible, consult with others who use that data set or similar data. Can you come to a consensus about efficient data entry in your situation?

2. Locate and visit an office or company where optical scanning of computer response sheets is done (e.g., see Figure 2.1). Notice how the data come in to the scanner and what is produced on the computer. Discuss with the data handlers what problems arise; for example, what happens if a scan sheet has a double-coded response (a student marks both A and B for a given item on a test)?

3. For the situation in question 1 above or for some other data-handling situation with which you are familiar, write up a data codebook. Show it to other people familiar with that data situation and obtain feedback. Revise the codebook and obtain feedback again. Repeat this process about three times and then compare the first draft of your codebook with the last draft. Everybody familiar with the data context should advise you on what variations in data are possible (e.g., the width of certain values for certain variables, new variable names that are more intuitive).

4. Describe any hierarchical data needs in your research and/or teaching settings. How does your preferred software handle such data?

5. At your setting, investigate the possibilities for data entry; seek help from local consultants or locally authored documentation or use the documentation provided with the software. Is optical scanning of data available? Can your software be used to construct data key-in templates? If so, how can you get data from the template into your preferred analytical software (e.g., SAS, SPSS)?

One data entry trick involves using SAS or SPSS to read multiple lines of data. For example, in SAS:

```
data demo;
    input name $ 18-26 /
          test1   18-21 /
          test2   18-21 /
cards;
Name of student: JUAN
          test1:   95
          test2:   84
Name of student: ANNA
          test1:   90
          test2:   91
Name of student: AHMED
          test1:   87
          test2:   90
    ;
run;
```

The field names to the left, though apparently part of the data set, are really ignored because the input command points to start-stop columns that are to the right of the colon in the data. You can make a template with your word processor or editor (e.g., the lines Name of student) and copy the template over and over again until you have sufficient templates to enter your data. Then you can key in the values and write a program to analyze it.

Investigate the implementation of SAS or SPSS at your setting and determine whether you can use this kind of a data entry trick.

NOTES

1. The EAI setting is just an example. As you read this book, you are free to translate the example into a setting or context more relevant to your work. For example, if you are more familiar with public schools, you might consider that EAI represents a school district and that the various EAI branches (which I talk about in later chapters) are schools within the district. The final exams and so forth that I define could just as easily be exams in your schools. Or you might consider that EAI is a central research project database on which you are working; each branch would be a phase or component of the project; each exam or person would be some data element of relevance to you. EAI is merely a convenient, straightforward context that allows me to illustrate common features of data handling.

2. There is a great deal of flexibility in the layout of a data codebook. Perhaps, for example, you would rather put the start-stop columns first:

```
START-STOP
   COLUMNS    VARIABLE NAME    TYPE    DESCRIPTION
   01-05      NAME             Char    Student's name
   08-12      COUNTRY          Char    Student's home country
   :

   :
etc.
```

There are other shorthand methods for elements in the codebook. The structure of the codebook is a decision the data handler makes. It is governed by readability, personal taste, and institutional consistency; that is, sometimes codebooks for many data sets within an institution need a common layout because many people work with the codebooks.

3. Entering numbers for class variables (e.g., SEX) could make sense from the standpoint of debugging, as I point out with Principle 4.1 in Chapter 4. Perhaps you could code SEX as 1 and 2 and request the computer to give you descriptive statistics on it. Then, if your maximum observed value were 3, you would know something was wrong. But the same objective can be achieved with M and F; you can request a frequency table of counts of each value (M and F), and if a third value pops up, then it is a data entry error. I illustrate such debugging tables in Chapter 3.

A special case that might justify numeric coding of a nonnumeric categorical variable is a two-category variable (e.g., SEX) that is coded 0 and 1. If, for example, females were coded zero, then a mean of .62 on that variable would indicate that the group is 62% female. Frequency tables available in both SAS and SPSS, however, give precisely the same information.

4. As I note in the "Implementation" discussion in Chapter 5, SPSS does not permit some statistical procedures to use alphanumeric character variables. Most critically, the categorical independent variables must be coded numeric. This is not the case in SAS. You might want to become aware of such subtle requirements of your software that condition data coding even at the early data input stages; I contend that distinction is a particular instance of Principle 2.1.

3 Data Manipulation

Overview/Outline

- Computers and Efficiency
- What Is Data Manipulation?
- Common Manipulations in Data Handling
- Computed Variables
- Recoding
- Value Codes
- Manipulation of Missing Data
- Data Relations
- Subsetting
- Catenation (Sometimes Called "Concatenation")
- Merging
- Hierarchical Relations: A Special Case of Merging
- Data Relations: A Summary
- Sorting
- Implementation
- Discussion Questions: Chapter 3

3.1. COMPUTERS AND EFFICIENCY

Unlike the (largely) inductive discussion of principles elsewhere in this book, in Chapter 3 we begin with a principle:

Principle 3.1: The Data Manipulation Principle

Let the computer do as much work as possible. Instruct it to do tasks such as recoding, variable computation, data set catenation, data set subsetting, data merging, and similar tasks that would, frankly, waste your time. Let the computer manipulate your data for you.

Data processing should benefit greatly from the power of a computer to do structured and repetitive tasks. The sheer presence of computers in our daily lives attests to this benefit. They can relieve us of painstaking drudgery. The challenge is not to justify a principle such as 3.1 above; rather, we must answer this: How can we take advantage of a computer's structured power to the greatest benefit when handling data? To answer this question, the sample data set from Chapter 2 is carried over into this chapter, and additional data structures are defined. I illustrate various means of data manipulation by description and then pseudocode. *Pseudocode* is structured language similar to the actual commands needed by a computer program, but not containing the commands themselves; it is often used as a first step in programming. Toward the end of the chapter, I present a full implementation of this data manipulation in SAS and SPSS to show this chapter's topics at operation.

The goal of this chapter is to instruct, at the level of principle, those features of data manipulation best left to the computer. Ask yourself the following question before attempting any change to your data: Is this contemplated change something I have to do manually, or can I achieve it more efficiently by instructing the computer to do it for me? That question is the heart of Principle 3.1.

3.2. WHAT IS DATA MANIPULATION?

The best way to define data manipulation is to clarify what it is not. Data manipulation is not the alteration of data in any way that may affect the substantive findings of your enterprise, be that education or research. Recall the data record for Juan, given in full here from Chapter 2:

```
                Name:  JUAN
      Native Country:  Mexico
     Native Language:  Spanish
                 Sex:  Male
   Time at Institute:  2 terms
      Term 1, Quiz 1:  29
      Term 1, Quiz 2:  32
      Term 1, Quiz 3:  44
  Term 1, Final Exam:  101
      Term 2, Quiz 1:  20
      Term 2, Quiz 2:  29
      Term 2, Quiz 3:  37
  Term 2, Final Exam:  99
      Term 3, Quiz 1:  [not applicable / missing]
      Term 3, Quiz 2:  [not applicable / missing]
      Term 3, Quiz 3:  [not applicable / missing]
  Term 3, Final Exam:  [not applicable / missing]
```

If we change the entry for the variable Term 2, Final Exam from the value 99 to the value 49, that is clearly unacceptable data manipulation. It implies that the data are being changed by the data analyst; this is an unethical and improper activity.[1]

3.3. COMMON MANIPULATIONS IN DATA HANDLING

The balance of this chapter illustrates common data manipulation scenarios: computed variables, recoding (and value codes), manipulation of missing data, and data relations (catenation, subsetting, merging, and sorting). These data manipulations are by no means a closed set of all possible manipulations you may need to do; however, they do represent the most common types I have encountered in many years of data handling.

3.3.1. COMPUTED VARIABLES

Suppose you want to know the average score Juan achieved on the final exams; that is, you want to add a variable called `Final Exam Average` as follows:

```
              Name:  JUAN
    Native Country:  Mexico
   Native Language:  Spanish
               Sex:  Male
 Time at Institute:  2 terms
   Term 1, Quiz 1:   29
   Term 1, Quiz 2:   32
   Term 1, Quiz 3:   44
Term 1, Final Exam:  101
   Term 2, Quiz 1:   20
   Term 2, Quiz 2:   29
   Term 2, Quiz 3:   37
Term 2, Final Exam:  99
   Term 3, Quiz 1:   [not applicable / missing]
   Term 3, Quiz 2:   [not applicable / missing]
   Term 3, Quiz 3:   [not applicable / missing]
Term 3, Final Exam:  [not applicable / missing]
Final Exam Average:  100
```

The new field was computed by adding the values of the final exam scores and dividing by the number of final exams, which in Juan's case is two.

You could, if you like, painstakingly calculate this by hand or with a calculator for each person in the database. You could create a blank field called `Final Exam Average` for each data entry template and then key in the average for each person. But there is an easier way, one that illustrates Principle 3.1. Ask the computer to determine:

1. How many final exams did Juan take?
2. What was the sum of scores on all those final exams?
3. What was the Final Exam Average? That is, divide (2) by (1).

This can be displayed as pseudocode as follows:

```
For each person in the data set, do the following:
    Count the number of final exams taken and store
        that count to a variable known as Number of
        Final Exams and then
    Add the scores for the final exams and then
    Divide the sum of the scores for the final exams by
        the number of final exams taken and store that
        in a new variable called Final Exam Average.
```

This procedure results in a *computed variable*, a variable that you did not key in but that you produced from existing variables. Most data-handling software can compute variables for you; you only need to know which variables are necessary to contribute to the computed variable and how to do the computation (what the mathematical operation will be). Once you have computed a variable, it becomes part of the data structure; in effect, it enters your data codebook even though it does not occupy columns in the data set that you keyed in.

Computed variables have a potential problem. Suppose a student takes a certain exam late, perhaps because the student was sick on the day of the exam. Is it necessary to rerun a statistical program to rerun the computed variables? Perhaps. The answer is dependent on the software you are using and the particular manner in which you access it. If you store the data in some simple row-by-column (RBC) file or a key-in template software package, it is quite likely that you will have to rerun some command language to get the computed variables for any latecomers.

You might want to compute several variables like average of final exams, shown above, and other averages, sums, or differences. These new computed variables may be of interest to you, and you might want to form a new data set that contains the original data plus the new data; that is, you might want to write a new RBC flat file onto computer storage that has all the information you keyed in plus the new variables you have computed. You might want to do this to store the data in a readable flat file format for later use by other programs or simply as a backup. One piece of advice:

Principle 3.2: The Original Data Principle

Always save a computer file copy of the original, unaltered data.

The examples of computed variables here are changes to a data set's structure that do not affect the content of the data, but rather add a variable by building upon the existing data values. It is clear why Principle 3.2 is needed: Perhaps you would build up a series of computed variables, add them to the data, write it all back out to a new file that is now somewhat cluttered up, and later want to look at the original uncluttered data. It would be nice to have the luxury of looking at the original data prior to the addition of the computed variables.

3.3.2. RECODING

There is a much more important reason to save a computer file copy of the original, unaltered data. One type of data manipulation is called *recoding*, the changing of a value on a variable. That practice may seem unethical, but in reality it is needed in many instances. We have a very real need to do some recoding in our data set from Chapter 2, p. 43, in which the field width is too narrow to adequately distinguish German as a language and as a country. If we recode the value for David's home country from German to Germany, we have not altered the substance of the data. Rather, we have made it better by clarifying the difference between the value on the Native Language variable German and the value on the Country variable Germany. There are several ways out of this problem via data manipulation.

What if you made a typographical mistake in the recoding instruction to the computer and accidentally recoded Language as Germany and Country as German? If you did not save a copy of the unaltered data set (Principle 3.2), then this mistake could never be recovered, and in fact perhaps it would never be noticed.[2]

In this instance, we want to recode instances of the word *German* appearing in a Native Country variable to read *Germany*. We assume we are working with a flat file RBC data set in which the *y* (from the original data key-in template) has been lost. This is because we made an error when we produced the flat file and did not allocate enough columns for that variable. Because we know that the variable indicates native country, however, we know that the value *German* does not mean a language, but rather a country. We can safely give the computer the following pseudo-code:

```
For each person in the data set, do the following:
    If the native country is 'German', then recode
        it to 'Germany'.
```

This may be done in two ways, and they depend on the type of recoding supported by the software you use. First, if the software allows you to "dynamically" change the width of a variable, simply translate the above pseudocode into the language of that software. *Dynamic width changes* refer to the ability to change the memory occupied by the variable Native Country by adding a seventh character. Perhaps your software is very intelligent and will let you do this with a single command. Perhaps two or more commands will be needed, along these lines:

```
For each person in the data set, do the following:
    Resize the width of the Native Country variable
        to a value wide enough to accommodate the
        widest country name you might have (see
        below), and then,
    If the native country is 'German', then recode
        it to 'Germany'.
```

Not all software permits this. Often, you have to do something rather involved and sometimes inelegant. For example, the current problem could also be solved by a pseudocode that reads as follows:

```
For each person in the data set, do the following:
    Create a computed variable called NC2 (Native
        Country two) and make it equal to all spaces
        for each record (let it be coded 'missing').
        Use as many spaces as the widest width of any
        country name in your data set. If you are not
        certain, guess and add a couple of spaces to
        be conservative.
    Copy Native Country as NC2. Make them equal for
        each record; that is, overwrite the NC2 spaces
        with the value of Native Country.
    Delete the variable Native Country.
    Rename the variable Native Country 2 (NC2) to
        Native Country.
    Then, if Native Country = 'German', change it
        to 'Germany'. If it is 'Zimbab', change it to
        'Zimbabwe', and so on, just as described
        above.
```

This solution creates the temporary variable NC2 solely for the purpose of widening the variable Native Country. Suppose the widest country name in your data set is Zimbabwe—eight characters. You would have a computed variable in your data set that is simply eight spaces, and you would create this for each person. Then, by copying Native Country into NC2, you would in effect make NC2 and Native Country equal. Let the software take care of issues such as what to do with left and right justification, for example, making ` Germany' the value for NC2, rather than `Germany ' (note the spaces). This solution is what computer programmers call a *kludge* (pronounced "KLOOGE"). A kludge is an inelegant, possibly wasteful solution, but it is a solution that works.

Principle 3.3: The Kludge Principle

Sometimes the best way to manipulate data is not elegant and seems to waste computer resources. A kludge is sometimes justifiable; the ends CAN justify the means.

Principle 3.3 reminds us that if recoding involves several extra steps, don't worry. If the results are what you want and if you can tolerate extra computing time, which is not a big problem with today's high-speed machines, then by all means write a kludge. For example, imagine you are programming late one afternoon and this width problem pops up with the LANGUAGE variable. You cannot return and redo the key in because the office with the key-in template computer is locked, and in any event, you have already been recoding the data and do not want to redo what you have already done. You suspect that a quick, dynamic, resizing command is someplace in your software to widen the field and thus permit you to simply recode German as Germany and Zimbab as Zimbabwe, but you cannot find it in the manual, the help files in the computer do not have it, and you are a bit under the gun to get the project done. Why not program six or seven inelegant extra steps (the kludge principle), rather than just one or two (the width-changing method)? It will work, and you can do it with the knowledge you currently have. In short, you patch together a series of computer commands from your own available repertoire and make the data do what you want. You write a kludge.

I write a lot of kludges. I suppose I should work more to become an elegant, efficient programmer, but usually I want to get things done so that I can get results and use them in the rest of my work. Later in the chapter, I discuss hierarchical relational data—that is, data in which many cases share a common set of values on a variable. My preferred recourse with such data is an avowed kludge.

3.3.3. VALUE CODES

There is one final way out of this native country value dilemma. Many data analysts would not key in full names of native countries. Rather, they would establish a second set of codes, called *value codes*, that might read as follows:

```
Native Country Value Codes.

    Albania  = 001
    Austria  = 002
    :

    :

    Germany  = 021
    Ghana    = 022
    :

    :

    Zimbabwe = 103
```

Then, when keying in data at the template, the keypuncher has a value code sheet and, on seeing Zimbabwe, would punch in 103, rather than Zimbab or Zimbabwe. On seeing Germany, the keypuncher would use 021, rather than German or Germany.

I advise against this type of solution for several reasons. Although it appears to standardize the width of the country variable to three characters/numerals, it requires later reprogramming to insert the value codes back into the data set. Furthermore, the keypuncher may slip up and put in the wrong number: 022 for Germany. This cannot be traced without resort to hard copy raw data; even if you catch the fact that somebody from Ghana probably does not speak German as a native language, can you be absolutely certain that the correct entry for Native Country is Germany? If the keypuncher uses more descriptive values and slips up and types "Ferman" instead of "German," however, later debugging (as described in Chapter 4) will clearly reveal this, and "Ferman" can be recoded without resort to the original hard copy; you can reason out that the keypuncher hit the F key instead of the G because they are adjacent on the keyboard. Finally, modern template-based data entry software can almost always accommodate long character fields, which are more natural and logical when naming attributes about persons in a flat file data set; that is, 021 is not a native country. Germany is.

3.3.4. MANIPULATION OF MISSING DATA

In our ongoing EAI data set, we have several instances of *missing data*, or variables on records without values. Missing data are very common in data handling on computers, and a coherent missing-data policy is always a good idea.

Our data set has two types of missing values. In one case, a missing value means the person was not measured on that variable; most typically, it means the student's score is not available—perhaps the student was sick on the day of the test. In the other case, a missing value means the variable is not relevant to a particular student. If a student has not yet reached the third term in the instructional sequence, then any third-term scores are irrelevant and therefore missing. It would be useful to obtain separate counts of both types of missing values.

To do this, it is essential that you be familiar with the computer software you use for data analysis. The issue is to know what your software does by default, because it may do what you want, and you might not have to engage in a kludge to handle your missing data. Modern statistical software such as SAS or SPSS is the product of many years of use and evolution. The default settings (e.g., missing value handling) represent common needs of a wide variety of users. The software publishers must do that if they are to market their products successfully. Hence, Principle 3.4 has two parts:

Principle 3.4: The Default Principle

Know your software's default settings. Know whether those settings meet your needs.

In particular, be aware of the default handling of missing values in your software.

Your software has many default settings. Some control the nature of data entry, some the appearance of your results. By far the most defaults concern missing data. One excellent way to illustrate the need for principled control of missing data is with a precise software example: dBase. dBase is a popular database program, currently in its fourth edition. Generally, this is superb software: It can be used for excellent key-in templates, for instance. But it fails in one important aspect: If you set up a template and designate a variable as numeric, then by default any key-puncher who simply skips over that field automatically produces a zero. The net effect can be a disaster (see Hudson, 1993). Assume that Juan's record is keyed in by using a dBase template and that every variable on which you will ultimately do arithmetic is designated as numeric—a practice I recommended in Chapter 2. Here is what you would get:

```
            Name:  JUAN
  Native Country:  Mexico
 Native Language:  Spanish
             Sex:  Male
Time at Institute:  2 terms
   Term 1, Quiz 1:  29
   Term 1, Quiz 2:  32
   Term 1, Quiz 3:  44
Term 1, Final Exam:  101
   Term 2, Quiz 1:  20
   Term 2, Quiz 2:  29
   Term 2, Quiz 3:  37
Term 2, Final Exam:  99
   Term 3, Quiz 1:  0
   Term 3, Quiz 2:  0
   Term 3, Quiz 3:  0
Term 3, Final Exam:  0
```

If you did not know that Juan was not present for the Term 3 variables—that is, if you did a simple average across all the Term 3 scores for all students—Juan's data would read in as a numeric zero and bring down the mean of the group. Put another way, it is not true that Juan took those three tests and scored zero. Fortunately, in dBase, you can create a template and designate all variables as characters. Then, if the keypuncher skips over a value, a space is left in that position; as we will see, a space can be considered to be a missing value. You could have dBase print out the data to an external file, and the spaces would appear wherever the data are missing. That data file could then be read in by software such as SAS or SPSS, which would properly interpret the spaces as missing.

Couldn't we simply permit those zeros and recode them later? Couldn't we simply ask the computer to change all zeros on any variable to some missing value indicator, such as 999 or some impossible score, and then tell later analyses to avoid records in which that indicator exists? Or more simply, couldn't we tell the computer to drop from any later arithmetic any persons with a score of zero?

That will not work. What if a student received a legitimate zero? Even if you recode all zeros to 999 or something else, bona fide zeros would be lost. A person who actually took a test and scored zero—however remote that possibility—would suddenly be re-coded as 999—missing. The issue here is that zero is not a good missing value indicator. It is a value that can be quite meaningful.

dBase's error is that no unique symbol (e.g., a dash, a dot) can indicate a missing numeric variable. The program, in a somewhat draconian fashion, enters a zero for you if you skip over a numeric field when keying into a template. The only way out of this dilemma is to know that it exists and therefore to seek alternative solutions (e.g., locate other data template keying software, key in data as characters and learn how to program character-to-numeric conversion later in the data analysis process). If you start out using dBase and do not know what it does to missing values, then you are running a great risk. Hence, Principle 3.4.[3]

Let's assume, then, you have used key-in software such as SAS that does permit a unique indicator of missing numeric values. SAS uses a dot, although you can reset this to a space or even to a value such as 999. Juan's record, if keyed in by using a SAS template, would then look like this:

```
              Name:  JUAN
   Native Country:  Mexico
  Native Language:  Spanish
              Sex:  Male
Time at Institute:  2 terms
   Term 1, Quiz 1:  29
   Term 1, Quiz 2:  32
   Term 1, Quiz 3:  44
Term 1, Final Exam:  101
   Term 2, Quiz 1:  20
   Term 2, Quiz 2:  29
   Term 2, Quiz 3:  37
Term 2, Final Exam:  99
   Term 3, Quiz 1:  .
   Term 3, Quiz 2:  .
   Term 3, Quiz 3:  .
Term 3, Final Exam:  .
```

If you then want to know the average score on the Term 3 Final Exam across all students, it is a simple process to ask your analysis software to ignore students for whom that variable is missing. In pseudocode:

> If the value on Term 3, Final Exam, equals a dot (the missing value indicator), then do not include that student in further analyses.

In fact, many software packages will do that for you; that is, if a person's value on a numeric variable is the missing value indicator, then that person is automatically dropped from arithmetic (e.g., the computation of averages).

Furthermore, if all four Term 3 variables are missing, you could compute a variable called TERM3 that would give you a count of the number of people in the database who have been in the system for three terms. The pseudocode for that would look like this:

> If Term 3, Quiz 1; and Term 3, Quiz 2; and Term 3, Quiz 3; and Term 3, Final Exam all equal a dot, then TERM3=' no'. Otherwise, TERM3='yes'.

If a person took at least one of the four Term 3 tests, we can assume that person was present during Term 3. Notice also one minor detail on this computed variable: the leading space on the value ` no' for TERM3. That automatically sets the computer field width to three to accommodate 'yes' as well as ` no'. In software such as SAS and SPSS, it is important to control the width of character variables with tricks like leading spaces (` no' instead of 'no').

Once all this has been done, later you could request a count of the values on the new computed variable, TERM3, and notice the number of people for whom its value is 'yes'. That number would indicate the number of people who have been in at least three terms of instruction.

3.3.5. DATA RELATIONS

The new variable introduced above, TERM3, is a computed variable that can be quite handy. Perhaps you want to know the average score on the three final exams only for those people who have been through the system for three terms. You would then want to analyze the data only for those people. This procedure is called *subsetting* and is one member of a family of data manipulation practices I call *data relations.* I use this term loosely because this family of data-handling practices also includes the construction of a hierarchical relational database, as described in Chapter 2. We explore data relations in this section of the chapter.

3.3.5.1. Subsetting

One way to grasp data relations is to conceive of a data set as a simple rectangle. Below is an expanded version of the flat file from Chapter 2. You may want to review Chapter 2 a bit to study the data definition (codebook).

```
01   JUAN   Mexico  Spanish M 2 29 32 44 101 20 29 37 99  .  .   .    .
01   ANNA   Italy   Italian  F 1 34 28 35  90  .  .  .  .  .   .    .
01  AHMED   Egypt   Arabic   M 3 23 23 39  97 28 29 36 99 18 21 40 103
:
:
02  JOSE   Mexico  Spanish M 3 39 32 42 102 19 29 30 90 14 15 22  88
02  MARIA  Italy   Italian F 1 45 21 35  88  .  .  .  .  .   .    .
02  DAVID  German  German  M 3 23 23 39  97 12 13 50 98 17 27 41 100
:
:
03
03 (etc. for other institutes and students)
03
```

Remember that the 01, 02, and so on in columns 1 and 2 represent the particular language institute branch these students attend. These variables could represent any variable in a data set that may eventually be used to divide the data into parts.

The data set above can be displayed graphically as a rectangle, like this:

```
(original data set)
┌──────────────────────────────────────────────────────┐
│  01   JUAN Mexico  Spanish M ................       │
│  01   ANNA Italy   Italian F ................       │
│  01 AHMED  Egypt   Arabic  M ................       │
│  :                                                  │
│  :                                                  │
│  02   JOSE Mexico  Spanish M ................       │
│  02 MARIA  Italy   Italian F ................       │
│  02 DAVID  German  German  M ................       │
│  :                                                  │
│  :                                                  │
│  03 ...............................................  │
│  03 (etc. for other institutes and students)        │
│  03 ...............................................  │
└──────────────────────────────────────────────────────┘
```

Generally, we have a data set organized as follows:

(original data set)

Branch 01
Branch 02
Branch 03

One possible operation to perform on this data set is to divide it into three subsets of data—that is, three separate data files. This process is called *subsetting*, the action of dividing data into smaller data sets. If we subsetted this data set into the three branches, we would then have three separate data sets.

(first subset)

Branch 01

(second subset)

Branch 02

(third subset)

Branch 03

When might we do this? Perhaps we want to save a copy of the Branch 03 data to return to that branch office. Perhaps we want to separate the data out only temporarily to run separate statistics on each subset.

Occasionally, it is necessary to subset data without using a subsetting variable. In the example above, BRANCH is the subsetting variable. We have broken the data into its constituent branch subsets. Sometimes one simply needs to use shorter data sets without breaking down the data set along logical lines (like the value of BRANCH). This situation occurs frequently when a data set is too large for some computer storage or transmission method, such as a floppy diskette or electronic mail. To do this, you could call up the large data set in your data entry software, or if it is a flat file from a word processor, you could block off a chunk and copy the chunk to an external file. You could then move to the next chunk and repeat the process until the entire data set had been divided into chunks and copied.

That would be an inelegant but workable solution—a kludge— and an excellent application of Principle 3.3. But there is a simpler way, and perhaps, in this instance, a kludge is just too awkward; what if you accidentally missed a line of data in the chunk-and-copy operation? Many data-handling software packages have *system variables*, reserved variable names that mean special things to that software. One might be CASE or RECORD (in SAS, it is OBS or _N_), a variable that is set to 1 for the first record, 2 for the second record, 3 for the third, and so on. The software writes in a value for RECORD and puts this in a seemingly hidden variable in your data set without your asking for it. You can usually take advantage of a system variable just as if you had created that variable yourself. You could then execute a set of software commands such as the following pseudocode:

```
For the whole data set:
    —Write to the first output file all cases for
    which 1<=RECORD<=300 (the variable RECORD is
    between 1 and 300, inclusive).
    —Write to the first output file all cases for
    which 301<=RECORD<=600.
    —Write to the first output file all cases for
    which 601<=RECORD<=900.
    :

    :

    (etc. Note: '<=' means 'less than or equal to,'
    hence 601<=RECORD<=900 means 'if the value of
    RECORD is between 601 and 900 inclusive.')
```

Other system variables in your software might include a designation of whether or not the data set is indexed or sorted and, if so, whether or not a given record is the last instance of a sort variable (e.g., if a certain student is the last case in the BRANCH=02 subset above).

3.3.5.2. Catenation
(Sometimes Called "Concatenation")

Catenation is the opposite of subsetting. Graphically, when one catenates data sets, one goes from this situation (three separate data files):

```
┌─────────────────────────────────────────┐
¦              Branch 01                   ¦
└─────────────────────────────────────────┘

┌─────────────────────────────────────────┐
¦              Branch 02                   ¦
└─────────────────────────────────────────┘

┌─────────────────────────────────────────┐
¦              Branch 03                   ¦
└─────────────────────────────────────────┘
```

to this situation (one single file):

```
┌─────────────────────────────────────────┐
¦              Branch 01                   ¦
├─────────────────────────────────────────┤
¦              Branch 02                   ¦
├─────────────────────────────────────────┤
¦              Branch 03                   ¦
└─────────────────────────────────────────┘
```

Catenation does not reorder the cases. It assumes that you want merely to take three smaller data sets and join them together into a single larger data set. Each subset is joined immediately after the preceding subset, and the order of records within each subset is retained.

3.3.5.3. Merging

Another common need when combining data subsets is to merge them. Assume that part of our data was entered at one time and the rest entered much later, by another person, using another computer file.

(Keypuncher 1 at Time 1 entered:)

```
              C
              O           T
              U           I
    N         N           M   T   T   T   T   T   T   T
    A         T       S   E   1   1   1   1   2   2   2
    M         R     L E   I   Q   Q   Q   F   Q   Q   Q
    E         Y     1 X   N   1   2   3   E   1   2   3
[LOG]    1        1       2       2       3       3       4       4
----5----0----5----0----5----0----5----0----5-

JUAN  Mexico Spanish 20 29 37  99  .   .    .    .
ANNA  Italy  Italian  .  .  .   .  .   .    .    .
AHMED Egypt  Arabic  28 29 36  99 18  21   40  103
```

(Keypuncher 2 at Time 2 entered:)

```
          T
          I
    N     M   T   T   T   T
    A S   E   3   3   3   3
    M E   I   Q   Q   Q   F
    E X   N   1   2   3   E
[LOG]    1       1       2
----5----0----5----0--

JUAN  M 2 29 32 44 101
ANNA  F 1 34 28 35  90
AHMED M 3 23 23 39  97
```

That is, the first keypuncher entered part of the data about the records, and the second keypuncher, at a later time, entered the rest. Notice the shared field between the two data sets: NAME. If the second keypuncher entered simply

```
2 29 32 44 101
1 34 28 35  90
3 23 23 39  97
```

we would have a risk. What if the data were accidentally reordered and we did not know that line 1 belonged to Juan, line 2 to Anna, and so on? It is important, therefore, to have a matching variable— one that appears on both data sets. Many software packages will require you to sort each data subset on that matching variable before merging.

Graphically, the situation is as follows. Before merging, you have two smaller data subsets arranged as follows:

```
┌─────────────────────────────────────────────────┐
¦ Matching Var.                        Subset 1   ¦
└─────────────────────────────────────────────────┘
```

```
┌─────────────────────────────────────────────────┐
¦ Matching Var.                        Subset 2   ¦
└─────────────────────────────────────────────────┘
```

After merging, you have one large data set that is arranged:

```
┌─────────────────────────────────────────────────┐
¦ Matching Var.                                    ¦
└─────────────────────────────────────────────────┘
```

Which actually represents:

```
┌─────────────────────────────────────────────────┐
¦                  (Formerly)    (Formerly)        ¦
¦ Matching Var.     Subset 1      Subset 2         ¦
└─────────────────────────────────────────────────┘
```

Notice that the matching variable is not duplicated on the large data set.

3.3.5.4. Hierarchical Relations:
A Special Case of Merging

In Chapter 2, we explored the nature of a hierarchical relational data set, or database. *Hierarchical relations* are really just a special case of merged relations, and I now illustrate a hierarchy as a merge.

Consider the data set from Chapter 2 displayed as rectangles. First, we have the student information. It is important to realize that these next boxes are conceptual and represent more than three students per branch.

```
r---------------------------------------┐
¦                Branch 01              ¦
├---------------------------------------┤
¦                Branch 02              ¦
├---------------------------------------┤
¦                Branch 03              ¦
L---------------------------------------┘
```

Next, we have information about each branch. Conceptually, we have one line of information for each branch (see Chapter 2):

```
01 CHICAGO 40 24 ENGLISH ASSOCIATES INCORPORATED: CHICAGO BRANCH
02   DALLAS 20 32 ENGLISH ASSOCIATES INCORPORATED: DALLAS BRANCH
03 MEMPHIS 22 30 ENGLISH ASSOCIATES INCORPORATED: MEMPHIS BRANCH
```

In reality, each student's record also possesses the information about the branch the student attends. That is the basic nature of a hierarchical relational database; each lower level of the database contains the information of the higher, more global levels. Conceptually, then, our student records now look like this:

```
r-------------------┐ CHICAGO 40 24 ENGL . . .
¦     Branch 01     ¦ CHICAGO 40 24 ENGL . . .
L-------------------┘ CHICAGO 40 24 ENGL . . .

r-------------------┐ DALLAS 20 32 ENGL . . .
¦     Branch 02     ¦ DALLAS 20 32 ENGL . . .
L-------------------┘ DALLAS 20 32 ENGL . . .

r-------------------┐ MEMPHIS 22 30 ENGL . . .
¦     Branch 03     ¦ MEMPHIS 22 30 ENGL . . .
L-------------------┘ MEMPHIS 22 30 ENGL . . .
```

Put more simply, we have merged and duplicated single-branch records with student records. This seems to be a waste of computer resources—and it is. Why waste all those columns of computer storage at the right of each record by copying all that information on each record's line? This motivates the second-to-last principle of this chapter:

Principle 3.5: The Complex Data Structure Principle

If your software can accommodate complex data structures (e.g., hierarchical relational databases), then you might benefit from using that software feature. Alternatively, you might prefer a kludge (e.g., copying the same information onto each record).

Principle 3.3 may seem to conflict with Principle 3.5. What if your software does indeed support relational databases, such that you could have three student data sets: Branch 01, Branch 02, and Branch 03, and only one Branch data set. If, while examining a student record, you wanted information about that student's branch, the software would know which record to access over in the Branch data set. That is much more efficient. But it may be more complex to learn and to implement. It would be easier to produce a kludge data set and live by Principle 3.3: Simply copy the branch information onto each data line. The choice is yours, and clearly you will have to consider the storage available in your computer as you make the decision, weighing that against any complexity in using your software's existing relational database capabilities.

The following pseudocode shows how to execute my kludge and produce the computed BRANCH variables for each record; you might enjoy implementing it in either SAS or SPSS:

```
For each record in the database, do:
    if BRANCH=01, then do these four commands:
        LOCATION=CHICAGO
        YEARS=40
        NUMTCHRS=24
            NAME=ENGLISH ASSOCIATES INCORPORATED:
            CHICAGO BRANCH
```

```
    else if BRANCH=02, then do these four commands:
        LOCATION=DALLAS
            YEARS=20 32
        NUMTCHRS=32
                NAME=ENGLISH ASSOCIATES INCORPORATED:
                    DALLAS BRANCH
    else if BRANCH=03 . . .
    :
    :
    (etc.)
```

3.3.5.5. Data Relations: A Summary

This segment of Chapter 3 has covered *data relations*, which I loosely defined as the possible global relations that any two or more data sets can take:

Four types of data relations:

For two or more data sets:
1. They can be derived from a larger data set (subsetted).
2. They can be joined together on an adjacent basis to form a larger data set (catenation).
3. They can be joined together on a case-by-case basis to form a larger data set (merging).
4. They can be joined together in a hierarchy (relational database construction—a special case of merging).

Generally, I contend that the above four possibilities form a fairly complete overview of what you might want to do to data sets as a whole. These four relations are at the level of principle, which is the stated goal of this book, but they are more on the order of definitions and not guidelines, as all other principles thus far have been. What principled guideline do these four relations imply? With respect to data relations, I submit that the most important thing is for you to know how your software does these four operations.

Principle 3.6:
The Software's Data Relations Principle

Know whether your software can perform the following four relations and, if so, what commands are necessary to do so: subsetting, catenation, merging, and relational database construction.

It is interesting that two of the principles in this chapter focus on your software: how it handles missing values (Principle 3.4) and how it performs data relations (Principle 3.6). There is a moral in that: If the software does not do what you want, and if you cannot write a kludge (Principle 3.3) to make it do what you want, perhaps it is time to switch to a different software package.

3.4. SORTING

Before closing this chapter and illustrating the principles I have discussed here, I present one more important form of data manipulation: sorting. Often, you have data keyed in by some more-or-less random order (e.g., the happenstance nature of the stack of hard copy). Once it is keyed in and debugged, you want to print it out to check it or possibly produce a report. But perhaps you want to sort the data so that the resulting printout is easier to read. In our ongoing sample data set introduced in Chapter 2, our data look like this:

```
          C
          O          T
          U          I
    N     N          M  T  T  T    T  T  T  T    T  T  T  T    T
    A     T        S E  1  1  1    1  2  2  2    2  3  3  3    3
    M     R      L E I  Q  Q  Q    F  Q  Q  Q    F  Q  Q  Q    F
    E     Y      1 X N  1  2  3    E  1  2  3    E  1  2  3    E
JUAN  Mexico Spanish M 2 29 32 44 101 20 29 37  99  .  .  .    .
ANNA  Italy  Italian F 1 34 28 35  90  .  .  .   .  .  .  .    .
AHMED Egypt  Arabic  M 3 23 23 39  97 28 29 36  99 18 21 40  103
```

Let's suppose other persons from each country took our tests. We might then have:

```
JUAN  Mexico Spanish M 3 40 39 47 110 31 31 42 103  .   .   .   .
MARIA Mexico Spanish F 2 29 32 44 101 20 29 37  99  .   .   .   .
ANNA  Italy  Italian F 1 34 28 35  90  .   .   .   .   .   .   .
OMAR  Egypt  Arabic  M 1 23 24 31  90  .   .   .   .   .   .   .
AHMED Egypt  Arabic  M 3 23 23 39  97 28 29 36  99 18 21 40 103
```

If this data set were very long, it might be difficult to read. Far easier would be to sort it somehow. Perhaps we might sort on the T1FE variable (Term 1, Final Exam), which would yield:

```
                        T1FE----->| | |
ANNA  Italy  Italian F 1 34 28 35  90  .   .   .   .   .   .   .
OMAR  Egypt  Arabic  M 1 23 24 31  90  .   .   .   .   .   .   .
AHMED Egypt  Arabic  M 3 23 23 39  97 28 29 36  99 18 21 40 103
MARIA Mexico Spanish F 2 29 32 44 101 20 29 37  99  .   .   .   .
JUAN  Mexico Spanish M 3 40 39 47 110 31 31 42 103  .   .   .   .
```

We have two persons with the same value on T1FE, and most software will produce the sorted data set in the order the data appears in the input: Anna before Omar.

Alternatively, we might want to do a "nested," or "double," sort. We might want to group the students by name within country. This would yield:

```
| | | | |<----NAME within...
    | | | | | |<-----COUNTRY
AHMED Egypt  Arabic  M 3 23 23 39  97 28 29 36  99 18 21 40 103
OMAR  Egypt  Arabic  M 1 23 24 31  90  .   .   .   .   .   .   .
ANNA  Italy  Italian F 1 34 28 35  90  .   .   .   .   .   .   .
JUAN  Mexico Spanish M 3 40 39 47 110 31 31 42 103  .   .   .   .
MARIA Mexico Spanish F 2 29 32 44 101 20 29 37  99  .   .   .   .
```

All the above sorts are ascending, from lowest value to highest. In the case of the T1FE sort, this *ascending sort* is simply numeric. In the case of the NAME within COUNTRY sort, it follows the alphabet.

It is also possible that you would want a *descending sort*. For example, you might want a descending sort on T1FE, which would look like the following (compare it with the sort above):

```
                    T1FE----->|||
JUAN  Mexico  Spanish M 3 40 39 47 110 31 31 42 103   .   .   .   .
MARIA Mexico  Spanish F 2 29 32 44 101 20 29 37  99   .   .   .   .
AHMED Egypt   Arabic  M 3 23 23 39  97 28 29 36  99 18 21 40 103
ANNA  Italy   Italian F 1 34 28 35  90   .   .   .   .   .   .   .
OMAR  Egypt   Arabic  M 1 23 24 31  90   .   .   .   .   .   .   .
```

All this seems like common sense, and it is. Sorting, at its most basic level, is nothing more than reorganization of the data along some ordered system. It is important to recall Principle 3.2 and be sure to save a copy of your original unsorted data. This is important in case you ever have to trace a bug back to a stack of hard copy in which the order of the hard copy might match the order of the original unsorted data. But beyond that, are there any benefits to sorting? Perhaps one, and it has to do with what I call *BY-groups*.

BY-group is actually a SAS term. Such groups are also known as *breaks* or *subsets* in other software (SPSS uses *break*). Essentially, a BY-group is a subset of data based on common values of some variable. Juan and Maria form a BY-group because the value on the variable COUNTRY is MEXICO for both of them. The same is true for Ahmed and Omar; they are both from Egypt. Anna and Omar, however, also form another BY-group on the variable T1FE because they both scored 90. In SAS, it is necessary to sort on BY-groups before you analyze on BY-groups. For example, if you wanted a set of average T1FE values for the Egyptian students separate from the Mexican students, you would have to sort on COUNTRY first. Furthermore, SAS requires that data be sorted into BY-groups before merging, as I illustrate in the implementation program below. So, I suggest the following principle for sorting:

Principle 3.7: The Software's Sorting Principle

Know how to perform a sort in your software and whether your software requires a sort before a BY-group analysis or before merging.

One interesting problem arises with BY-groups that is a good illustration of Principle 3.7. What happens if you merge two data sets using the match-merge variable and one data set contains BY-groups that the other does not? Suppose you merge data from two schools along grade level. School A has kindergarten through sixth grade, and School B has kindergarten through eighth. The merged data should contain all the data, and there will be no cases from School A in seventh or eighth grade. But cases for kindergarten through sixth will include data from both schools. There are related analogous problems; for example, what happens when one data set has cases with missing values on BY-group variables (or match-merge variables, for that matter)? The spirit of Principles 3.6 and 3.7 apply in all cases: I advise you to try out your software's sorting and merging capabilities and find out what happens. Part of data handling is an experiment: learning your software.

3.5. IMPLEMENTATION

In this segment of Chapter 3, I present some SAS and SPSS code to demonstrate implementation of some of the principles and issues discussed here. Review the "Implementation" section of Chapter 2 before studying these examples so that you can refresh yourself on RBC data input in SAS and SPSS.

The implementations below follow the order of topics in this chapter. First, I illustrate reading some data and producing computed variables in SAS and SPSS. Assume we have the same data set as in Chapter 2, from which I delete the NAME variable because it is not really relevant to this illustration. In deleting the NAME variable, I have also made the data set more abstract so that you can relate it to your setting (imagine variables in your context that might have values such as those used below).

In SAS, we could read in the data and compute the average and sum of the three scores, x1, x2, and x3, as follows:

```
*---------------------------------------------------------------*
    Name of input program: ch3.sas (SAS)
                Function: demonstrate various data
                         manipulations:
                             -computed variables
                             -recoding
                             -manipulation of missing data
                             -data relations:
                             -catenation
                             -merging
                             -subsetting
                             -sorting
    Name of input ASCII data set(s): internal to program
  Name of output PC-SAS data set(s): none
                Program written by: Fred Davidson
*---------------------------------------------------------------*;

title1 'Chapter 3 Demo. Program SAS';

*-----------Demonstrate Computed Variables (SAS)------------;
data compute;
    input x1 x2 x3;
    xavg=(x1+x2+x3)/3;
    xsum=x1+x2+x3;
cards;
3 4 4
1 4 5
2 3 4
1 1 4
3 5 1
3 3 3
1 3 4
1 3 4
;
run;
proc print data=compute;
    title2 'Illustrate data set with computed variables added';
run;
```

The code above is quite similar to that in Chapter 2, except for a few important additions. First, the lines xavg= . . . and xsum= . . . produce two computed variables. The /3 denominator works only if all students took all three tests: Remember that it is important to keep track of your missing data. If that is not the case, then the computed variables (xsum and xavg) will be automatically designated as missing in SAS.

In addition, there are two titles and an extensive comment box. In SAS, anything beginning with an asterisk is ignored until the next command terminator—the semicolon—so the entire box above is a remark. I use commenting extensively in my programming to aid in readability and control (Principle 2.1). The comment box refers to all of the implementation in this chapter; if you like, you can copy all the SAS or SPSS codes given here into single programs.

The results of the above SAS code would look like this:

Chapter 3 Demo. Program SAS
Illustrate dataset with computed variables added

OBS	X1	X2	X3	XAVG	XSUM
1	3	4	4	3.66667	11
2	1	4	5	3.33333	10
3	2	3	4	3.00000	9
4	1	1	4	2.00000	6
5	3	5	1	3.00000	9
6	3	3	3	3.00000	9
7	1	3	4	2.66667	8
8	1	3	4	2.66667	8

Compare the input code to the output, noticing in particular the use of two titles and the level of precision of XAVG.

In SPSS, the above functions could be accomplished with similar input code. My SPSS sample also includes similar titling and commenting:

```
*-------------------------------------------------------------*
|      Name of input program: ch3.sps (SPSS)                  |
|                  Function: demonstrate various data         |
|                            manipulations:                   |
|                            -computed variables              |
|                            -recoding                        |
|                            -manipulation of missing data    |
|                            -data relations:                 |
|                            -catenation                      |
|                            -merging                         |
|                            -subsetting                      |
|                            -sorting                         |
|    Name of input ASCII data set(s): internal to program     |
| Name of output SPSS-PC data set(s): none                    |
|                  Program written by: Fred Davidson          |
|                                                             |
| title 'Chapter 3 Demo. Program SPSS'.                       |
*-------------------------------------------------------------*.

*----------Demonstrate Computed Variables (SPSS)-----------.
data list list
   / x1 x2 x3.
begin data
3 4 4
1 4 5
2 3 4
1 1 4
3 5 1
3 3 3
1 3 4
1 3 4
end data.
   compute xavg=(x1+x2+x3)/3.
   compute xsum=x1+x2+x3.
   save outfile=compute.
execute.

get file=compute.
   subtitle 'Illustrate data set with computed variables added'.
   list.
execute.
```

There are two differences regarding computed variables. First, SAS computes a variable by direct arithmetic, for example:

```
xsum=x1+x2+x3;
```

whereas SPSS requires a command word before an algebraic formula, for example:

```
compute xsum=x1+x2+x3.
```

Second, the computation formulas precede the input data in SAS, whereas they follow the data in SPSS.

The results of the above SPSS code would look similar to those below. Notice that the title and subtitle are printed both before and after the result of the list command. (I have never been able to discern the rules by which SPSS locates its titles on output; sometimes they appear before, sometimes after, and sometimes as here: in both locations. Most frequently, it is after the particular results to which the titles directly apply, as is the case for the balance of the SPSS results in this chapter.)

Chapter 3 Demo. Program SPSS
Illustrate data set with computed variables added

X1	X2	X3	XAVG	XSUM
3.00	4.00	4.00	3.67	11.00
1.00	4.00	5.00	3.33	10.00
2.00	3.00	4.00	3.00	9.00
1.00	1.00	4.00	2.00	6.00
3.00	5.00	1.00	3.00	9.00
3.00	3.00	3.00	3.00	9.00
1.00	3.00	4.00	2.67	8.00
1.00	3.00	4.00	2.67	8.00

Number of cases read: 8   Number of cases listed: 8

Chapter 3 Demo. Program SPSS
Illustrate data set with computed variables added

Another common manipulation is recoding. Suppose we have a data set with the following information:

```
VIKTOR GERMAN GERMAN
 MARIA ITALY  ITALIA
  JOSE SPAIN  SPANIS
```

for which the codebook would be:

VARIABLE	TYPE	DESCRIPTION	COLUMNS
NAME	Character	Student Name	1-6
COUNTRY	Character	Home Country	8-13
NL	Character	Native Language	15-20

You can see the problem: The field to hold L1 is not wide enough, so that ITALIAN and SPANISH (the names of the languages) are truncated. Recoding is needed to fix this problem. And as above, I illustrate the fix without using the NAME variable; it is really not relevant to the topic.

The code to read in the data and repair the problem in SAS could be:

```
*-----------Demonstrate Recoding (SAS)-----------;
data recode1;
   input country $ language $;
cards;
GERMAN GERMAN
 ITALY ITALIA
 SPAIN SPANIS
run;

proc print data=recode1;
   title2 'Illustrate problematic country and language values';
run;

data recode2;
   * Make data set recode2 an exact duplicate of recode1;
   set recode1;
   length nc2 nl2 $ 10;
   nc2=country;
   nl2=language;
   drop country language;
run;
```

```
data recode3;
   set recode2;
   country=nc2;
   language=nl2;
   drop nc2 nl2;
   if country='GERMAN' then country='GERMANY';
   if language='ITALIA' then language='ITALIAN';
   if language='SPANIS' then language='SPANISH';
run;

proc print data=recode3;
   title2 'Illustrate repaired country and language values';
run;
```

The SAS code above is a good opportunity to introduce two bits of SAS jargon: the data step and the proc[edure] step. SAS is a *procedural language,* meaning that commands, subcommands, and command options (words that can change within a command or subcommand) are all arranged within program blocks. A block of commands that reads in data is called a *data step;* a group of commands that does statistics is called a *proc step.* Three data steps and two proc steps are included in the example above. Procedural languages are quite common in computing. They represent Principle 2.1 in action at the level of computer command syntax because the programmer can organize procedures into program blocks. Program blocks are like the "paragraphs" of a computer program.

SPSS does not use terminology like *data step* or *proc step,* but it is possible to program SPSS in a procedural grouped manner, and I prefer to do so. That is not a requirement of the SPSS language, and indeed, you can be much looser in your SPSS programming. Bear in mind that the SAS and SPSS examples shown in this book are my stylistic preferences and that as you work with either language, you will develop your own preferences; I return to that topic in Chapter 6.

Let's now examine the example above a bit more closely. First, the original (wrong) data are read in and named recode1. A printout is requested, and then another data step follows. The set subcommand copies the data set recode1 and renames it recode2. The length command defines two new variables, NC2 and NL2, which are of type character ($) and defined to a width of 10; you would need a number as wide as the widest value in your data set, and by choosing 10, I am assuming that EAI can distinguish the native languages and home countries of its students with 10 or fewer characters. NC2 and NL2 are computed variables assigned the values of the original COUNTRY and NL variables. The original COUNTRY and NL variables are then removed from the data set (the drop command). In the final data step, a third copy of the data set is created and called recode3, in which the COUNTRY and NL variables are re-created and assigned the values of NC2 and NL2. A series of if statements then recodes COUNTRY and LANGUAGE to the appropriate values; clearly, we have examined the data and become aware of the precise incorrect values to be able to do this. If all of this seems rather roundabout, it is. But it works, and that is an illustration of Principle 3.3. My solution to this particular recoding need is something of an inelegant solution—a kludge. (And notice that I did not, of course, delete the original unaltered data—as I recommend in Principle 3.2.)

The output for the above SAS code would look like this:

Chapter 3 Demo. Program SAS
Illustrate problematic country and language values

OBS	COUNTRY	LANGUAGE
1	GERMAN	GERMAN
2	ITALY	ITALIA
3	SPAIN	SPANIS

Chapter 3 Demo. Program SAS
Illustrate repaired country and language values

OBS	COUNTRY	LANGUAGE
1	GERMANY	GERMAN
2	ITALY	ITALIAN
3	SPAIN	SPANISH

The recoding in SPSS is quite similar, although it takes a bit more code to make it work:

```
*-----------Demonstrate Recoding (SPSS)-----------.
data list list
   / country (a6) language (a6).
begin data
GERMAN GERMAN
 ITALY ITALIA
 SPAIN SPANIS
end data.
save outfile=recode1.
execute.

get file=recode1.
   subtitle 'Illustrate problematic country and language
            values'.
   list.
execute.

get file=recode1.
   save outfile=recode2.
execute.

get file=recode2.
   string nc2 (a10) / nl2 (a10).
   compute nc2=country.
   compute nl2=language.
   if country='GERMAN' /*then*/ nc2='GERMANY'.
   if language='ITALIA' nl2='ITALIAN'.
   if language='SPANIS' nl2='SPANISH'.
   save outfile=recode2.
execute.

get file=recode2 / drop=country language.
   save outfile=recode2.
execute.

get file=recode2.
   string country (a10) / language (a10).
   compute country=nc2.
   compute language=nl2.
   save outfile=recode3.
execute.
```

```
get file=recode3 / drop nc2 nl2.
    subtitle 'Illustrate repaired country and language
             values'.
    list.
execute.
```

The SPSS code is longer because, to copy a data set, you must first get it and then resave it under the new name. Other differences also exist. For example, the if statements require the word then in SAS, but then is not required in SPSS. Consider the line in SPSS, above:

```
if country='GERMAN' /*then*/ nc2='GERMANY'.
```

/*then*/ is an alternate comment format for SPSS, permitting an ignored remark within a command. It lets me show you where then would appear if SPSS required it. You can thus compare the syntax with its SAS counterpart:

```
if country='GERMAN' then country='GERMANY';
```

Interestingly, the order of commands differs somewhat. In SPSS, I set the length of the new variable with the string command, as I did with length in SAS. I then copied the old values into the new variable (e.g., NC2 had the value ITALIA). I then applied an SPSS if statement to recode the new variable, and in the next copy of the data set (after dropping the old variables), I re-created the original variables. This is somewhat the reverse of SAS, in which it seemed to work better to apply the if statements to the new variables NL2 and NC2. I have found many such peculiarities in creating data-handling programs in SAS and SPSS.

Following are the SPSS results for the above code:

```
COUNTRY  LANGUAGE

GERMAN   GERMAN
ITALY    ITALIA
SPAIN    SPANIS
```

Number of cases read: 3   Number of cases listed: 3

Chapter 3 Demo. Program SPSS
Illustrate problematic country and language values

```
COUNTRY  LANGUAGE

GERMANY  GERMAN
ITALY    ITALIAN
SPAIN    SPANISH
```

Number of cases read: 3   Number of cases listed: 3

Chapter 3 Demo. Program SPSS
Illustrate repaired country and language values

Next, let's look at the handling of missing data. Suppose we have a data set similar to the exam data we have seen in the chapter (suppose EAI is branching out into foreign language teaching within the United States; this explains the Anglo-sounding names):

```
N    T    T    T    T    T    T    T    T    T    T    T    T
A    1    1    1    1    2    2    2    2    3    3    3    3
M    Q    Q    Q    F    Q    Q    Q    F    Q    Q    Q    F
E    1    2    3    E    1    2    3    E    1    2    3    E

[LOG]     1    1    2    2    3    3    4    4    5    5
----5----0----5----0----5----0----5----0----5----0----5

BILL    20   23   21   89    .    .    .    .    .    .    .    .
DEBI    19    .   29   88   34   34   40   90   20   22   22   77
TERI    20   22   24   91   30   29   34   80    .    .    .    .
DOUG    29   30   30   99    .    .    .    .   30   25   25   88
GILL     .    .    .    .    .    .    .    .    .    .    .    .
```

This data set was keyed in with the assumption that it would be analyzed in SAS, so the keypuncher used the SAS default missing value indicator—a dot—to indicate a missing value; perhaps the keypuncher was applying Principle 3.4. This is fortunate because we can read the data in with freefield input; that is, we do not have to specify start-stop columns.

To illustrate some issues of missing data with the above data set in SAS, let's examine the following program:

```
*-------Demonstrate Handling of Missing Values (SAS)-------;
data miss1;
   input name $ t1q1 t1q2 t1q3 t1fe t2q1 t2q2 t2q3 t2fe
                t3q1 t3q2 t3q3 t3fe;
cards;
BILL 20   23   21   89   .    .    .    .    .    .    .    .
DEBI 19   .    29   88   34   34   40   90   20   22   22   77
TERI 20   22   24   91   30   29   34   80   .    .    .    .
DOUG 29   30   30   99   .    .    .    .    30   25   25   88
GILL .    .    .    .    .    .    .    .    .    .    .    .
;
run;

proc print data=miss1;
   title2 'Original data for missing value demonstration';
run;

data miss2;
   set miss1;
   * initialization of the three TERM variables;
   TERM1='???';
   TERM2='???';
   TERM3='???';
   if (t1q1=. and t1q2=. and t1q3=. and t1fe=.) then do;
      TERM1=' NO';
      TERM2=' NO';
      TERM3=' NO';
   end;
   else if (t2q1=. and t2q2=. and t2q3=. and t2fe=.) then do;
      TERM1='YES';
      TERM2=' NO';
      TERM3=' NO';
   end;
   else if (t3q1=. and t3q2=. and t3q3=. and t3fe=.) then do;
      TERM1='YES';
      TERM2='YES';
      TERM3=' NO';
   end;
   else do;
      TERM1='YES';
      TERM2='YES';
   end;
```

```
* Do you see the error? What if TERM refers to proficiency
  level and not sequential term attended—i.e., what if
  DOUG skipped over TERM2 and went from TERM1 to TERM3?
  What would happen to his data? Let's see . . .;
run;

proc print data=miss2;
   title2 'Illustrate data after handling of missing values';
   title3 'Note problem with DOUG';
run;

* Turn off the third title;
title3;
proc freq data=miss2;
   tables term1 term2 term3;
   title2 'Frequency tables for the variables TERM1, TERM2,
          and TERM3';
run;
```

Before I discuss the particular missing value problem here, notice
the initialization of the TERM variables to '???'. *Initialization* is creation of a computed variable with some default value that
is under your control: Principle 2.1 again. If all goes well, that
default value should never appear in the results of the program; in
a sense, this is a form of debugging, the topic of the next chapter.

In this case, the problem here is with Doug. In the input data,
it is clear that he took the tests for Term 1 and Term 3, but not
Term 2, presumably because he took some sort of proficiency exam
and was permitted to skip over that instructional level. Suppose
we want to know which terms a student has attended and to store
that information in the variables TERM1, TERM2, and TERM3.
Unless we figure out what is going on with Doug, we might (for
example) erroneously assume he attended for three full terms.
Hence, all the complex if statement code. The purpose of those
commands is to compute the correct values for three new variables
called TERM1, TERM2, and TERM3, which contain 'YES' if the
student attended that term or ' NO' (notice the leading space)
otherwise. Work through the if statements logically, and you will
see the potential problem I note in my comment above.

The SAS output clarifies whether that problem is real or not, and indeed it is quite real as the TERM values for Doug illustrate. He did attend Term 3, but his TERM3 value is ` NO`. And what's more, because ` NO` appears rather than `????`, we know that the various if-then code is working, but that it is working incorrectly:

Chapter 3 Demo. Program SAS

Original data for missing value demonstration

OBS	NAME	T1Q1	T1Q2	T1Q3	T1FE	T2Q1	T2Q2	T2Q3	T2FE	T3Q1	T3Q2	T3Q3	T3FE
1	BILL	20	23	21	89	.	.	.	.	.	.	.	.
2	DEBI	19	.	29	88	34	34	40	90	20	22	22	77
3	TERI	20	22	24	91	30	29	34	80	.	.	.	.
4	DOUG	29	30	30	99	.	.	.	.	30	25	25	88
5	GILL	.	.	.	.	.	.	.	.	.	.	.	.

Chapter 3 Demo. Program SAS

Illustrate data after handling of missing values

Note problem with DOUG

	N A M E	T Q 1 1	T Q 1 2	T Q 1 3	T F 1 E	T Q 2 1	T Q 2 2	T Q 2 3	T F 2 E	T Q 3 1	T Q 3 2	T Q 3 3	T F 3 E	T E R M 1	T E R M 2	T E R M 3
O B S																
1	BILL	20	23	21	89	.	.	.	.	.	.	.	.	YES	NO	NO
2	DEBI	19	.	29	88	34	34	40	90	20	22	22	77	YES	YES	YES
3	TERI	20	22	24	91	30	29	34	80	.	.	.	.	YES	YES	NO
4	DOUG	29	30	30	99	.	.	.	.	30	25	25	88	YES	NO	NO
5	GILL	.	.	.	.	.	.	.	.	.	.	.	.	NO	NO	NO

I illustrate pseudocode method to solve the above problem after first showing you the analogous code in SPSS. Notice, in particular, that the input data contain spaces—not dots—to represent missing values, and therefore it was necessary to use start-stop columns when reading the data into SPSS and not specify list to indicate freefield data:

```
*---Demonstrate Handling of Missing Values (SPSS)---.
data list
    / name    1-4  (a)
      t1q1    8-9
      t1q2    12-13
      t1q3    16-17
      t1fe    20-21
      t2q1    24-25
      t2q2    28-29
      t2q3    32-33
      t2fe    36-37
      t3q1    40-41
      t3q2    44-45
      t3q3    48-49
      t3fe    52-53.
begin data
BILL    20  23  21  89
DEBI    19      29  88  34  34  40  90  20  22  22  77
TERI    20  22  24  91  30  29  34  80
DOUG    29  30  30  99                  30  25  25  88
GILL
end data.
    save outfile=miss1.
execute.

get file=miss1.
    subtitle 'Original data for missing value
             demonstration'.
    list.
execute.

get file=miss1.
    string term1 (a3) / term2 (a3) / term3 (a3).
    compute TERM1='???'.
    compute TERM2='???'.
    compute TERM3='???'.
    do if (sysmis(t1q1) and sysmis(t1q2) and sys mis(t1q3)
        and sysmis(t1fe)).
      compute TERM1=' NO'.
      compute TERM2=' NO'.
      compute TERM3=' NO'.
```

```
    else if (sysmis(t2q1) and sysmis(t2q2) and sysmis(t2q3)
          and sysmis(t2fe)).
  compute TERM1='YES'.
  compute TERM2=' NO'.
  compute TERM3=' NO'.
    else if (sysmis(t3q1) and sysmis(t3q2) and sysmis(t3q3)
          and sysmis(t3fe)).
  compute TERM1='YES'.
  compute TERM2='YES'.
  compute TERM3=' NO'.
    else.
  compute TERM1='YES'.
  compute TERM2='YES'.
  compute TERM3='YES'.
  end if.
  save outfile=miss2.
execute.
```

*Do you see the error? What if TERM refers to proficiency
level and not sequential term attended—i.e. what if
DOUG skipped over TERM2 and went from TERM1 to TERM3?
What would happen to his data? Let's see.

*Note: SPSS permits only one 'title' and one 'subtitle'
at a single time, and what is more, a title or subtitle
cannot have more than 60 characters. This means we
have to be creative to title what will happen next.

```
get file=miss2.
  subtitle 'Illustrate data after handl. miss. vals:
          Note prob. w/ DOUG'.
  list.
execute.

get file=miss2.
  subtitle 'Frequency tables for the variables
          TERM1, TERM2, and TERM3'.
  frequencies variables=term1 term2 term3.
execute.
```

The SPSS code above is again quite similar to SAS, with some minor differences. For example, checking for a missing value in SPSS involves the `sysmis` function, whereas in SAS you can check for it with an algebraic equation on the default missing value designator of a dot (if `term1=.`). Look through the SPSS example and see what other differences you can detect.

One minor problem concerns the length of SPSS titles. The limit is 60 characters, which is why I had to use the awkward abbreviations on the first `subtitle` above.

The SPSS code would produce output similar to that shown below; recall that SPSS often places its titles below the particular output to which the title applies:

```
NAME T1Q1 T1Q2 T1Q3 T1FE T2Q1 T2Q2 T2Q3 T2FE T3Q1 T3Q2 T3Q3 T3FE


BILL  20   23   21   89   .    .    .    .    .    .    .    .
DEBI  19   .    29   88   34   34   40   90   20   22   22   77
TERI  20   22   24   91   30   29   34   80   .    .    .    .
DOUG  29   30   30   99   .    .    .    .    30   25   25   88
GILL  .    .    .    .    .    .    .    .    .    .    .    .

Number of cases read: 5   Number of cases listed: 5

Chapter 3 Demo. Program SPSS
Original data for missing value demonstration
```

													TERM	TERM	TERM
NAME	T1Q1	T1Q2	T1Q3	T1FE	T2Q1	T2Q2	T2Q3	T2FE	T3Q1	T3Q2	T3Q3	T3FE	1	2	3
BILL	20	23	21	89	.	.	.	.	.	.	.	.	YES	NO	NO
DEBI	19	.	29	88	34	34	40	90	20	22	22	77	YES	YES	YES
TERI	20	22	24	91	30	29	34	80	.	.	.	.	YES	YES	NO
DOUG	29	30	30	99	.	.	.	.	30	25	25	88	YES	NO	NO
GILL	.	.	.	.	.	.	.	.	.	.	.	.	NO	NO	NO

```
Number of cases read: 5   Number of cases listed: 5

Chapter 3 Demo. Program SPSS
Illustrate data after handl. miss. vals: Note prob. w/ DOUG
```

Let's return to the problem with Doug, who attended Terms 1 and 3 but not Term 2. One solution would be to avoid the `else` command—for example, in pseudocode:

```
TERM1='YES'
TERM2='YES'
TERM3='YES'
if T1FE is missing, then TERM1=' NO'
if T2FE is missing, then TERM2=' NO'
if T3FE is missing, then TERM3=' NO'
```

This solution is less of a kludge than the complex code I present in the SAS and SPSS recoding examples above. That is rather common: In the first pass through a program, you might write something overly complex, create a dilemma, and solve it with something more elegant. We need not live by Principle 3.3 all the time. As I note in discussion question 8, I encourage you to implement the more elegant pseudocode in SAS or SPSS on your own.

Next, I illustrate some data relations. Before you study the next programming examples, review the descriptions of catenation, merging, subsetting, and sorting given here in Chapter 3.

Catenation in SAS is handled in a manner like that shown in the following example:

```
*------------Demonstrate Catenation (SAS)------------;
data c1;
    input a1 a2;
cards;
1 3
4 5
;
run;

data c2;
    input a1 a2;
cards;
2 4
6 7
;
run;

data catenate;
    set c1 c2;
run;
```

```
proc print data=catenate;
    title2 'Illustrate catenated data';
run;
```

The above SAS code uses the set statement, with which you are already familiar as a data copying operation. Here, it both copies data and catenates it: set c1 c2 appends data set C2 after data set c1 in the new data set named CATENATE.

The SAS output of the above code would be:

```
          Chapter 3 Demo. Program SAS
            Illustrate catenated data
              OBS    A1    A2
               1      1     3
               2      4     5
               3      2     4
               4      6     7
```

In SPSS, catenation code would be something like this:

```
*-----------Demonstrate Catenation (SPSS)-----------.
data list list
    / a1 a2.
begin data
1 3
4 5
end data.
    save outfile=c1.
execute.

data list list
    / a1 a2.
begin data
2 4
6 7
end data.
    save outfile=c2.
execute.

add files file=c1 / file=c2.
    save outfile=catenate.
execute.
```

```
get file=catenate.
  subtitle 'Illustrate catenated data'.
  list.
execute.
```

The SPSS output would be as follows:

A1	A2
1.00	3.00
4.00	5.00
2.00	4.00
6.00	7.00

Chapter 3 Demo. Program SPSS
Illustrate catenated data

We might encounter merging in SAS in a situation such as the following:

```
*-------------Demonstrate Merging (SAS)-------------;
data m1;
   input name $ sex $ s1 s2;
cards;
TOM M 33 55
SUE F 45 10
JOE M 34 11
;
run;

data m2;
   input name $ t1 t2;
cards;
TOM 88 89
JOE 78 78
SUE 80 90
;
run;
```

```
proc sort data=m1;
   by name;
run;

proc sort data=m2;
   by name;
run;

data merge;
   merge m1 m2;
   by name;
run;

proc print data=merge;
   title2 'Illustrate merged data';
run;
```

Which would produce SAS output such as:

Chapter 3 Demo. Program SAS
Illustrate merged data

OBS	NAME	SEX	S1	S2	T1	T2
1	JOE	M	34	11	78	78
2	SUE	F	45	10	80	90
3	TOM	M	33	55	88	89

In SPSS, merging is handled quite similarly, though again, it is necessary to write something rather longer because one must get a file before copying it and saving it under another name:

```
*-------------Demonstrate Merging (SPSS)-------------.
data list list
   / name (a3) sex (a1) s1 s2.
begin data
TOM M 33 55
SUE F 45 10
JOE M 34 11
end data.
    save outfile=m1.
execute.
```

```
data list list
   / name (a3) t1 t2.
begin data
TOM 88 89
JOE 78 78
SUE 80 90
end data.
   save outfile=m2.
execute.

get file=m1.
   sort cases by name.
   save outfile=m1.
execute.

get file=m2.
   sort cases by name.
   save outfile=m2.
execute.

match files file=m1 / file=m2 / by name.
   save outfile=merge.
execute.

get file=merge.
   subtitle 'Illustrate merged data'.
   list.
execute.
```

And the SPSS results would be:

NAME	SEX	S1	S2	T1	T2
JOE	M	34.00	11.00	78.00	78.00
SUE	F	45.00	10.00	80.00	90.00
TOM	M	33.00	55.00	88.00	89.00

Number of cases read: 3   Number of cases listed: 3

Chapter 3 Demo. Program SPSS
Illustrate merged data

Notice that, in both SAS and SPSS, it is necessary to sort the data on the merging variable before actually merging the data sets into a new data set. I discuss some more particulars of sorting below.

Subsetting is also similar in SAS and SPSS. In SAS, a subsetting situation might be as follows, and assume that this code is in the same program as the merging example above because its set command copies the merged data set:

```
*------------Demonstrate Subsetting (SAS)------------;
data subset;
    set merge;
    if sex='M';
run;

proc print data=subset;
    title2 'Illustrate subsetted data';
run;
```

Which would yield the following SAS results:

Chapter 3 Demo. Program SAS
Illustrate subsetted data

OBS	NAME	SEX	S1	S2	T1	T2
1	JOE	M	34	11	78	78
2	TOM	M	33	55	88	89

The SPSS input would be:

```
*-----------Demonstrate Subsetting (SPSS)-----------.
get file=merge.
    select if (sex='M').
    save outfile=subset.
execute.

get file=subset.
    subtitle 'Illustrate subsetted data'.
    list.
execute.
```

And the SPSS results would be:

NAME	SEX	S1	S2	T1	T2
JOE	M	34.00	11.00	78.00	78.00
TOM	M	33.00	55.00	88.00	89.00

Number of cases read: 2   Number of cases listed: 2

Chapter 3 Demo. Program SPSS
Illustrate subsetted data

The final data manipulation to demonstrate is sorting, which is both a manipulation and a convenience for producing BY-groups for data analysis. As with the merging example, we use a data set we have already created in this ongoing program: the compute data set produced above with the variables X1, X2, and X3. Suppose we wanted to do some sorts on those variables and produce BY-group analyses. In SAS, this could be accomplished as follows:

```
*-------------Demonstrate Sorting (SAS)-------------;
proc sort data=compute out=sort1;
   by x1;
run;

proc sort data=compute out=sort2;
   by x1 x2;
run;

proc print data=sort1;
   title2 'COMPUTE data set: demonstrate sorting by
          X1';
run;

proc print data=sort2;
   title2 'COMPUTE data set: demonstrate nested/double
          sorting by X2 within X1';
run;

proc means data=sort1;
   by X1;
   var X2 X3;
   title2 'COMPUTE data set: demonstrate analysis
          with BY-group on X1';
run;

* End of SAS program;
```

The above SAS code introduces several new elements. First, we see some actual statistical procedures (proc means) for the first time; in addition, proc print is used to illustrate the unsorted and sorted data sets by the use of data=sort1 and data=sort2. The proc means command, by default, gives you the statistics shown below—*n* size, mean, standard deviation, observed minimum value, and observed maximum value.

As I have noted, all the SAS or SPSS examples in this chapter could be strung together into one long program; I display them in chunks only to make my explanations easier. In the above SAS program—that is, all the above SAS code examples strung together into one single program—each data set (e.g., compute, sort1) is temporary and is automatically deleted when the program terminates, and so I use another element of my style: an end-of-program SAS comment that can go wherever I want to quit. As we will see, this is not the case with SPSS, in which you must be a bit more careful to delete your temporary data sets. This matter—controlling the naming and flow of temporary data sets—is another example of Principle 2.1. As you program in SAS and SPSS, you will develop your own style and preferences, a point to which I return at the end of Chapter 6.

The SAS output of this sorting demonstration is as follows:

Chapter 3 Demo. Program SAS
COMPUTE data set: demonstrate sorting by X1

OBS	X1	X2	X3	XAVG	XSUM
1	1	4	5	3.33333	10
2	1	1	4	2.00000	6
3	1	3	4	2.66667	8
4	1	3	4	2.66667	8
5	2	3	4	3.00000	9
6	3	4	4	3.66667	11
7	3	5	1	3.00000	9
8	3	3	3	3.00000	9

Chapter 3 Demo. Program SAS
COMPUTE data set:
demonstrate nested/double sorting by X2 within X1

OBS	X1	X2	X3	XAVG	XSUM
1	1	1	4	2.00000	6
2	1	3	4	2.66667	8
3	1	3	4	2.66667	8
4	1	4	5	3.33333	10
5	2	3	4	3.00000	9
6	3	3	3	3.00000	9
7	3	4	4	3.66667	11
8	3	5	1	3.00000	9

Chapter 3 Demo. Program SAS
COMPUTE data set:
demonstrate analysis with BY-group on X1

---------------------------------------$X1=1$---------------------------------------

Variable	N	Mean	Std Dev	Minimum	Maximum
X2	4	2.7500000	1.2583057	1.0000000	4.0000000
X3	4	4.2500000	0.5000000	4.0000000	5.0000000

---------------------------------------$X1=2$---------------------------------------

Variable	N	Mean	Std Dev	Minimum	Maximum
X2	1	3.0000000	.	3.0000000	3.0000000
X3	1	4.0000000	.	4.0000000	4.0000000

---------------------------------------$X1=3$---------------------------------------

Variable	N	Mean	Std Dev	Minimum	Maximum
X2	3	4.0000000	1.0000000	3.0000000	5.0000000
X3	3	2.6666667	1.5275252	1.0000000	4.0000000

The results of the proc means yield descriptive statistics on X2 and X3 for each BY-group of X1.

These operations are quite similar in SPSS, except for the complexity of the subcommands of the report command:

```
*-------------Demonstrate Sorting (SPSS)-------------.
get file=compute.
    sort cases by x1.
    save outfile=sort1.
execute.

get file=compute.
    sort cases by x1 x2.
    save outfile=sort2.
execute.

get file=sort1.
    subtitle 'COMPUTE data set: demonstrate sorting by
            X1'.
    list.
execute.

get file=sort2.
    subtitle 'COMPUTE data set: demo. nested/double
            sorting by X2 within X1'.
    list.
execute.

get file=sort1.
    subtitle 'COMPUTE data set: demonstrate analysis
            with BY-group on X1'.
    report
        / variables=x2 x3
        / break=x1
        / summary=mean
        / summary=stddev
        / summary=min
        / summary=max.
execute.

*------------End-of-program housecleaning------------.
```

```
*clear working file.
new file.

*erase temporary files created by this program.
erase file='compute'.
erase file='recode1'.
erase file='recode2'.
erase file='recode3'.
erase file='miss1'.
erase file='miss2'.
erase file='c1'.
erase file='c2'.
erase file='catenate'.
erase file='m1'.
erase file='m2'.
erase file='merge'.
erase file='subset'.
erase file='sort1'.
erase file='sort2'.

* End of SPSS program.
```

Here we see the SPSS temporary file handling I noted above. If all the SPSS examples in this chapter were strung together into one program, you would need the above erase statements to delete the temporary working data sets created by the program. SAS, as I noted, does not require such erasure. Put another way, as you read in data and manipulate it in SAS, it is stored temporarily for the life of the program's execution; if you want to save a permanent copy, you need to actively do so (see the file command, which I discuss in Appendix B). In SPSS, however, any temporary data set created by a program is stored in your computer, and you need to remember that fact or else various small data sets will proliferate.

Following is the SPSS output of the sorting example. Notice the slightly different layout of the BY-group descriptive statistics:

X1	X2	X3	XAVG	XSUM
1.00	4.00	5.00	3.33	10.00
1.00	1.00	4.00	2.00	6.00
1.00	3.00	4.00	2.67	8.00
1.00	3.00	4.00	2.67	8.00
2.00	3.00	4.00	3.00	9.00
3.00	4.00	4.00	3.67	11.00
3.00	5.00	1.00	3.00	9.00
3.00	3.00	3.00	3.00	9.00

Number of cases read: 8   Number of cases listed: 8
Chapter 3 Demo. Program SPSS

COMPUTE data set: demonstrate sorting by X1

X1	X2	X3	XAVG	XSUM
1.00	1.00	4.00	2.00	6.00
1.00	3.00	4.00	2.67	8.00
1.00	3.00	4.00	2.67	8.00
1.00	4.00	5.00	3.33	10.00
2.00	3.00	4.00	3.00	9.00
3.00	3.00	3.00	3.00	9.00
3.00	4.00	4.00	3.67	11.00
3.00	5.00	1.00	3.00	9.00

Number of cases read: 8   Number of cases listed: 8
Chapter 3 Demo. Program SPSS

COMPUTE data set: demo. nested/double sorting by X2
         within X1

X1	X2	X3
1.00		

	X2	X3
Mean	2.75	4.25
StdDev	1.26	.50
Minimum	1.00	4.00
Maximum	4.00	5.00

2.00

Mean	3.00	4.00
StdDev	.	.
Minimum	3.00	4.00
Maximum	3.00	4.00

3.00

Mean	4.00	2.67
StdDev	1.00	1.53
Minimum	3.00	1.00
Maximum	5.00	4.00

Chapter 3 Demo. Program SPSS
COMPUTE data set: demonstrate analysis with BY-group on X1

3.6. DISCUSSION QUESTIONS: CHAPTER 3

1. In your research or instructional setting, locate and describe at least three instances in which you have to compute variables, recode values for variables, subset data, catenate data, and match-merge data. Do not think about doing these on the computer; try to find real-world needs for them. For example: Do you work in an institute where you have to match data on the same students from different classes (match-merge)? Are you in a research project in which you have to combine data on the same test from two groups of people (catenate)?

2. If you have missing data in any of your data sets, what caused it? Can your missing data be retrieved? How? What is the default policy for handling missing values in your software, and is it satisfactory? Generally, try to come up with a unified policy for handling missing data. Remember Principle 1.3 as you explore this problem.

3. Follow some data handling from hard copy to online copy. Do a time-usage study of the process. Try to locate manual tasks that would be better done on the computer (e.g., sorting a stack

of hard copy). Implement that task on the computer and consider whether you are better off doing it online or "offline" (manually). What is the efficiency trade-off of each method?

4. In your data-handling situation, what could be the consequences of not saving a copy of the original unaltered data?

5. In your preferred software, how do you do the following operations: compute variables, recode variables, assign value codes, and perform data relations (subsetting, catenation, merging)? Can your software handle hierarchical databases? If so, how?

6. If you have access to SAS or SPSS at your setting, try using some of the code given in "Implementation" above. Apply it to your data. Note: If software at your setting is available on a mainframe or some shared-use computer, you may have access to a statistical consultant and/or SAS/SPSS Site Manager. Identify that person and establish a cordial, productive relationship. That will help later on. Guaranteed!

7. If you do not have SAS or SPSS at your setting, identify the support personnel for whatever software you will use. And . . . you guessed it: Establish a cordial, productive relationship!

8. Assuming you can access SAS or SPSS, try running the programs given above. Once you have one of my programs typed in, try altering some of the code slightly. First, change the code in a way that will not produce an error; for example, delete all titles and comments (you will find that the program still runs but is hard to understand—Principle 2.1 again). Next, try changing something that does produce an error; for example, leave out a line or misspell a word. Notice how the system reacts to the error. Then correct the error and rerun the program. I particularly recommend that you play around with the "Doug Problem" noted above. Try various if-then solutions and see whether you can produce an alternative to my pseudocode suggestion.

NOTES

1. Assuming, of course, that the 99 was a legitimate score and not an error (data bug). This is a topic we explore in Chapter 4.

2. Actually, you can guess that this would be detected. We happen to have a person in this data set, Anna, who is from Northern Italy, perhaps Bolzano, where German is widely spoken in addition to Italian. Assuming that you had added a field to the database to identify other foreign languages, if you accidentally recoded every instance of German for any language (rather than country) variable to Germany, then Anna's data would look odd:

```
                Name:  ANNA
     Native Country:  Italy
   Language, Native:  Italian
 Language, Other, 1:  Germany <<----Notice the problem!
 Language, Other, 2:  [not applicable / missing]
 Language, Other, 3:  [not applicable / missing]
                Sex:  Female
  Time at Institute:  1 term
    Term 1, Quiz 1:   34
    Term 1, Quiz 2:   28
    Term 1, Quiz 3:   35
  Term 1, Final Exam:  90
    Term 2, Quiz 1:   [not applicable / missing]
    Term 2, Quiz 2:   [not applicable / missing]
    Term 2, Quiz 3:   [not applicable / missing]
  Term 2, Final Exam:  [not applicable / missing]
    Term 3, Quiz 1:   [not applicable / missing]
    Term 3, Quiz 2:   [not applicable / missing]
    Term 3, Quiz 3:   [not applicable / missing]
  Term 3, Final Exam:  [not applicable / missing]
```

In Chapter 4, I address the issue of detection of problems like this via debugging analysis.

3. This book avoids evaluative comments about particular software, but in this situation an exception is being made. Missing value handling for numerics in dBase is very poorly thought out. I have not done an extensive survey of software to determine whether other data entry and analysis programs make the same mistake. SAS and SPSS do not.

Data Debugging

Overview/Outline

- Debugging Versus Money Runs
- Stressing Your Data: Computerized Debugging
- Implausibility and Impossibility
- Data Sensibility
- Manual Checking: Another Set of Eyes
- Criticality (A Priori Versus A Posteriori Checking)
- How to Check Manually
- Error Typology (or "Bug Species")
- Implementation
- Discussion Questions: Chapter 4

4.1. DEBUGGING VERSUS MONEY RUNS

The activity of analyzing data for the specific purpose of seeking errors ("bugs") and then fixing them is known as *debugging*. *To debug* is a verb that refers to the process of consciously and deliberately studying a data set to see that it is correctly relaying the information it is supposed to relay. Analysts often speak also of debugging a program; I prefer to use the term *debug* for both uses: to detect and correct errors in command line programs or data analyses, as well as in data sets themselves.

If the data contain bugs, then data values need to be corrected. Both the act of searching for errors and the act of fixing the errors are part of the debugging process. That process also includes searching for errors in your programming, a special topic I address later in the chapter. Some debugging can be facilitated by the computer; some must be done by the analyst. Typically, a debugging session is a fusion of the two; debugging is really like a detective's job because clues are uncovered, are followed, fail, or pan out. Eventually, a sort of threshold of confidence is reached. The analyst thinks the data are clean enough to proceed to substantive study of the data, or what I call a *money run.*

In computer data analysis, a *money run* is a computer analysis that is "for the money," or intended to produce results that answer questions of substantive importance. The money run may address administrative issues, student progress issues, or research issues. Often, what starts out as a money run ends up being a debugging session; often, the data set is thought to be clean, and unfortunately, while examining the output of a substantive analysis, some oddity will come up that will require a return to an earlier stage. One of the most frustrating experiences of a data analyst is to get very near the end of a project only to have to go all the way back to the very beginning and re-input data, all because of a bug.

It may seem, then, that the healthy skeptical attitude advocated at the end of Chapter 3 needs to become even firmer. Perhaps the analyst should be constantly pessimistic, constantly suspicious. I disagree. I sense a middle ground, where the analyst follows standardized debugging practices without becoming overly delayed and suspicious. My purpose in this chapter is to sketch some of those middle-ground practices—to give you, in effect, a repertoire of debugging/analytical principles that can help you build confidence in your data. I must emphasize that the middle ground is a fairly conservative, cautious terrain. For example, it would be embarrassing to publish a paper or submit a report with some sort of data bug that you had missed but that an alert reviewer is able to catch. Learn to be healthily skeptical; the first form of skepticism is to submit your data to stress—to run it through analyses designed to detect problems.

4.2. STRESSING YOUR DATA: COMPUTERIZED DEBUGGING

One way to approach debugging is to consider your data set to be an entity that must be stressed by use of the computer; that is, you should use the computer to help you debug your data. It must be put through rigorous computerized analyses to determine whether it is within acceptable boundaries. I classify those computerized data tests into two general families: testing for implausibility/ impossibility, and data sensibility.

4.2.1. IMPLAUSIBILITY AND IMPOSSIBILITY

From the standpoint of computerized debugging, data can be one of three types: (a) possible, (b) impossible, or (c) possible but implausible. (Again, a data value could also be completely wrong, but if it is wrong but possible, you cannot detect it with computer stress tests. That would require manual checking, to which I turn later on.) *Impossible data* refers to a data value on a variable that simply cannot exist. For example, if you have the variable AGE and you suddenly see a value of zero, you know that is impossible. If a person actually exists and is in your data set, then the person must have a non-zero age. Notice, interestingly, that this is one instance in which you could safely recode zeros to missing values; perhaps you do not know that person's age and somehow keyed in a zero. Unlike the example I discussed in Chapter 3, here recoding of zero as missing would be acceptable.

Implausible data refers to values that are possible but highly unlikely. Let me illustrate two types of data implausibility: situationally implausible and generally implausible. Let's envision our ongoing situation—EAI—and here assume that the student group is all adults who are enrolled concurrently with full-time employment in the downtown of each city (e.g., Chicago, Memphis). If

AGE is a variable in that data set and suddenly you see an age value of 10, you might become suspicious. A 10-year-old does not fit the pattern of an adult learning EFL in a major urban area. You would have sufficient cause to trace down that entry and see whether it is a typographical error. Another type of implausibility is not so situationally bound: I refer to it as generally implausible. For example, regardless of the usual age of the learners in that setting, an AGE value of 98 is generally implausible because it is very near the upper range limit for human life. If the data set contained an age of 98, I would be motivated to return to the original hard copy and check that entry.

Possibility, implausibility, and impossibility can interact during the detective job of debugging data. A good example is the type of scores used in the United States by the Educational Testing Service (ETS) in Princeton, New Jersey: In this scoring system, the average score for the national norming group is 500, and the standard deviation is 100. Tests like the ETS's TOEFL are also fixed at a restricted range (Educational Testing Service, 1993).[1] Hence, a student receiving a TOEFL score of 188 is impossible and represents a data bug. A TOEFL score of 387 is possible, but 25 scores of 387 out of a group of 100 people is implausible because the scores should be normally distributed about a mean of 500. The closer you get to the mean score of 500, the greater likelihood that many people will have received that score. Therefore, if all 100 people score between 470 and 530 on the TOEFL, you might not worry; indeed, I have worked with data sets with score ranges like that and have trusted the data. But if I worked with a set of TOEFL data for 100 people and the scores were normally distributed from about 350 to 450, I would be suspicious.

Checking data in this manner need not be time-consuming; a principle is warranted:

Principle 4.1: The Impossibility/Implausibility Principle

Use the computer to check for impossible and implausible data.

It is wise to apply Principle 4.1 routinely, without even asking whether it is really needed. The application of this principle involves pseudocode that is fairly simple:

```
For the whole data set:

Run simple descriptive statistics on each variable
and determine whether some value exists that is
implausible or impossible. If it does, search through
the data set for records that contain that value for
the variable under question and correct the bug.
```

Another application of Principle 4.1 is to enter data twice—in two separate computer files, and then have each file read by your software. Then you could run some simple statistics to check comparability of results. SAS has a procedure to do this (PROC COMPARE) for you. This is time-consuming debugging, but it is a process often followed in high-stakes data situations.

4.2.2. DATA SENSIBILITY

A professor of mine in graduate school was fond of chiding his students: "Get a sense of the order of magnitude of your data." Knowing your data's likely values is critical to becoming a good data handler. To illustrate it, I present a hypothetical project. Suppose EAI is interested in the role of student attitude and motivation in ultimate success at learning a foreign language. Management figures that if it could detect which attitudes and motivations characterize a successful learner of languages, then their faculty could adjust the teaching methodology to foster those conditions (and because EAI is a for-profit corporation, make more money). Before detailed research on this topic, management first wants to confirm a strong relationship between attitude/motivation and language learning. To do so, EAI researchers randomly select 300 students from nine world branches and obtain the students' permission to use (anonymously) the full data record of standard tests, quizzes, and final exams used in all EAI schools. They also give these 300 students several attitude and motivation questionnaires—some they have designed themselves, and some based on review of literature on this subject. All the questionnaires are in the students' native languages to control for variability in whatever language is being studied. These questionnaires include items such as:

> Foreign language learning is important in the modern industrialized world.
> strongly disagree — disagree — neutral — agree — strongly agree

> Learning a foreign language is difficult.
> strongly disagree — disagree — neutral — agree — strongly agree

This special project comes to be called the EAI-AM study, for EAI-Attitude and Motivation. The first phase of the project—determining whether the relationship exists—involves simple correlation coefficients among all the variables. The team assigns a value to each response in the questionnaires such that 1 = strongly disagree, 2 = disagree, and so forth. They then sum up all the items on each questionnaire and correlate the sums with the various language ability measures.

Let's suppose two types of findings. First, let's suppose the EAI-AM team uncovers a high positive relationship between the attitude/motivation questionnaires and performance on classroom tests. This kind of finding makes sense; it seems logical that people who agree with motivational statements (e.g., the two items above) will do better on tests of the learning material. If the EAI-AM team got such correlations, they would probably report back to their supervisors something like the following: "Yes, attitude and motivation appear to play a role in our schools. They correlate highly with our standard achievement tests. We should investigate them further and figure out ways to maximize them in our learners."

Suppose, however, the EAI-AM team got a totally different finding. Suppose the attitudinal measures were weakly correlated with the achievement measures, or even negatively correlated. That is what my professor was worried about when he urged his students to get a sense of the order of magnitude of our data. More generally, he was encouraging us to actually carry out our analyses, but not for real. We would do a "pseudo" money run, of sorts, and carry our data all the way down the road to the final output and then ask ourselves: Is this likely? Does what I have make sense?

A principle can summarize this need. I call it Burstein's data sensibility principle in memory of Professor Leigh Burstein of UCLA, who brought it up in his challenging course in multiple regression.

Principle 4.2: Burstein's Data Sensibility Principle

Run your data all the way through to the final computer analysis and ask yourself whether the results make sense. Be prepared to decide that they do not, and hence be prepared to treat the analysis not as final, but as another debugging step.

It is important to emphasize one epistemological point about Principle 4.2. Maybe the weird results are right. Maybe this EAI research has made a serious and important discovery that attitude and motivation are not as closely related to achievement as the EAI-AM team expected. More likely, some subtle bug does exist, and being good debuggers, the EAI-AM team would do everything they could to stress the data (computerized checking), check the syntax in their program code, and even manually compare the computer files to the original hard copy test booklets and questionnaire forms.

4.3. MANUAL CHECKING: ANOTHER SET OF EYES

Testing for impossibility/implausibility and running a pseudo money run to check the sensibility of results both involve the computer. The computer may not catch some data bugs. For example, if a value on a variable is possible and sensible but wrong, neither a computerized impossibility/implausibility check nor a computerized sensibility check can catch it. If, for instance, Jose got a 99 on the Term 1 final exam and it was entered into the data set as a 98, and if both 99 and 98 are possible and within the expected order of magnitude of our ultimate findings, then we would not catch the problem.

The impossibility/implausibility check and the sensibility check, each of which led to a principle above, were intended to locate an error. In the present instance, we have no computerized means to locate a 98 substituted for a 99. We must assume that errors like that exist and go after them by other means. To emphasize this, I present two principles, side by side:

Principle 4.3: The Extant Error Principle

Data bugs exist.

Principle 4.4: The Manual Check Principle

Nothing can replace another set of eyes to check over a data set. Either check your data entry, input, and manipulation yourself, or get somebody else to help you do it.

Determine the criticality of your data set before expending human resources to check it manually. Highly critical data sets require manual checking regardless, possibly a priori, certainly a posteriori.

Ideally, all data sets require manual checking.

You should debug data by computer (Principle 4.1) before you check it manually so that manual checking is easier.

Principle 4.4 might, at first glance, seem to contradict advice I give elsewhere (e.g., Principle 3.1 or 4.1). Both Principles 3.1 and 4.1 advise you to use the computer to do the work for you (3.1) and to check your data (4.1). Actually, those two principles can coexist with 4.4. The key is to use the computer to help out first and then to check data manually. The cleaner the data are before the manual check (because you used the computer to debug them), the quicker the manual check will be over.

In my data stories in Chapter 7 and Appendix C, I present some tales of data gone awry. Somehow, somewhere, data are always buggy. There are always wrong values, transposed values, and flipped columns. Reversed data sets even pop up; it is very easy to misname a data set on a computer, and when handling many data sets of a similar nature, the analyst can accidentally name a data set incorrectly and therefore call the wrong data set into an analytical procedure. Furthermore, archives of data files and programs can grow and become hard to manage, and it can be very easy to run the wrong program on the right data. (I suggest some remedies to this dilemma in Chapter 6.)

Bugs exist. Even after you have run the data set through elegant and clever implausibility/impossibility and sensibility checks, bugs will still exist, and you should have a healthy attitude of healthy skepticism even after you have stressed the data with programs to test impossibility/implausibility and sensibility.

One interesting spinoff of checking data visually is that you can begin to analyze it. Suppose EAI has two data sets:

```
        Data Set A                      Data Set B
     5    10   15   20   25          5    10   15   20   25
 ----|----|----|----|----|       ----|----|----|----|----|
 0001 00001000101000100001       0101 01111110111111101111
 0002 00110000000010100001       0102 11110111111110101111
 0003 11100100000001000000       0103 10111111111011111011
 0004 01010000011000000001       0104 11111111101111101111
 0005 01110100001000000000       0105 11110111111111101111
 0006 00110100000000001010       0106 11111111111111101011
 0007 00110100101000000000       0107 01111111111111101111
 0008 00010000001011100000       0108 11111111111111101011
 0009 10011000010000000010       0109 01111111111111101111
 0010 11100000100100000000       0110 11111110111111101111
 0011 01100000000010100001       0111 11110111111111101111
 0012 01010110001001000000       0112 01111111111111101111
 0013 01010000101010100000       0113 01111111111111101111
 0014 00110000111000100000       0114 01111111111111101111
 0015 00110000011100000100       0115 11110111111111101111
```

In each data set, 15 students were tested on 20 language test items, and each item was scored right or wrong: 1 or 0. An ID number is given in columns 1 to 4, and the item scores are in columns 5 to 25. Students 0001 through 0015 did not do as well as students 0101 to 0115; there are more 1s in Data Set B than in Data Set A. Even though you have not run any analyses to confirm that Group B performed better, it is apparent that they did because of the larger number of 1s in Data Set B. Looking at the data in the debugging process often begins to uncover substantive patterns such as these. (For tips on producing binary "zero-one" data sets from raw "A,B,C,D" responses, see Appendix B.)

Principle 4.4 is long and carefully worded. It refers to a very logical means of debugging: to have another look at your data. I now present some organized and systematic procedures for manual data integrity checking, a crucial part of the debugging process.

4.3.1. CRITICALITY (A PRIORI VERSUS A POSTERIORI CHECKING)

Professional data entry services use professional data debugging. Entering a 99 for Juan's final exam—when in fact he received a 98—is precisely the type of error they wish to guard against. Such professionalism includes a manual checking routine, as well as extensive computerized debugging.

An assumption those services make is that every data set they work with is equally important. It would be best for all of us to adopt that attitude too; we should consider all our data sets to be as equally important as the most important data set. If we did, we would be logically drawn to manual checking of data entry. As it stands, however, that attitude is not practical and certainly not cheap.

I advocate, therefore, a "criticality metric" in which data types are plotted against the need for manual checking. This metric is a written scale stating what kinds of data most merit manual checking. It might look something like the following, for the EAI situation:

Sample Data Criticality Metric

Data Level	Amount of Debugging
Most Important	
(1) High-Stakes Final Exams	Computer debugging and a priori manual checking
(2) Classroom Exams	Computer debugging and either a priori or a posteriori manual checking
(3) Quizzes, Worksheets	Computer debugging and a posteriori manual checking
(4) All other data	Computer debugging and optional a posteriori manual checking
Least Important	

Data can be checked manually at two possible time points: before any computer debugging (a priori) and after computer debugging (a posteriori). Clearly, a posteriori manual checking has the advantage that any problems caught by computer debugging will not also turn up in the manual checking; they will have been fixed. I maintain, however, that a priori manual checking is still a good idea when data are most critical.

In this example, Level 1 is the most critical. If data are entered into the school's record base incorrectly and if those data reflect high-stakes final exams, then a student might be misjudged—and that worries me (see Principle 1.3). I advocate, in this topmost level, data entry and manual checking of the data before any computerized debugging. We should not trust the computer for all debugging, and a priori debugging might fall prey to a sentiment such as: "Well, we'll skip that kind of bug for now. We'll use the computer to hunt for those problems later." If the data are high on the criticality metric, then all persons involved with the data should become aware of the criticality, and enforcing a priori manual checking is a splendid means to do so.

Level 4 in the example above is the least critical data type. It might include optional assignments and other data sources that the institution researchers think are not as important as those at Levels 1, 2, and 3. Manual checking at this data level is still a good idea, but cost considerations may require the researchers to rely on computer debugging only.

The two intermediate levels represent a mix of possibilities. Manual checking is still wise, but it need not be prioritized and emphasized in the administrative structure to the extent it is at Level 1. A good group exercise for any teaching institute or large-scale research project is to gather together the staff members and brainstorm a criticality metric such as that shown above.

For example, in the Cambridge-TOEFL Comparability Study (CTCS; see Bachman, Davidson, Ryan, & Choi, 1995), in which I participated, we did so, although our brainstorming was via electronic mail. We decided there was only one level of data importance in our project: Level 1 above (*very important*). As a result, we budgeted for data entry and a priori manual checking before any computer debugging procedures. We hired temporary "data enterers," or to use an older term, "keypunchers," and asked them to serve as both primary data entry and a priori data-checking personnel. We developed a schedule to allow the keypunchers to swap off from primary data entry to checking and thereby provide some task variety; we also rented seven computers and leased some special rooms to isolate the data entry and checking staff from any distraction. The data entry phase lasted about 3 weeks, and I moved my office to our rented quarters during that time. The rented rooms became a single-purpose data-processing center.

Data entry and debugging such as our CTCS has an affective dimension. I would like to claim that a sense of familial joviality also pervaded that place, but I do recall that the staff seemed to vanish at the lunch hour. Do not overstress your staff and colleagues. Asking people to bang away at computers and/or check data for 7 or 8 hours a day is itself a source of bugs. Fatigue breeds problems, and if I were to work on a massive project like that again, I would probably budget a longer data-entry phase and use personnel half-days or possibly contract the data entry to a professional data company.

In any event, even if such staff discussions determine that no manual checking is needed or (as is often the case) that few personnel resources can be allocated to manual checking, I maintain that Principles 4.1 and 4.2 must still hold and computerized debugging is always wise.

4.3.2. HOW TO CHECK MANUALLY

Once a decision to perform manual checking has been made, some sort of checking procedure is needed. These employ common sense, regardless of whether the checking is a priori or a posteriori. Two pairs of eyes are better than one. It is better to use a different person as checker than as the initial data entry keypuncher because as one enters data, one acquires a familiarity with it, and errors might be harder to spot. If that is not possible, then the same person might check his or her data entry but at a later time.

During all manual checking, the data entry staff should be encouraged to develop a sense of what types of errors are likely. Manual checking becomes easier the longer one does it. Gradually, the checker develops a sixth sense for the most typical key-in errors that are made. In the CTCS, we kept an informal written log of common typographical errors, and by the halfway point of data entry, the staff had become (a) more accurate because the same people were doing data entry as checking and (b) quicker at checking. Manual checking actually helps develop an error typology for each data set.

4.4. ERROR TYPOLOGY (OR "BUG SPECIES")

Whether detected by computer (impossibility/implausibility and sensibility checks) or by manual checking, errors belong to categories; bugs have species, so to speak. I describe two general error types: entry errors and logic errors.

The first type of error is an *entry error*. This is the most common-sense type of error, and once you have detected it, it is the easiest to fix. The bulk of this chapter is devoted to the detection of entry errors.

Another type of bug is a *logic error*. Sometimes software commands can create data bugs. In the language/attitude example above, it is possible that the computer command to read in data was incorrect and variable values were transposed, such that *strongly disagree* was uniformly entered as the value 5 and *strongly agree* as 1. In such a case, computer programs cannot reveal the fault. The results are logical but wrong, and hence the name: logic error. As another example, notice the SAS input command in the sample program at the end of Chapter 3. If that line were mistyped to read input name $ sex $ s2 s1;, then a bug would be introduced into the data. Values of s2 would appear in the output for values of s1 and vice versa; this is the type of error I would suspect with the language/aptitude example above. An error such as that, assuming that the values of s2 and s1 were possible and sensible, could be located only by manual checking. In this case, you would have to check the entry program manually, as well as the data itself.

Bugs do not exist only in data; they can also exist in data-handling programs. If we made a logic error in our SAS program, SAS would run properly if we did make that error, but the result would be wrong. However, what if we made the following mistake on the input line: input name $ sex $ s1 s2 without the required terminating semicolon? SAS would return an error message because we had violated a requirement of its command language. This is known in computer programming as a *syntactic error*. It is an error in which the syntax rules of a command language have been violated. Usually, your software will alert you to syntactic errors. (And by the way, I have found in teaching and using SAS that the most common error in SAS is to forget the terminating semicolon, and I would suspect that the terminating period in SPSS is forgotten often too!) Logic errors do not cause a program to stop and display some sort of error or warning. Syntactic errors do cause a program to abort, or "bomb." Therefore, logic errors are much harder to detect than syntactic errors.

This brief discussion of error types suggests a principle:

Principle 4.5: The Error Typology Principle

Debugging includes detection and correction of errors. To ease correction, try to classify each error as you uncover it.

4.5. IMPLEMENTATION

The data sets in the program segments below contain various bugs (remember Principle 4.3: Bugs exist) of several types: impossible data, implausible data, and checking sensibility. I show some methods in SAS and SPSS to detect bugs and examine magnitude of your findings. As always, you will benefit from these examples if you quickly review "Implementation" in the previous chapters. Remember also that the particular variables and settings used in this book are but examples; try to generalize these data to settings relevant to you (e.g., what kind of data might you have that can occupy only two columns per value, but for which somebody might accidentally key in a third—as in the example below?).

As with Chapters 2 and 3, the SAS and SPSS code below could be strung together into a single contiguous program. And as in all "Implementation" sections in this book, I strive to maximize readability and make the program clear and comprehensible. Hence, the first thing that should appear in the sample programs for this chapter are the following two comment boxes and titles, first, in SAS:

```
*----------------------------------------------------------*
| Name of input program: ch4.sas (SAS)                     |
|               Function: demonstrate various data         |
|                         debugging                        |
|   Name of input ASCII dataset(s): internal to program    |
| Name of output PC-SAS dataset(s): none                   |
|               Program written by: Fred Davidson           |
*----------------------------------------------------------*;
title1 'Chapter 4 Demo. Program SAS';
```

and in SPSS:

```
*----------------------------------------------------*
|                                                    |
|   Name of input program: ch4.sps                   |
|             Function: demonstrate various data      |
|                       debugging                     |
|     Name of input ASCII dataset(s): internal to program
| Name of output SPSS-PC dataset(s): none             |
|             Program written by: Fred Davidson        |
*----------------------------------------------------*.
title 'Chapter 4 Demo. Program SPSS'.
```

The first situation we examine is that of impossible data. Suppose that an RBC data set contains the variable AGE and that, in a keypunching error, an impossibly high value has been entered. How might you detect it? Following is a data step from SAS and some repair code to show that problem:

```
*------------ Demonstrate Impossible Data -----------;
data imposs;
    input name $ exam1 exam2 age;
cards;
ANNA 24 34 29
BILL 22 30 26
JOSE 25 29 278
;
run;

proc print data=imposs;
    title2 'Illustrate an impossible data value
           (a typographical error)';
run;

data fix1;
    input name $ exam1 exam2 age;
cards;
ANNA 24 34 29
BILL 22 30 26
JOSE 25 29 27
;
run;
```

```
proc print data=fix1;
   title2 'Illustrate repair of the impossible data
          value';
run;
```

The example above is not earth-shattering in its programming complexity. Basically, the first data step had a bad data value for Jose's age: 278, and in the second data step it was retyped and corrected. Once we determine Jose's correct age from other sources (e.g., asking Jose himself), it is possible to use the SAS set command and make a copy of the imposs data set and correct the original data value, for example:

```
data fix1;
   set imposs;
   if name='JOSE' then age=27;
run;
```

With very large data sets, I have done tricks like that when it is exceedingly painful to trace the precise error in the raw data. In some of my operational data analysis programs, I know of data bugs that I have tried to correct but that proved too time-consuming to track down. In such cases, I have not been able to find the proper values for the incorrect data, so my regular analyses include recoding commands that set those values to missing—an application of Principle 4.3 (known bugs) using an inelegant solution (Principle 3.3: a kludge).

The SAS results for the impossible age example above would look something like the following. Principle 4.1 is at play because you can simply scan down the AGE column in the first table in the results and detect quickly and easily the single aberrant value:

Chapter 4 Demo. Program SAS
Illustrate an impossible data value (a typographical error)

OBS	NAME	EXAM1	EXAM2	AGE
1	ANNA	24	34	29
2	BILL	22	30	26
3	JOSE	25	29	278

Chapter 4 Demo. Program SAS
Illustrate repair of the impossible data value

OBS	NAME	EXAM1	EXAM2	AGE
1	ANNA	24	34	29
2	BILL	22	30	26
3	JOSE	25	29	27

In SPSS, the input code to demonstrate this impossible age example might be:

```
* ----------- Demonstrate Impossible Data -----------.
data list list
    / name (a4) exam1 exam2 age.
begin data.
ANNA       24      3429
BILL       22      3026
JOSE       25      29278
end data.
    save outfile=imposs.
execute.

get file=imposs.
    subtitle 'Illustrate an impossible data value
              (a typographical error)'.
    list.
execute.

data list list
    / name (a4) exam1 exam2 age.
begin data
ANNA 24 34 29
BILL 22 30 26
JOSE 25 29 27
end data.
    save outfile=fix1.
execute.
```

```
get file=fix1.
    subtitle 'Illustrate repair of the impossible data
            value'.
    list.
execute.
```

Typical SPSS command language is used above to input the incorrect data, print it, and then input the corrected data and print it. The SPSS output would look something like this:

Chapter 4 Demo. Program SPSS
Illustrate repair of the impossible data value

NAME	EXAM1	EXAM2	AGE
ANNA	24.00	34.00	29.00
BILL	22.00	30.00	26.00
JOSE	25.00	29.00	278.00

Number of cases read: 3 Number of cases listed: 3

Chapter 4 Demo. Program SPSS
Illustrate an impossible data value (a typographical error)

NAME	EXAM1	EXAM2	AGE
ANNA	24.00	34.00	29.00
BILL	22.00	30.00	26.00
JOSE	25.00	29.00	27.00

Number of cases read: 3 Number of cases listed: 3

Notice that the error is also easily detected in the SPSS printout.

The next example is of *implausible data values,* which are data that could be true but likely are not. Suppose EAI has a data set of some of its students, both those studying English as a foreign language and some of the students in the newer programs in the United States to teach languages other than English. Suppose the following appears in a SAS program; there are three variables: student name, student home country, and student native language:

```
* ---------- Demonstrate Implausible Data ---------- ;
data implaus;
   input name $ country $ language $;
cards;
YOSHI JAPAN  SPANISH
JUAN   SPAIN JAPANESE
BILL     USA  ENGLISH
;
run;

proc print data=implaus;
   title2 'Illustrate implausible data values
          (value transposition)';
run;
```

And the SAS results look like this:

Chapter 4 Demo. Program SAS
Illustrate implausible data values (value transposition)

OBS	NAME	COUNTRY	LANGUAGE
1	YOSHI	JAPAN	SPANISH
2	JUAN	SPAIN	JAPANESE
3	BILL	USA	ENGLISH

Clearly, something is wrong. For a student from Japan named Yoshi, the data show a native language of Spanish although his home country is Japan. Furthermore, for a student called Juan, who is from Spain, the native language is apparently Japanese. These two situations are theoretically possible but highly implausible, unlike the human age of 278 in the first error example, which is totally impossible. Suppose EAI researchers study this error, determine it is a keypunching fault, and correct it. The fixed SAS code would look like this:

```
data fix2;
    input name $ country $ language $;
cards;
YOSHI JAPAN JAPANESE
JUAN SPAIN SPANISH
BILL USA ENGLISH
;
run;

proc print data=fix2;
    title2 'Illustrate repair of the implausible data
            value';
run;
```

And the corrected SAS results would be:

Chapter 4 Demo. Program SAS
Illustrate repair of the implausible data values

OBS	NAME	COUNTRY	LANGUAGE
1	YOSHI	JAPAN	SPANISH
2	JUAN	SPAIN	JAPANESE
3	BILL	USA	ENGLISH

In SPSS, the input code, both that containing the error and the repaired data, would appear as follows:

```
* ---------- Demonstrate Implausible Data ---------- .
data list list
    / name (a5) country (a5) language (a8).
begin data
YOSHI JAPAN  SPANISH
JUAN  SPAIN JAPANESE
BILL     USA  ENGLISH
end data.
    save outfile=implaus.
execute.
```

```
get file=implaus.
   subtitle 'Illustrate implausible data values
          (value transposition)'.

list.
execute.

data list list
   / name (a5) country (a5) language (a8).
begin data
YOSHI JAPAN JAPANESE
JUAN  SPAIN  SPANISH
BILL    USA   ENGLISH
end data.
   save outfile=fix2.
execute.

get file=fix2.
   subtitle 'Illustrate repair of the implausible
          data value'.
   list.
execute.
```

And the SPSS output of the above code would be:

NAME	COUNTRY	LANGUAGE
YOSHI	JAPAN	SPANISH
JUAN	SPAIN	JAPANESE
BILL	USA	ENGLISH

Number of cases read: 3   Number of cases listed: 3

Chapter 4 Demo. Program SPSS
Illustrate implausible data values (value transposition)

NAME	COUNTRY	LANGUAGE
YOSHI	JAPAN	JAPANESE
JUAN	SPAIN	SPANISH
BILL	USA	ENGLISH

Number of cases read: 3   Number of cases listed: 3

Chapter 4 Demo. Program SPSS
Illustrate repair of the implausible data value

Let's now turn to an example of Principle 4.2: the examination of data sensibility. Suppose EAI researchers want to compare two teaching methodologies for foreign language education: audiolingual and communicative. *Audiolingual language teaching* is highly rote-based, drill-intensive, teacher-dominated pedagogy. *Communicative language teaching* is something of an umbrella term for more modern, student-centered, eclectic teaching methods, which can include drilling if deemed necessary. Suppose EAI has two classes of similar students, one being instructed in the audiolingual method and the other in the looser communicative pedagogy. After a period of instruction, EAI researchers administer an achievement test designed for communicative language teaching; that is, the test is designed for use in communicative teaching classrooms, not audiolingual classrooms.

In the following SAS code, CTSCORE is the variable for the communicative language test:

```
*-----------Demonstrate Sensibility Checking---------;
data compare;
      length method $13;
      input name $ method $ ctscore;
cards;
ANNA   Audiolingual 48        <--Notice the generally
BILL Communicative 12             high CTSCORE values
JOSE Communicative 20             for the audiolingual
JUAN   Audiolingual 37            group. It is not likely
GILL   Audiolingual 39            that audiolingual
SUE  Communicative 22             methodology would cause
DOUG   Audiolingual 37            a high score on a test
DAVE Communicative 18             created for use in a
LARS Communicative 19             communicative classroom.
HANS   Audiolingual 45            This is also an illustra-
FRED   Audiolingual 44            tion of Principle 4.4:
TOM  Communicative 25             We can learn much just by
JIM    Audiolingual 40            looking at the data.
MIKE Communicative 20
;
run;
```

```
proc sort data=compare;
   by method;
run;

proc means data=compare;
   by method;
   title2 'Illustrate findings which are not sensible';
run;
```

My note in the above program is not part of the SAS language. Rather, I call your attention to the data set: It looks like the keypuncher systematically reversed the values for the teaching method because the audiolingual scores are usually high and the communicative scores low. But to be certain, I have requested a proc means with BY-groups, and the results below seem to confirm my suspicions; the mean for audiolingual is unexpectedly high, and that for communicative is unexpectedly low:

Chapter 4 Demo. Program SAS
Illustrate findings which are not sensible

Analysis Variable : CTSCORE

------------------------------ METHOD=Audiolingual ------------------------------

N Obs	N	Minimum	Maximum	Mean	Std Dev
7	7	37.000000	48.0000000	41.4285714	4.2761799

-------------------------- METHOD=Communicative --------------------------

N Obs	N	Minimum	Maximum	Mean	Std Dev
7	7	12.0000000	25.0000000	19.4285714	3.9940432

Granted, these results could be real. As I note in this chapter, Principle 4.2 is not cut-and-dried. Sometimes you do make a real discovery, and in this case, maybe we have discovered that our supposedly communicative test is really loaded with a lot of drills; perhaps it is an audiolingual wolf in communicative sheep's clothing. Alternatively, let's suppose we look at the test and determine that it is indeed correctly attuned to communicative methodology and that the keypuncher did regularly reverse the values for teaching method. We can use a search-and-replace function (very common in all computer editors and word processors) to do the following:

```
In the data set:
1. Change all instances of 'Audiolingual' to 'xxxxx',
   then
2. Change all instances of 'Communicative' to
   'Audiolingual', then
3. Change all instances of 'xxxxx' to 'Communicative'
```

The 'xxxxx' is another type of what programmers call a *wild card*, and it serves to edit the file and make the necessary change. Other types of wild cards exist in programming—for example, the '*' and '?' permitted in IBM/compatible filenames.

Once we have made the changes, the repaired SAS code would look like this:

```
data fix3;
    length method $13;
    input name $ method $ ctscore;
cards;
ANNA Communicative 48       <--The audiolingual and
BILL  Audiolingual 12          communicative values
JOSE  Audiolingual 20          have been reversed.
JUAN Communicative 37
GILL Communicative 39
 SUE  Audiolingual 22
DOUG Communicative 37
DAVE  Audiolingual 18
LARS  Audiolingual 19
HANS Communicative 45
FRED Communicative 44
 TOM  Audiolingual 25
 JIM Communicative 40
MIKE  Audiolingual 20
;
run;
```

```
proc sort data=fix3;
   by method;
run;

proc means data=fix3;
   by method;
   title2 'Illustrate repair based on sensibility
         check';
run;
```

And the repaired SAS output would show us that all is now well
in the ideal language teaching land of EAI:

Chapter 4 Demo. Program SAS
Illustrate repair based on sensibility check

Analysis Variable : CTSCORE

---------------------------- METHOD=Audiolingual ----------------------------

N Obs	N	Minimum	Maximum	Mean	Std Dev
7	7	12.0000000	25.0000000	19.4285714	3.9940432

--------------------------METHOD=Communicative--------------------------

N Obs	N	Minimum	Maximum	Mean	Std Dev
7	7	37.0000000	48.0000000	41.4285714	4.2761799

Following is the analogous code in SPSS:

```
*  --------- Demonstrate Sensibility Checking --------.
data list list
   / name (a4) method (a13) ctscore.
begin data
ANNA  Audiolingual 48
BILL Communicative 12
JOSE Communicative 20
JUAN  Audiolingual 37
```

```
GILL  Audiolingual 39
 SUE Communicative 22
DOUG  Audiolingual 37
DAVE Communicative 18
LARS Communicative 19
HANS  Audiolingual 45
FRED  Audiolingual 44
 TOM Communicative 25
 JIM  Audiolingual 40
MIKE Communicative 20
end data.
    save outfile=compare.
execute.

get file=compare.
    sort cases by method.
    save outfile=compare.
execute.

get file=compare.
    subtitle 'Illustrate findings which are not
             sensible'.
    report
       / variables ctscore
       / break=method
       / summary=mean
       / summary=stddev
       / summary=min
       / summary=max.
execute.

data list list
    / name (a4) method (a13) ctscore.
begin data
ANNA Communicative 48
BILL  Audiolingual 12
JOSE  Audiolingual 20
JUAN Communicative 37
GILL Communicative 39
 SUE  Audiolingual 22
DOUG Communicative 37
DAVE  Audiolingual 18
```

```
LARS   Audiolingual 19
HANS Communicative 45
FRED Communicative 44
 TOM   Audiolingual 25
 JIM Communicative 40
MIKE   Audiolingual 20
end data.
    save outfile=fix3.
execute.

get file=fix3.
    sort cases by method.
    save outfile=fix3.
execute.

get file=fix3.
    subtitle 'Illustrate repair based on sensibility
            check'.
    report
        / variables ctscore
        / break=method
        / summary=mean
        / summary=stddev
        / summary=min
        / summary=max.
execute.

* ---------- End-of-program housecleaning ----------.

*clear working file.
new file.

*erase temporary files created by this program.
erase file='imposs'.
erase file='fix1'.
erase file='implaus'.
erase file='fix2'.
erase file='compare'.
erase file='fix3'.

* End of program.
```

This is the final example of the chapter, so as usual, if all the SPSS code in this chapter were in one single program, it would be necessary to manually delete the temporary files with the SPSS `erase` commands above.

Following is the SPSS output of this particular problem and its fix:

```
METHOD          CTSCORE

Audiolingual

Mean            41.43
StdDev           4.28
Minimum         37.00
Maximum         48.00

Communicative

Mean            19.43
StdDev           3.99
Minimum         12.00
Maximum         25.00
```

Chapter 4 Demo. Program SPSS
Illustrate findings which are not sensible

```
METHOD          CTSCORE

Audiolingual

Mean            19.43
StdDev           3.99
Minimum         12.00
Maximum         25.00

Communicative

Mean            41.43
StdDev           4.28
Minimum         37.00
Maximum         48.00
```

Chapter 4 Demo. Program SPSS
Illustrate repair based on sensibility check

4.6. DISCUSSION QUESTIONS: CHAPTER 4

1. Identify (a) impossible data values for your setting and (b) implausible data values for your data setting. What are some acceptable findings of your research or administrative data analysis? What would you accept without question, and what would cause you to suspect bugs? How would Principle 4.2 apply to your setting?

2. Use your software to search some of your databases and see whether you do indeed have some impossible and implausible data values. Use the computer to check also for other possible data bugs.

3. Sometimes a seeming bug is not really a problem, but some larger systemic flaw with which you must live. When I worked as a researcher and statistician for the state of Illinois, I did analyses of data on more than 57,000 ESL and bilingual education students. The database recorded each student's last name and first initial. A catenation of the last name, first initial, and date of birth formed the only unique identity (ID) variable for each case. I discovered that I had three instances of duplicate records on the unique identifier and one instance of three records with identical ID values; that is, these records were duplicated on ID values, but all other data—test scores and such—did not match.

   The problem was that Illinois had three sets of twins for whom English was a second language, who had (clearly) the same last name, and who had a first name beginning with the same initial. And . . . you guessed it . . . there was one set of similarly named triplets! I remember calling the data entry people in the state capitol about this. They agreed that the problem existed—for those nine children out of 57,000.

   What do you think the state of Illinois should do about this? How does Principle 1.3 affect your opinion?

4. This is not really a discussion question. Rather, it is a challenge. During the next few months, listen for the varying degrees to which people believe or do not believe that data bugs exist. In real research and administrative situations, do you meet people who are:

   A. solidly convinced that their databases are perfectly clean?

   B. firmly convinced that their databases are hopelessly buggy?

   C. people who are amazed when they learn that data actually can be buggy?

5. Data input and debugging are a cyclical process. In your next project, keep track of when you fix bugs. Do you tend to debug after you enter a batch of records? After you write some initial programs (so that you can also debug computed variables)? What are your preferences—your personal principles in this regard? As I note in Chapter 7, it is a good idea to develop your own principles of data handling.

6. Jump ahead and have a look at discussion question 1 for Chapter 6. After you have read Chapter 6, review Chapter 4's principles briefly and then answer discussion question 1 for Chapter 6; it relates to both chapters. Be certain you ask the professional data analyst how his or her company debugs data. What is his or her data criticality metric?

NOTE

1. The TOEFL is the Test of English as a Foreign Language. This is the world's largest test of English as a second/foreign language. Produced by Educational Testing Service, it is probably administered to more than 1 million people per year, counting both its international and locally licensed tests (Bachman et al., 1995). In addition, TOEFL scores can only end in zero, 3, or 7, so a TOEFL score of, for example, 506 would be an impossible data bug due to my knowledge of the TOEFL score manuals.

Data Aspects of Statistical Analysis

Overview/Outline

- Introduction
- The Worn Path Phenomenon
  (The Know Yourself Principle)
- Some Statistical Terminology:
  A Review
- Descriptive Statistics and Data
  Handling: The Ubiquitous Table 1
- Correlation and Regression
- t Tests and the Analysis of
  Variance (ANOVA): Univariate
  Versus Multivariate Data Modes
- Frequency Data and the
  Chi-Square Test: More on
  Univariate Versus Multivariate
  Data Modes
- Implementation
- Discussion Questions: Chapter 5

5.1. INTRODUCTION

The purpose of this chapter is to present information that almost, but not quite, goes beyond the goal of this book. This book is about statistical data handling. My purpose is to explore the nature and management of statistical data and not really to dwell on its analysis. Statistical research does not deal with data without dealing with its ultimate purpose, however, and to be realistic, a researcher is probably thinking about his or her analysis with each data-handling keystroke. The analysis is, after all, what the enterprise is about; we are in this business for what data can tell us—not for the data themselves.[1]

This chapter is not a treatise on statistics. As I cautioned in Chapter 1, I do not discuss such topics as checking assumptions or accommodating complex changes in a statistical procedure (e.g., random vs. fixed effects in ANOVA). I recommend that you read this chapter with an eye toward understanding how to get data ready for these procedures, and not the full-blown complexity of the procedures themselves.

This chapter has a second purpose. In addition to illustrating data preparation for statistics, I want you to consider your personal preferences for and against certain statistical tests. Those preferences can be seen in your data structures. In that regard (and with a nod to Eudora Welty's famous story of the same name), let me describe a phenomenon in data handling I call the *worn path*.

5.1.1. THE WORN PATH PHENOMENON
(THE KNOW YOURSELF PRINCIPLE)

A senior scholar in second/foreign language acquisition, Barry McLaughlin (1987), has noted that research requires close attention to one's data structures: "There is a sense that as descriptions of learners' [language acquisition] accumulate, answers will emerge to the larger questions about second-language acquisition. This 'bottom-up' strategy requires careful attention to the limitations of one's database" (p. 80). I believe that by this he is warning us that anyone working with data perceives the world in certain terms and establishes a philosophical preference on how the world is structured and therefore how it operates. McLaughlin is reminding us of a critical part of researcher preference for statistical procedure and that it begins at the point of data structuring.

Data can be like a worn path. This tendency can be felt by empirical researchers, as well as by persons who use administrative databases. For example, educational administrators may also come to view a database in a simple and familiar form. Recall the following figure from Chapter 2:

```
        C
        O        T
        U        I
    N   N        M  T  T  T    T  T  T  T    T  T  T  T    T
    A   T        S  E  1  1  1    1  2  2  2    2  3  3  3    3
    M   R        L  E  I  Q  Q  Q    F  Q  Q  Q    F  Q  Q  Q    F
    E   Y        1  X  N  1  2  3    E  1  2  3    E  1  2  3    E
[LOG]   1    1   2     2     3     3     4     4     5     5     6     6
----5----0----5----0----5----0----5----0----5----0----5----0----5
JUAN  Mexico Spanish M 2 29 32 44 101 20 29 37  99  .   .   .   .
ANNA  Italy  Italian F 1 34 28 35  90  .   .   .   .   .   .   .   .
AHMED Egypt  Arabic  M 3 23 23 39  97 28 29 36  99 18 21 40 103
```

It is quite easy to structure a school and organize its data just like the figure above, year in and year out, and miss a lot of useful information.

That ease bothers me. It has for years. I worry about the tendency of instructional program administrators to structure their perceptions of students into rows and columns. "What is being lost?" I ask myself. What might we know about Anna, Ahmed, or Juan that is absent in this simple RBC computer file? Do we capture, for instance, that Juan is a fanatic about football? That Anna wants to fly commercial airplanes? That Ahmed has already been published, with distinction, in an Arab-language history journal? That Juan is sleeping poorly because his apartment is noisy? That Anna's mother is seriously ill with cancer?

Are those facts important? For instance, could they explain a sudden drop or rise in a student's scores? How can EAI management know unless it records them as variables? The issue is not whether such information will help devise better instruction (or better answer research questions). The issue is that I am bothered by the fact that EAI has not recorded such information. And EAI has not recorded it because its data structures are in a *worn path*—a structure that is most comfortable and familiar.

The people at EAI who set up the above data set may have considered a background questionnaire or an interview to determine more about each student as the term progresses. Or they may have not. But what I bet they did say is something like this: "Sure, stuff like that is important, but our database is not set up to handle it." This is truly an example of the tail wagging the dog; the institutional preference for data structures is prohibiting certain information. I alluded to this phenomenon in Principle 2.2, but I state it slightly differently here because Principle 2.2 was more mechanical, more aimed at the simple nuts and bolts of data entry. I propose something more philosophical here:

Principle 5.1: The Know Yourself Principle

Know yourself. Know your own preferences about data structure. Know your worn path in analysis of data and ask yourself whether you might be interested in other paths, other data types, and other analyses. Balance this principle against Principle 6.1, the Reinvented Wheel Principle.

I leave it to better philosophers of science to explore this topic further. For starters, I strongly recommend Runkel's 1990 book. It gets the mind working on assumptions about reality and inquiry in a remarkable manner, but at the same time, Runkel does not go far enough. He is rightly worried about a particular aspect of the worn path phenomenon—namely, researchers who have forgotten that although any individual may be a member of a group, all individuals have singular characteristics, and we must attend to those unique characteristics in psychological research. I would also suggest that the tendency to record each person's characteristics as the same as those of all members of a group derives from the easy, familiar worn path by which we prefer to structure data. If we break the inquiry loop at the tangent point of data structuring, other epistemological innovation will follow, such as the innovations Runkel supports.

Although I worry about missing information in databases, I am not advocating collecting data for data's sake. I do not support harvesting any and all data that might be available to an administrative unit or a researcher. We should not simply gather all the variables we can and then fish around for answers to our questions. Data are purposive—as I argue in my definition in Chapter 1—and we must be purposive in obtaining it.

When things work right—when the process is at its ideal, finely tuned best—here is how I think data handlers can leave their worn paths. Whether researchers or administrative users of data, the personnel involved have questions about the world. Those questions will be answered by extant data (as in the use of ongoing administrative databases), specially collected data (as in an experiment), or some hybrid (as in the attitude/motivation study in Chapter 4). In each case, a question or hypothesis is formed and the data are consulted to answer that question. All I ask is that we stop at that moment and ask ourselves very simple questions: Is our view of the world being colored by the types of data we most prefer? Are we about to set out on a worn path? Or can we gather other information that will help answer our questions better? My suggestion is simply to think about your data at that point when you think about your questions about the data.

It is not ipso facto unwise to pursue your worn path. If, for example, all your research is done on data sets that ultimately yield multiple regression or if your administrative setting wants only information on student test scores and not background information, that is fine, provided that's available; see my discussion of Principle 6.1. If other data are available and can enhance the answers to your data-based questions, even correct some answers, that is all the better. (Remember, data about people are about people. Data can have social consequences [Principle 1.3].)[2]

5.1.2. SOME STATISTICAL TERMINOLOGY: A REVIEW

The notion of a worn path resurfaces in the "Implementation" scenario later in the chapter. Before we can get to that story, I need to go through the data structures for several common statistical tests that I illustrate in this chapter. As I discuss in Chapter 1, this is not a book about statistical analysis on computers (e.g., Cody & Smith, 1991). My goal in this chapter is to show you how to prepare data for some common statistical tests; this is why this chapter is not entitled, for example, "Data Analysis." Hence, before we begin, you might want to consult your favorite statistics book and review these concepts:

ANOVA (analysis of variance): statistical procedure to study change in mean performance across several groups or interacting combination of groups. ANOVAs are of various designs—for example, between-subjects, repeated-measures, and mixed designs.

Independent Variables: the variables over which the researcher has some control, either by random assignment (as in an experiment) or by selection of intact groups (as with available groupings in an educational setting, like class groups). Classically, the latter definition—intact groups—is not part of the notion of independent variables. The classic notion is that an independent variable is one for which no confounding values exist. It is a unique category and therefore must be randomly assigned. My experience has taught me, however, that it is also used with intact groups, and in data handling (the focus of this book) both intact groups and randomly assigned independent variables are handled the same way in software like SAS or SPSS.

Dependent Variable: the variable that should change if there is an effect among the independent variables.

Correlation: an index of the degree to which two variables covary, or tend to rank observations similarly. The index is called a coefficient, and it can range from -1.00 to $+1.00$, where -1.00 is a perfect inverse relationship (as one variable goes up, the other goes down) and +1.00 is a perfect positive relationship (as one goes up, so does the other). A coefficient of 0.00 indicates no substantive agreement of rank between the two variables.

Regression: a statistical procedure to determine whether a dependent variable can be predicted by one or more independent variables. In this case, *predicted* refers to the construction of a mathematical formula to yield estimated values on the dependent variable(s) when only the independent variables have been measured. ANOVA and regression are both forms of general linear modeling (often called GLM, as SAS does), in which an dependent variable is analyzed as the linear combination of independent variable(s).

Chi-Square: a statistical procedure to determine the degree of relationship between two or more categorical variables. The categories of the variables are arranged in a frequency crosstable (for which I give examples in the "Implementation"), and the chi-square test tells you whether the cell crossfrequencies are greater than expected by chance.

5.2. DESCRIPTIVE STATISTICS AND DATA HANDLING: THE UBIQUITOUS TABLE 1

Descriptive statistics are results that paint a picture of the data without drawing any conclusions. They include results such as the mean, standard deviation, range, and simple frequency tables. Virtually every research project I have been involved in has had a "Table 1" (or set of first tables) that simply describes the data. Such tables are important because they provide general background to the reader about the nature of the study. Following is one example, excerpted from Table 1 of Davidson (1988).

In that study, I examined 21 language-testing data sets from nine world sources. I thought the first thing I should report was simple, descriptive information about all the data sets. The column heads were n = number of subjects, k = number of items in the test, mean, s.d. for standard deviation, range, and reliab(ility) coefficient. Most Table 1s have columns such as that, but the precise information contained in descriptive tables varies widely and should be a decision made by you, the report writer. My Table 1 example includes some explanatory notes about special circumstances governing the data and analyses, linked to the table through asterisks. Such notes often help the reader understand special circumstances behind some of the descriptive statistics. The ubiquitous Table 1 should almost stand by itself as a straightforward description of the data, and such footnotes help with that goal.[3]

Table 1   Descriptive Statistics and Reliabilities on 21 Language Test Data Sets

Dichotomous (0=wrong, 1=correct) items unless noted.
Missing=0=wrong in all data sets.

Code	Data Set	n	k	mean	s.d.	range	reliab.
(1a)	Alderson: both parts	1014	160	97.649	21.650	57-157	.945
(1b)	Alderson: Part 1	1014	120	79.140	14.249	52-117	.904
(1c)	Alderson: Part 2	1014	40	18.509	9.581	1-40	.940
(1d)	Alderson: Continuous	1014	13	60.241	15.301	6-98	.805**
(2a)	ACTFL, Lev.1	305	94	53.505	12.464	27-83	.906
⋮							
⋮							
(8b)	Jones/Southam Literacy, v.2	1186	39	26.656	9.115	0-39	.935
(9)	1985 TOEFL	5000	146	93.074	28.847	7-146	.970

*Four of the seven ACTFL data sets had . . . zero or near-zero sample proportions (proportions of persons scoring correct) [on some items, which were therefore deleted]

Code	Data Set	Original k	# items deleted	k as reported
(2b)	ACTFL Lev.2	117	6	111
(2c)	ACTFL Lev.3	127	16	111
(2d)	ACTFL Lev.4	141	31	110
(2f)	ACTFL Lev.6	103	16	87

**Data set (1d) is the only one containing continuous, nondichotomous items. Strictly speaking, the alpha reliability figure may be spurious because the items were designed with differing maximum possible points. . . . Furthermore, it is not entirely accurate to treat each of the Alderson data sets as separate. The test was administered across two days: Part 1 on day 1 and Part 2 on day 2. The 13 continuous items are mixed into both parts.

Sometimes the Table 1 is not a single table, but rather a series of tables. This is particularly true if the data include character variables that will not be submitted to mathematics and that therefore seem out of place in a table of means and standard deviations. Furthermore, if your study includes various groups of subjects (BY-groups), you might have several initial tables: one for all subjects in the study, and several for each subgroup.

Principle 4.2 is also relevant at this stage, and I suggest you review it and its discussion in Chapter 4. One way to debug data is to examine the descriptive tables and see whether the results make sense. Suppose, for example, I had gotten these results for the Alderson Part 1 data in my study:

Code	Data Set	n	k	mean	s.d.	range	reliab.
(b)	Alderson: Part 1	1014	120	79.140	14.249	52-127	.904

I know that data set and the test on which it is based, and it has only 120 items ($k = 120$). I also know that each item is scored right-wrong, with a value of 1 for right and 0 for wrong. Therefore, the maximum possible score, the right-hand value of the range, should be 120. How can I have a value of 127 for the upper end of the range? This would cause me to go back to the data and try to figure out what is happening; in this case, I would first suspect a value of 6 or something equally out of the ordinary somewhere in the test item values, some value that boosted the score for one item above 1 as a maximum value. A good technique would be to use the computer to calculate the mean of each item and see whether any mean is over 1.00; it should not be, and if it is, I would suspect that for that item somebody has a value over 1. From there, I could edit the data file and have a look, correct the problem, and regenerate Table 1. That is Principle 4.2 in action.

5.3. CORRELATION AND REGRESSION

Suppose we had an EAI data set like this:

```
        T   T   T   T   T   T   T   T   T
    N   E   E   E   E   E   E   E   E   E
    A   S   S   S   S   S   S   S   S   S
    M   T   T   T   T   T   T   T   T   T
    E   1   2   3   4   5   6   7   8   9
 [LOG]      1       1       2       2       3
----5----0----5----0----5----0----
 JUAN   7   2   1   5   4   4   3   4   5
 ANNA   6   3   3   4   3   5   5   4   3
 AHMED  5   5   6   4   3   2   4   4   1
  :
  :
(etc.)
```

Some EAI students took nine tests—perhaps nine quizzes over the course of an academic term or nine parts to a larger test. We want to know how student ranking compares on any pairwise test comparison (test1 with test2, test1 with test3, and so forth). The appropriate statistic would be a correlation, and the above data layout is sufficient to calculate correlation coefficients in software such as SAS or SPSS. The rows are observations; the columns are continuous, numeric variables. Data layout to compute correlations really has no special needs. Hence, Principle 5.2:

Principle 5.2: The Correlative Data Principle

Data structure for correlation-based statistics (e.g., correlations and regression) is easy. That does not mean such statistical analyses are always appropriate.

I have only two warnings about Principle 5.2. First, I must emphasize that although the statistical procedures themselves are complex, the data structure for these procedures is quite easy. For instance, mathematical assumptions hold for the statistics, and these must be examined. Just because you can arrange your data in a manner befitting regression does not mean that regression is appropriate, and you should always consult a good statistics book to assure yourself that you have met the requirements for any statistical analysis (e.g., Hedrick, Bickman, & Rog, 1993; Kerlinger, 1986; Minium et al., 1993).

Second, a problem could arise with phenomena like data polarity. *Polarity* in data refers to the expected high value if the trait being measured is strong. Suppose—for some reason—one of the tests above is scored like the game of golf: A high value means you did not do as well. A lower value means you did; you were closer to or even exceeded par. In correlational analysis, including a variable like that will produce some negative correlations when paired with variables of the opposite polarity. For example, if we assume the games of golf and bowling rank people similarly, then the coefficient between golf and bowling will be negative because a high score in golf is a low number, whereas in bowling a high score is the number of points made (pins knocked over). It will be a strong relationship, but a strong inverse relationship. If you do not want that to happen, you have to reverse one of the variables (and explain that you did so in the writeup of your project, clearly).

Perhaps you were taught that the sign of the correlation coefficient does not really matter (I tend to agree), that the magnitude is critical (whether or not the coefficient is close to an absolute value of 1). Sometimes, however, there are other reasons to reverse polarity; perhaps you need to compute an accurate total. Suppose you wanted to add the scores in bowling and golf such that a high combined score meant the person did well in both games. In that case, you would have to reverse the numbers on one game or the other. The reversal is quite easy; you simply form a computed variable by subtracting the observed value from the maximum possible plus 1. I illustrate how to do this in the "Implementation," but I offer the following principle because I think this issue is easy to forget:

Principle 5.3: The Expected Data Principle

Modify your data to control for expected direction of results (e.g., polarity). But remember Principle 3.2 and always keep a copy of the original unaltered data.

Principle 5.3 does not mean we can alter data to get the results we want to get (I do not intend to suggest we alter data to, for example, make it statistically significant). But in some instances—such as the example in the "Implementation"—we need to legitimately change data values.

5.4. *t* TESTS AND THE ANALYSIS OF VARIANCE (ANOVA): UNIVARIATE VERSUS MULTIVARIATE DATA MODES

Let's look at our data set above and expand it a bit:

```
        T   T   T   T   T   T   T   T   T               T
    N   E   E   E   E   E   E   E   E   E       C   O
    A   S   S   S   S   S   S   S   S   S       O   E
    M   T   T   T   T   T   T   T   T   T       N N F
    E   1   2   3   4   5   6   7   8   9       L T L
 [LOG]    1     1     2     2     3     3     4     4
 ----5----0----5----0----5----0----5----0----5----
 JUAN   7   2   1   5   4   4   3   4   5 Spanish y 540
 ANNA   6   3   3   4   3   5   5   4   3 Italian n 517
 AHMED  5   5   6   4   3   2   4   4   1 Arabic  n 523
 MARIA  4   5   5   4   4   5   4   3   1 Spanish y 523
 IMAN   6   6   5   4   5   2   3   3   1 Arabic  n 540
    :
    :
 (etc.)
```

We still have the nine test scores, and assuming that polarity is the same on all tests (Principle 5.3), we could also compute a total test score as I discuss in Chapter 3. We now also have two categorical character variables: first is NL, or native language, and second is

CONTinue, which is yes if the student has attended EAI before and no if not. Finally, we have a score on the TOEFL, which is the large international test of English. This data set as it is shown above is directly amenable to ANOVA, between-subjects, repeated-measures, and mixed designs (between/repeated or fixed plus random effects). I illustrate how to run such designs in the "Implementation" example, but before that, a data layout problem needs attention.

A tricky aspect of handling ANOVA data is related to the idea of between-subjects versus repeated-measures (within subjects) designs or mixed designs (between and repeated). Suppose we treat the nine tests above as repeated measures of the same trait, such that we want to include them as a repeated (within-subjects) ANOVA factor. An excellent explanation of the data needs for repeated measures is in the SAS manual itself (SAS Institute, 1990, pp. 951-952):

SUBJ	GROUP	TIME	Y
1	1	1	15
1	1	2	19
1	1	3	25
2	1	1	21
2	1	2	18
2	1	3	17
1	2	1	14
1	2	2	12
1	2	3	16
2	2	1	11
2	2	2	20
2	2	3	21
	.		
	.		
	.		
10	3	1	14
10	3	2	18
10	3	3	16

Repeated Measures Data in "univariate mode"

SOURCE: SAS Institute, 1990, p. 951

The above data set is the true conceptual layout for a repeated-measures ANOVA. There are 10 subjects (people). Each SUBJ (person) is a member of a GROUP called 1, 2, or 3. Each person was measured three TIMEs: 1, 2, and 3. A member of Group 1 at Time 1, Subject 1 had a score (on the dependent variable) of 15. At Time 2, Subject 1 (still a member of Group 1) had a score of 19, and at Time 3, 25. Subject 2 was also a member of Group 1, and his or her respective scores (at Times 1, 2, and 3) were 21, 18, and 17. Subject 3 was a member of Group 2, and his or her scores on the dependent variable are given above. The pattern continues through 10 subjects. The 10th and final case was a member of Group 3, as shown, and received the dependent variable scores shown.

All this complex business is by way of saying that the real case—the true observation—in a repeated-measures data set appears not to be a human being, but rather is a human being at a unique instance of measurement. Subject 1, for example, actually appears to constitute three cases in the data set. I suggest that, as an exercise, you try to fill out sample data lines for the missing people above: Subjects 3 through 9.

The above data layout is what SAS calls *univariate mode.* It is not the most likely way to lay out repeated measures data. Rather, as the SAS manual notes (SAS Institute, 1990, p. 952), "a more complete and efficient repeated measures" data set might look like this:

GROUP	Y1	Y2	Y3
1	15	19	25
1	21	18	17
2	14	12	16
2	11	20	21
		.	
		.	
		.	
3	14	18	16

Repeated Measures "multivariate" data layout

SOURCE: SAS Institute, 1990, p. 952

In the above figure, each row of the data set is a unique set of data points for a given subject. It says that Person 1, a member of Group 1, was measured three times (now called Y1, Y2, and Y3) and received the scores 15, 19, and 25. As the data set stands, two persons are in Group 1, two in Group 2, and one in Group 3. Again, as an exercise, you could fill out the data set with additional people in Groups 1, 2, and 3.

Fortunately, both SAS and SPSS allow repeated-measures and mixed (repeated and between-subject) ANOVA from data in multivariate mode, which is a far easier way to enter the data. Indeed, in SAS it is easier to program an ANOVA from a multivariate mode data layout than a univariate data layout, although you could do the ANOVA either way and obtain the same results.

Now let's return to our sample data set, which is arranged in multivariate mode:

```
        T   T   T   T   T   T   T   T   T               T
    N   E   E   E   E   E   E   E   E   E           C   O
    E   S   S   S   S   S   S   S   S   S           O   E
    M   T   T   T   T   T   T   T   T   T         N N   F
    E   1   2   3   4   5   6   7   8   9         L T   L
[LOG]       1       1       2       2       3       3       4       4
----5----0----5----0----5----0----5----0----5----
 JUAN  7   2   1   5   4   4   3   4   5 Spanish y 540
 ANNA  6   3   3   4   3   5   5   4   3 Italian n 517
AHMED  5   5   6   4   3   2   4   4   1 Arabic  n 523
MARIA  4   5   5   4   4   5   4   3   1 Spanish y 523
 IMAN  6   6   5   4   5   2   3   3   1 Arabic  n 540
 :

 :
(etc.)
```

The univariate analog to our data would be as follows. The variable T represents TEST, on which we have measured nine repeated times:

NAME	CONT	NL	T	TOEFL
Juan	y	Spanish	7	540
Juan	y	Spanish	2	540
Juan	y	Spanish	1	540
Juan	y	Spanish	5	540
Juan	y	Spanish	4	540
Juan	y	Spanish	4	540
Juan	y	Spanish	3	540
Juan	y	Spanish	4	540
Juan	y	Spanish	5	540
Juan	y	Spanish	6	540
Anna	y	Italian	3	517
Anna	y	Italian	3	517
Anna	y	Italian	4	517

.

.

.

(etc., see if you can fill in some more lines)

A principle that evolves in this discussion is somewhat relevant to repeated-measures analysis, but it is generalizable to a lot of other data gathering as well, as I illustrate for chi-square in the next section.

Principle 5.4: The Unit of Observation Principle

The unit of observation is not always the unit of analysis.

Principle 5.4 reminds us that although we may key in the data in multivariate mode, if we do a repeated-measures study in SAS or SPSS, the software actually converts it to univariate mode.

5.5. FREQUENCY DATA AND THE CHI-SQUARE TEST: MORE ON UNIVARIATE VERSUS MULTIVARIATE DATA MODES

This univariate/multivariate distinction is also relevant to the analysis of frequency data. Suppose EAI also wishes to conduct a study in which the dependent variable is some assessment of complexity in learner writing—for example, the average length of clauses in a student essay. In this case, what is the unit of observation—and therefore the unit of analysis? It is a value—the average clause length—for each student for each essay. Each student would be measured several times: once for each essay she or he writes. Now suppose the EAI staff want to know something about the characteristics of individual clauses: Do they or do they not contain a subordinate clause? To do so, they intend to sample five clauses randomly from each student essay and to ask the question: Does the sampled clause contain a subordinate clause? For each clause that each student produces within each essay, the question is posed: Does it have a subordinate clause—yes or no? The unit of observation is clause within essay within subject.

The above clause example can serve as a good illustration for chi-square data layout. It might be conceived as a univariate mode data set that looks like this:

NAME	ESSAY	CLAUSE	SUB
Juan	1	1	y
Juan	1	2	y
Juan	1	3	n
Juan	1	4	y
Juan	1	5	y
Juan	2	1	n
Juan	2	2	y
Juan	2	3	n
Juan	2	4	y
Juan	2	5	n
Juan	3	1	n
Juan	3	2	y
Juan	3	3	y
Juan	3	4	y
Juan	3	5	y

Anna	1	1	n
Anna	1	2	n
Anna	1	3	y
Anna	1	4	y
Anna	1	5	y
Anna	2	1	n
Anna	2	2	y
Anna	2	3	n
Anna	2	4	y
Anna	2	5	y
Anna	3	1	y
Anna	3	2	n
Anna	3	3	n
Anna	3	4	n
Anna	3	5	y
.			
.			
.			
Ahmed	3	5	n

Sample clause data: univariate mode

NOTE: SUB is y if the clause contains a subordinate clause, n otherwise.

Software varies in the required data structuring for data sets such as these. For example, if we are to do chi-square analysis in SAS (which is handled by PROC FREQ), we have no choice about data layout. We must enter the data in the above univariate format or go through some fairly complex programming to get it into such a format before we run a chi-square. This requirement suggests an important data-handling principle that follows from Principle 5.4:

Principle 5.5: The Software Unit Principle

Because the unit of observation is not always the unit of analysis (see Principle 5.4), know whether your software requires you to key in data in univariate or multivariate mode. This affects the complexity of data entry.

Principle 5.5 would suggest that if you are headed toward a SAS chi-square analysis, it is important to key in data in the univariate form. But if you are to do ANOVA in SAS, you can use a more comfortable data multivariate layout. You need to know this before you begin data entry in your software.

5.6. IMPLEMENTATION

Let's construct a scenario to illustrate data preparation for statistical analysis. Suppose a researcher, R, is employed at EAI. She is also pursuing a doctorate at a major university, and she has an internship at EAI's world headquarters. As part of her internship, she has approached the EAI management to investigate some questions in which she thinks EAI is quite interested. After some negotiation, a research focus emerges for which EAI will pay her and which her Ph.D. committee has endorsed as a dissertation.

The question that interests both parties—R and EAI—concerns a new language-teaching methodology with which EAI is experimenting at some of its schools: proactive immersion (or PI; there really is no such thing, although if there were, I wonder what it would be). The PI method interests EAI because of one of its key claims: It is purported to work in classrooms with widely varying preinstruction student ability. In the world of commercial language teaching, it is difficult to monitor student progress through a suite of courses and ensure that students remain in homogeneous classrooms. EAI's clients—the students—have their own agendas and time frames, and the EAI administrators have long wished for a teaching method that would permit a wider variety of ability in the classroom. The PI method is supposed to do precisely that, and if true, would make it much easier for EAI to accept and promote students because the administration would not be restricted to the periodicity of strict level-placement procedures.

EAI staff are interested in many features of the PI methodology, but after negotiation, they and R decide to focus on a few key points that reflect R's main academic interest: student attitude toward language learning. They decide to investigate the following questions:

Is there a difference across NL in attitude about the PI method? That is, do students from certain language backgrounds tend to prefer the PI system more or less than students from other language backgrounds? (Note: The independent variable is NL; the dependent variable is a measure of preference about the PI system.)

Is there a difference in attitude across prior study? That is, do people who have studied the target language before arriving at EAI prefer the PI method more or less than those who have not had prior study? (Note: Here, prior study is the independent variable; attitude is the dependent variable.)

Do NL and prior study interact? Does some combination of native language background and prior study affect student attitude toward the PI method? (Note: This is a classic ANOVA question: We have two independent variables—prior study and NL—and one dependent: attitude.)

PI's proponents claim that their system can work in classes with widely varying preinstruction ability. Is student ability also a factor in the NL/prior study effect on attitude? (Note: This is a new variable in the ANOVA—an independent variable that is measured on a continuous scale [ability], rather than a categorical scale such as NL.)

R perceives that she has three independent variables: NL, prior study, and proficiency level. One more twist: R correctly reasons that she may have more than one dependent variable. She has a 10-item attitude survey, with questions such as:

A. The PI method made me study harder.

strongly agree   agree   neutral   disagree   strongly disagree

B. The PI method was tiring.

strongly agree   agree   neutral   disagree   strongly disagree

and so forth. Can she simply add up the items and form a total score? Can she also analyze them as 10 separate dependent variables? Or should she treat the 10 items as repeated measures on a single abstract attitudinal variable; that is, does she have a within-subjects factor in her ANOVA? Furthermore, what about the fact that the expected response under the positive (alternative) hypothesis is sometimes *strongly disagree* and sometimes *strongly agree*? Notice, for example, that if the PI method is favorable, then the answer to question A above would be *agree*, whereas it would be *strongly disagree* for question B. What should she do about this polarity problem?

Let's assume R is well versed in the literature on foreign language acquisition in particular and on human learning in general. She had several statistics classes some years back, including one about ANOVA in which she learned some SAS. She keeps up with literature on language learning and attitude, and she needs help putting her data into the form of what she sees as the most common approach to questions in that discipline: ANOVA. R is beset with data questions. She does not know how to make a computer tell her the answers she needs because she sees many complex data-related problems in her way.

Let's also assume this is a pilot study allowing R to work out design bugs and generally test the waters for feasibility of a much larger project (and allowing me to present a rather small data set to save space). I use SAS and SPSS to illustrate several analyses of R's data other than the one in which she is most interested: ANOVA. One of these other procedures—chi-square—is another approach she wants to try. The others—correlation, regression, and the *t* test—are here to help me teach some SAS and SPSS and (I admit) represent too much of a fishing expedition in the data, although you may disagree. (We return to R and her project in discussion question 6, where I pose the question: Is her work following a worn path?)

As always, the SAS and SPSS examples here could be linked into one contiguous program, and as before, I recommend that you review the "Implementation" in previous chapters before studying these examples.

As you work through these examples, compare the SAS and SPSS results. They are uniformly the same within rounding. *Rounding*, or level of precision, is a decision made by software designers.

The first programming I illustrate is data input and computation of correlations. Let's assume that R has data on 14 variables: student name, prior study (y/n), NL (native language), 10 attitude variables, and the TOEFL score. The SAS code to read in the data and run correlations is given below, and as a bonus, it will yield some output that she could use to form her Table 1 of descriptive statistics. Notice the use of start-stop column designators in SAS, the shorthand for reading in the 10 attitude variables (@21 (att01-att10) (2.)), and the computation to reverse the polarity on two variables.

```
*----------------------------------------------------------*
|                                                          |
| Name of input program: ch5.sas (SAS)                     |
|              function: demos for Chapter 5:              |
|                        data setup for:                   |
|                        -correlation                      |
|                        -regression                       |
|                        -t tests                          |
|                        -ANOVA: between-subjects           |
|                               and mixed                  |
|                        -chi-square                       |
| Name(s) of input data sets: in the program, see below.   |
|        Program written by: Fred Davidson                 |
*----------------------------------------------------------*;

title1 'Chapter 5 Demo. Program SAS';

data rdat;

  input name    $  1-5
        prior   $  7
        nl      $  9-20
        @21 (att01-att10) (2.)
        toefl      41-44;

* Reverse polarity for ATT5 and ATT9. (We assume a
  five-point attitude scale where 1=strongly disagree,
  2=disagree, 3=neutral, 4=agree, and 5=disagree.
  Hence, to reverse some items, it is necessary to
  subtract from six.);
  att05=6-att05;
  att09=6-att09;
```

```
* Computed variable: the ATT total (after reversal);
atot=sum(of att01-att10);

cards;
```

JUAN	y	Spanish	5	4	4	5	1	3	4	4	1	5	480
ANNA	y	Italian	4	5	5	4	2	4	5	5	2	3	510
AHMED	n	Arabic	5	5	4	4	3	4	4	4	1	3	550
S04	y	Spanish	5	4	3	3	2	3	4	4	1	3	501
S05	n	Arabic	4	3	4	2	2	3	4	4	1	3	537
S06	y	Spanish	5	3	5	4	1	3	4	3	1	3	607
S07	n	Italian	4	4	4	4	2	3	4	4	1	4	570
S08	n	Italian	5	5	4	4	3	4	3	2	1	3	600
S09	y	Italian	4	5	4	4	1	4	3	2	1	4	605
S10	n	Spanish	4	3	4	4	3	5	3	4	2	4	490
S11	y	Arabic	3	4	4	3	4	5	3	4	2	4	507
S12	n	Arabic	4	5	5	4	1	4	3	4	1	4	577
S13	y	Spanish	5	3	5	3	2	4	3	5	3	5	490
S14	n	Italian	4	4	5	4	2	4	5	4	1	5	550
S15	n	Italian	3	5	5	4	2	5	4	4	2	4	600
S16	n	Arabic	4	4	4	5	3	5	4	5	2	5	610
S17	y	Arabic	5	4	5	4	1	5	3	4	2	5	637
S18	y	Spanish	4	4	4	5	2	5	5	4	1	4	630
S19	n	Arabic	5	4	5	5	1	5	4	5	2	3	597
S20	n	Italian	5	4	4	5	2	4	4	4	2	4	577
S21	y	Spanish	4	5	4	4	3	4	5	5	2	4	537
S22	n	Italian	5	4	4	3	2	4	4	5	2	5	590
S23	y	Italian	4	4	4	4	1	5	5	4	2	5	597
S24	n	Arabic	5	5	5	5	1	5	5	5	1	5	657
S25	n	Arabic	4	5	4	4	2	4	3	4	2	5	547
S26	y	Arabic	5	4	5	5	1	4	5	4	2	5	557
S27	n	Spanish	3	4	3	5	1	4	5	3	2	5	540
S28	n	Spanish	4	5	4	5	1	5	4	5	1	5	533
S29	y	Arabic	5	4	5	4	1	4	4	5	1	5	537
S30	n	Spanish	4	4	5	4	1	4	4	5	1	3	540
S31	y	Arabic	5	4	3	4	1	4	4	4	3	3	557
S32	n	Italian	4	5	4	4	2	4	4	4	3	3	550
S33	y	Italian	5	4	5	4	1	4	4	4	1	3	547
S34	n	Spanish	5	5	4	4	3	4	4	4	2	4	497
S35	y	Spanish	4	5	4	4	2	4	5	3	2	3	500
S36	n	Italian	5	4	5	4	2	3	3	4	1	5	507
S37	y	Arabic	4	5	4	4	2	4	4	5	2	4	517

```
    S38   n   Spanish   3  5  3  4  2  3  4  5  2  4  527
    S39   y   Italian   5  5  4  5  1  4  4  5  2  4  530
    S40   y   Arabic    4  5  4  5  1  4  4  4  1  5  537
;
run;

proc print data=rdat;
    title2 'DEBUG: printout of data';
run;

proc print data=rdat;
    var att05 att09;
    title2 'Check polarity reversal compare to input data';
run;

proc corr data=rdat;
    var att01-att10;
    title2 'DEMO: Correlations of ATT variables';
run;
```

The SAS results of the above code would be the following:

Chapter 5 Demo. Program SAS
DEBUG: printout of data

		P		A	A	A	A	A	A	A	A	A	A	T	
	N	R		T	T	T	T	T	T	T	T	T	T	O	A
O	A	I		T	T	T	T	T	T	T	T	T	T	E	T
B	M	O	L	0	0	0	0	0	0	0	0	0	1	F	O
S	E	R	1	1	2	3	4	5	6	7	8	9	0	L	T
1	JUAN	y	Spanish	5	4	4	5	5	3	4	4	5	5	480	44
2	ANNA	Y	Italian	4	5	5	4	4	4	5	5	4	3	510	43
3	AHMED	n	Arabic	5	5	4	4	3	4	4	4	5	3	550	41
4	S04	y	Spanish	5	4	3	3	4	3	4	4	5	3	501	38
5	S05	n	Arabic	4	3	4	2	4	3	4	4	5	3	537	36
	:														

: [some cases deleted to save space]

38	S38	n	Spanish	3	5	3	4	4	3	4	5	4	4	527	39
39	S39	y	Italian	5	5	4	5	5	4	4	5	4	4	530	45
40	S40	y	Arabic	4	5	4	5	5	4	4	4	5	5	537	45

Chapter 5 Demo. Program SAS
Check polarity reversal compare to input data

OBS	ATTO5	ATTO9
1	5	5
2	4	4
3	3	5
4	4	5
5	4	5
:	:	:
39	5	4
40	5	5

Chapter 5 Demo. Program SAS
DEMO: Correlations of ATT variables

Correlation Analysis

10 'VAR' Variables: ATTO1   ATTO2   ATTO3   ATTO4   ATTO5
                       ATTO6   ATTO7   ATTO8   ATTO9   ATT10

Simple Statistics

Variable	N	Mean	Std Dev	Sum	Minimum	Maximum
ATTO1	40	4.3500	0.6622	174.0000	3.0000	5.0000
ATTO2	40	4.3250	0.6558	173.0000	3.0000	5.0000
ATTO3	40	4.2500	0.6304	170.0000	3.0000	5.0000
ATTO4	40	4.1250	0.6864	165.0000	2.0000	5.0000
ATTO5	40	4.2250	0.8002	169.0000	2.0000	5.0000
ATTO6	40	4.0750	0.6558	163.0000	3.0000	5.0000
ATTO7	40	4.0000	0.6794	160.0000	3.0000	5.0000
ATTO8	40	4.1500	0.7696	166.0000	2.0000	5.0000
ATTO9	40	4.3750	0.6279	175.0000	3.0000	5.0000
ATT10	40	4.0750	0.8286	163.0000	3.0000	5.0000

Pearson Correlation Coefficients / Prob R under Ho: Rho=0 / N = 40[4]

	ATT01	ATT02	ATT03	ATT04	ATT05
ATT01	1.00000	-0.20960	0.27641	0.07052	0.23469
	0.0	0.1943	0.0843	0.6655	0.1449
ATT02	-0.20960	1.00000	-0.13954	0.30615	-0.04519
	0.1943	0.0	0.3905	0.0547	0.7819
ATT03	0.27641	-0.13954	1.00000	0.04444	0.24142
	0.0843	0.3905	0.0	0.7854	0.1334
ATT04	0.07052	0.30615	0.04444	1.00000	0.36761
	0.6655	0.0547	0.7854	0.0	0.0196
ATT05	0.23469	-0.04519	0.24142	0.36761	1.00000
	0.1449	0.7819	0.1334	0.0196	0.0
ATT06	-0.18008	0.12072	0.20155	0.32039	-0.08183
	0.2662	0.4581	0.2123	0.0438	0.6157
ATT07	-0.11400	0.11510	-0.05987	0.32991	0.18866
	0.4837	0.4794	0.7136	0.0376	0.2437
ATT08	0.04528	0.00254	0.18497	0.06067	0.02706
	0.7814	0.9876	0.2532	0.7100	0.8683
ATT09	0.10793	0.00778	0.21053	0.06693	0.18499
	0.5074	0.9620	0.1923	0.6815	0.2531
ATT10	-0.04907	-0.04601	0.11045	0.29868	0.16725
	0.7636	0.7780	0.4975	0.0612	0.3023

	ATT06	ATT07	ATT08	ATT09	ATT10
ATT01	-0.18008	-0.11400	0.04528	0.10793	-0.04907
	0.2662	0.4837	0.7814	0.5074	0.7636
ATT02	0.12072	0.11510	0.00254	0.00778	-0.04601
	0.4581	0.4794	0.9876	0.9620	0.7780
ATT03	0.20155	-0.05987	0.18497	0.21053	0.11045
	0.2123	0.7136	0.2532	0.1923	0.4975
ATT04	0.32039	0.32991	0.06067	0.06693	0.29868
	0.0438	0.0376	0.7100	0.6815	0.0612
ATT05	-0.08183	0.18866	0.02706	0.18499	0.16725
	0.6157	0.2437	0.8683	0.2531	0.3023

ATT06	1.00000	0.05755	0.18034	-0.25685	0.22531
	0.0	0.7243	0.2655	0.1096	0.1622
ATT07	0.05755	1.00000	0.19616	0.00000	0.00000
	0.7243	0.0	0.2251	1.0000	1.0000
ATT08	0.18034	0.19616	1.00000	-0.22551	0.22316
	0.2655	0.2251	0.0	0.1618	0.1663
ATT09	-0.25685	0.00000	-0.22551	1.00000	-0.00616
	0.1096	1.0000	0.1618	0.0	0.9699
ATT10	0.22531	0.00000	0.22316	-0.00616	1.00000
	0.1622	1.0000	0.1663	0.9699	0.0

In the SAS results above, we first see a printout of the entire data set, followed by a printout of only the two variables that were reversed: an example of Principle 5.3. (I deleted some of the cases because the results in this chapter are rather long.) Following the listing of the data are the results of SAS proc corr: We have a full set of descriptive statistics for each variable to be correlated, and R could easily cut and paste the descriptive statistics into her preliminary report to EAI as her ubiquitous Table 1. We next have a complete correlation matrix. A *correlation matrix* is a square table in which rows and columns are the same variables. The cells are the correlations (and observed probabilities of the correlations) between each variable and each other variable. For example, the correlation between ATT01 (the first attitude question) and ATT02 (the second) is -0.20960, which has an observed probability of 0.1943. By definition, the correlation of any variable with itself is +1.00; the 1s are on the diagonal, as often stated in correlational parlance. The matrix is too large to fit in the 80-column-width default of SAS output, so it has been truncated and continued below; to see what I mean, study the matrix at the upper left and find the diagonal of 1s, then follow it into the next segment of the matrix just below. A correlation matrix is symmetric, so values above the diagonal are the same as those below.

In SPSS, the input code to do the above procedures is quite similar to that for SAS. The correlation code has a minor difference: SPSS has a subcommand to request descriptive statistics (/ statistics=descriptives), whereas SAS provides that information by default. Notice also the familiar differences in file handling (the SPSS get statement):

```
*-------------------------------------------------------*
| Name of input program: ch5.sps (SPSS)                 |
|              function: SPSS demos for Chapter 5:       |
|                        data setup for:                |
|                        -correlation                   |
|                        -regression                    |
|                        -t tests                       |
|                        -ANOVA: between-subjects        |
|                                and mixed              |
|                        -chi-square                    |
| Name(s) of input data sets: in the program, see below.|
|      Program written by: Fred Davidson                |
*-------------------------------------------------------*.
```

```
title 'Chapter 5 Demo. Program SPSS'.

data list fixed
   / name          1-5  (a)
     prior           7  (a)
     nl           9-20  (a)
     att01 to att10 (10F2.0)
     toefl       41-44.
begin data
  JUAN y Spanish      5 4 4 5 1 3 4 4 1 5 480
  ANNA y Italian      4 5 5 4 2 4 5 5 2 3 510
 AHMED n  Arabic      5 5 4 4 3 4 4 4 1 3 550
   S04 y Spanish      5 4 3 3 2 3 4 4 1 3 501
   S05 n  Arabic      4 3 4 2 2 3 4 4 1 3 537
   S06 y Spanish      5 3 5 4 1 3 4 3 1 3 607
   S07 n Italian      4 4 4 4 2 3 4 4 1 4 570
   S08 n Italian      5 5 4 4 3 4 3 2 1 3 600
   S09 y Italian      4 5 4 4 1 4 3 2 1 4 605
   S10 n Spanish      4 3 4 4 3 5 3 4 2 4 490
   S11 y  Arabic      3 4 4 3 4 5 3 4 2 4 507
   S12 n  Arabic      4 5 5 4 1 4 3 4 1 4 577
   S13 y Spanish      5 3 5 3 2 4 3 5 3 5 490
   S14 n Italian      4 4 5 4 2 4 5 4 1 5 550
   S15 n Italian      3 5 5 4 2 5 4 4 2 4 600
   S16 n  Arabic      4 4 4 5 3 5 4 5 2 5 610
   S17 y  Arabic      5 4 5 4 1 5 3 4 2 5 637
```

```
S18 y Spanish      4 4 4 5 2 5 5 4 1 4 630
S19 n Arabic       5 4 5 5 1 5 4 5 2 3 597
S20 n Italian      5 4 4 5 2 4 4 4 2 4 577
S21 y Spanish      4 5 4 4 3 4 5 5 2 4 537
S22 n Italian      5 4 4 3 2 4 4 5 2 5 590
S23 y Italian      4 4 4 4 1 5 5 4 2 5 597
S24 n Arabic       5 5 5 5 1 5 5 5 1 5 657
S25 n Arabic       4 5 4 4 2 4 3 4 2 5 547
S26 y Arabic       5 4 5 5 1 4 5 4 2 5 557
S27 n Spanish      3 4 3 5 1 4 5 3 2 5 540
S28 n Spanish      4 5 4 5 1 5 4 5 1 5 533
S29 y Arabic       5 4 5 4 1 4 4 5 1 5 537
S30 n Spanish      4 4 5 4 1 4 4 5 1 3 540
S31 y Arabic       5 4 3 4 1 4 4 4 3 3 557
S32 n Italian      4 5 4 4 2 4 4 4 3 3 550
S33 y Italian      5 4 5 4 1 4 4 4 1 3 547
S34 n Spanish      5 5 4 4 3 4 4 2 4 3 497
S35 y Spanish      4 5 4 4 2 4 5 3 2 3 500
S36 n Italian      5 4 5 4 2 3 3 4 1 5 507
S37 y Arabic       4 5 4 4 2 4 4 5 2 4 517
S38 n Spanish      3 5 3 4 2 3 4 5 2 4 527
S39 y Italian      5 5 4 5 1 4 4 5 2 4 530
S40 y Arabic       4 5 4 5 1 4 4 4 1 5 537
end data.

    * Reverse polarity for ATT5 and ATT9.
    compute att05=6-att05.
    compute att09=6-att09.

    * Computed variable: the ATT total
      (after reversal).
    compute atot=sum(att01 to att10).
    save outfile=rdat.
execute.

get file=rdat.
    subtitle 'DEBUG: printout of data'.
    list.
execute.
```

```
get file=rdat.
    subtitle 'Check polarity reversal compare to input
            data'.
    list variables=att05 att09.
execute.

get file=rdat.
    subtitle 'DEMO: Correlations of ATT variables'.
    correlations variables=att01 to att10
        / statistics=descriptives.
execute.
```

And the SPSS output listing is as follows:

Chapter 5 Demo. Program SPSS
DEBUG: printout of data

NAME	P R I O R	NL	A T T 0 1	A T T 0 2	A T T 0 3	A T T 0 4	A T T 0 5	ATT06	ATT07	ATT08	ATT09	ATT10	TOEFL	ATOT
JUAN	y	Spanish	5	4	4	5	5	3	4	4	5	5	480	44.00
ANNA	y	Italian	4	5	5	4	4	4	5	5	4	3	510	43.00
AHMED	n	Arabic	5	5	4	4	3	4	4	4	5	3	550	41.00
S04	y	Spanish	5	4	3	3	4	3	4	4	5	3	501	38.00
S05	n	Arabic	4	3	4	2	4	3	4	4	5	3	537	36.00
S06	y	Spanish	5	3	5	4	5	3	4	3	5	3	607	40.00
S07	n	Italian	4	4	4	4	4	3	4	4	5	4	570	40.00
S08	n	Italian	5	5	4	4	3	4	3	2	5	3	600	38.00
S09	y	Italian	4	5	4	4	5	4	3	2	5	4	605	40.00
S10	n	Spanish	4	3	4	4	3	5	3	4	4	4	490	38.00
S11	y	Arabic	3	4	4	3	2	5	3	4	4	4	507	36.00
S12	n	Arabic	4	5	5	4	5	4	3	4	5	4	577	43.00
S13	y	Spanish	5	3	5	3	4	4	3	5	3	5	490	40.00
S14	n	Italian	4	4	5	4	4	4	5	4	5	5	550	44.00
S15	n	Italian	3	5	5	4	4	5	4	4	4	4	600	42.00
S16	n	Arabic	4	4	4	5	3	5	4	5	4	5	610	43.00
S17	y	Arabic	5	4	5	4	5	5	3	4	4	5	637	44.00

S18	y	Spanish	4	4	4	5	4	5	5	4	5	4	630	44.00
S19	n	Arabic	5	4	5	5	5	5	4	5	4	3	597	45.00
S20	n	Italian	5	4	4	5	4	4	4	4	4	4	577	42.00
S21	y	Spanish	4	5	4	4	3	4	5	5	4	4	537	42.00
S22	n	Italian	5	4	4	3	4	4	4	5	4	5	590	42.00
S23	y	Italian	4	4	4	4	5	5	5	4	4	5	597	44.00
S24	n	Arabic	5	5	5	5	5	5	5	5	5	5	657	50.00
S25	n	Arabic	4	5	4	4	4	4	3	4	4	5	547	41.00
S26	y	Arabic	5	4	5	5	5	4	5	4	4	5	557	46.00
S27	n	Spanish	3	4	3	5	5	4	5	3	4	5	540	41.00
S28	n	Spanish	4	5	4	5	5	5	4	5	5	5	533	47.00
S29	y	Arabic	5	4	5	4	5	4	4	5	5	5	537	46.00
S30	n	Spanish	4	4	5	4	5	4	4	5	5	3	540	43.00
S31	y	Arabic	5	4	3	4	5	4	4	4	3	3	557	39.00
S32	n	Italian	4	5	4	4	4	4	4	4	3	3	550	39.00
S33	y	Italian	5	4	5	4	5	4	4	4	5	3	547	43.00
S34	n	Spanish	5	5	4	4	3	4	4	4	4	4	497	41.00
S35	y	Spanish	4	5	4	4	4	4	5	3	4	3	500	40.00
S36	n	Italian	5	4	5	4	4	3	3	4	5	5	507	42.00
S37	y	Arabic	4	5	4	4	4	4	4	5	4	4	517	42.00
S38	n	Spanish	3	5	3	4	4	3	4	5	4	4	527	39.00
S39	y	Italian	5	5	4	5	5	4	4	5	4	4	530	45.00
S40	y	Arabic	4	5	4	5	5	4	4	4	5	5	537	45.00

Number of cases read: 40   Number of cases listed: 40

Chapter 5 Demo. Program SPSS
DEBUG: printout of data

ATT05	ATT09
5	5
4	4
3	5
4	5
4	5
5	5
4	5
3	5
5	5
3	4
2	4

5	5
4	3
4	5
4	4
3	4
5	4
4	5
5	4
4	4
3	4
4	4
5	4
5	5
4	4
5	4
5	4
5	5
5	5
5	5
5	3
4	3
5	5
3	4
4	4
4	5
4	4
4	4
5	4
5	5

Number of cases read: 40   Number of cases listed: 40

Chapter 5 Demo. Program SPSS
Check polarity reversal compare to input data

Variable	Cases	Mean	Std Dev
ATTO1	40	4.3500	.6622
ATTO2	40	4.3250	.6558
ATTO3	40	4.2500	.6304
ATTO4	40	4.1250	.6864
ATTO5	40	4.2250	.8002

ATTO6	40	4.0750	.6558
ATTO7	40	4.0000	.6794
ATTO8	40	4.1500	.7696
ATTO9	40	4.3750	.6279
ATT10	40	4.0750	.8286

Chapter 5 Demo. Program SPSS
DEMO: Correlations of ATT variables

- - Correlation Coefficients - -

	ATTO1	ATTO2	ATTO3	ATTO4	ATTO5	ATTO6
ATTO1	1.0000	-.2096	.2764	.0705	.2347	-.1801
	(40)	(40)	(40)	(40)	(40)	(40)
	P= .	P= .194	P= .084	P= .665	P= .145	P= .266
ATTO2	-.2096	1.0000	-.1395	.3061	-.0452	.1207
	(40)	(40)	(40)	(40)	(40)	(40)
	P= .194	P= .	P= .390	P= .055	P= .782	P= .458
ATTO3	.2764	-.1395	1.0000	.0444	.2414	.2016
	(40)	(40)	(40)	(40)	(40)	(40)
	P= .084	P= .390	P= .	P= .785	P= .133	P= .212
ATTO4	.0705	.3061	.0444	1.0000	.3676	.3204
	(40)	(40)	(40)	(40)	(40)	(40)
	P= .665	P= .055	P= .785	P= .	P= .020	P= .044
ATTO5	.2347	-.0452	.2414	.3676	1.0000	-.0818
	(40)	(40)	(40)	(40)	(40)	(40)
	P= .145	P= .782	P= .133	P= .020	P= .	P= .616
ATTO6	-.1801	.1207	.2016	.3204	-.0818	1.0000
	(40)	(40)	(40)	(40)	(40)	(40)
	P= .266	P= .458	P= .212	P= .044	P= .616	P= .
ATTO7	-.1140	.1151	-.0599	.3299	.1887	.0575
	(40)	(40)	(40)	(40)	(40)	(40)
	P= .484	P= .479	P= .714	P= .038	P= .244	P= .724
ATTO8	.0453	.0025	.1850	.0607	.0271	.1803
	(40)	(40)	(40)	(40)	(40)	(40)
	P= .781	P= .988	P= .253	P= .710	P= .868	P= .265

ATT09	.1079	.0078	.2105	.0669	.1850	−.2569
	(40)	(40)	(40)	(40)	(40)	(40)
	P= .507	P= .962	P= .192	P= .682	P= .253	P= .110

ATT10	−.0491	−.0460	.1104	.2987	.1673	.2253
	(40)	(40)	(40)	(40)	(40)	(40)
	P= .764	P= .778	P= .497	P= .061	P= .302	P= .162

(Coefficient / (Cases) / 2-tailed Significance)

" . " is printed if a coefficient cannot be computed

Chapter 5 Demo. Program SPSS
DEMO: Correlations of ATT variables

- - Correlation Coefficients - -

	ATT07	ATT08	ATT09	ATT10
ATT01	−.1140	.0453	.1079	−.0491
	(40)	(40)	(40)	(40)
	P= .484	P= .781	P= .507	P= .764
ATT02	.1151	.0025	.0078	−.0460
	(40)	(40)	(40)	(40)
	P= .479	P= .988	P= .962	P= .778
ATT03	−.0599	.1850	.2105	.1104
	(40)	(40)	(40)	(40)
	P= .714	P= .253	P= .192	P= .497
ATT04	.3299	.0607	.0669	.2987
	(40)	(40)	(40)	(40)
	P= .038	P= .710	P= .682	P= .061
ATT05	.1887	.0271	.1850	.1673
	(40)	(40)	(40)	(40)
	P= .244	P= .868	P= .253	P= .302
ATT06	.0575	.1803	−.2569	.2253
	(40)	(40)	(40)	(40)
	P= .724	P= .265	P= .110	P= .162
ATT07	1.0000	.1962	.0000	.0000
	(40)	(40)	(40)	(40)
	P= .	P= .225	P=1.000	P=1.000

ATT08	.1962	1.0000	–.2255	.2232
	(40)	(40)	(40)	(40)
	P= .225	P= .	P= .162	P= .166
ATT09	.0000	–.2255	1.0000	–.0062
	(40)	(40)	(40)	(40)
	P=1.000	P= .162	P= .	P= .970
ATT10	.0000	.2232	–.0062	1.0000
	(40)	(40)	(40)	(40)
	P=1.000	P= .166	P= .970	P= .

(Coefficient / (Cases) / 2-tailed Significance)

" . " is printed if a coefficient cannot be computed

Chapter 5 Demo. Program SPSS
DEMO: Correlations of ATT variables

The SPSS output above is similar to SAS, but for the notable exception that by default SPSS gives the *n* size in each cell of the correlation matrix. That is helpful if you have missing data.

The next example is a simple two-variable regression. Suppose R wants to know whether TOEFL scores can be predicted by the total of the attitude scale. This could be programmed in SAS with the following simple code (remember, the polarity of ATT05 and ATT09 was reversed before computing the total ATT value).

A new feature here is that we must use both run and quit to terminate the SAS regression procedure because proc reg (ression) is an interactive routine. That means you can run it and interrupt it, trying different regression models. SAS has several such interactive routines (e.g., proc glm [general linear models]), which I illustrate for ANOVA below. Following is the SAS regression code:

```
proc reg data=rdat;
   model toefl=atot;
   title2 'DEMO: Simple two-variable regression';
run;
quit;
```

And the SAS output would be:

Chapter 5 Demo. Program SAS
DEMO: Simple two-variable regression

Model: MODEL1
Dependent Variable: TOEFL

Analysis of Variance

Source	DF	Sum of Squares	Mean Square	F Value	ProbF
Model	1	9001.64089	9001.64089	5.093	0.0298
Error	38	67157.33411	1767.29827		
C Total	39	76158.97500			

Root MSE	42.03925	R-square	0.1182
Mean	553.22500	Adj R-sq	0.0950
C.V.	7.59894		

Parameter Estimates

Variable	DF	Parameter Estimate	Standard Error	T for H0: Parameter=0	Prob|T|
INTERCEP	1	338.601774	95.32988978	3.552	0.0010
ATOT 1	1	5.116167	2.26693380	2.257	0.0298

The SAS regression output contains the regression formula, which in its generic form is:

```
predicted value of the dependent variable = intercept
parameter plus (regression coefficient parameter
times independent variable raw value)
```

Or in this case:

```
Predicted TOEFL = 338.60 + (5.12*ATOT)
```

See whether you can find the appropriate values in the above output; you will probably find it helpful at this point to review two-variable regression in your favorite statistics book. The formula indicates that if we had an observed value of 39 on the ATOT variable, the formula would be:

```
Predicted TOEFL = 338.60 + (5.12*39)
                = 338.60 + 199.68
                = 538.28
                ≅ 538 [integer rounding]
```

This is a predicted TOEFL score and not a real result, so if I were running this analysis, I would not worry about a value ending in 8.

In SPSS, the code to run the regression would be as follows. SPSS code for regression is different from the SAS code, in that you must specify both the independent and dependent variables on one line (/ variables=...) and designate the dependent variable again on the next line (/ dependent=toefl). It is also necessary to specify the method of regressing, which in this case is enter, the appropriate designation for two-variable regression.

```
get file=rdat.
subtitle 'DEMO: Simple two-variable regression'.
regression
   / variables=toefl atot
   / dependent=toefl
   / method=enter.
execute.
```

The SPSS output would be:

* * * * M U L T I P L E   R E G R E S S I O N * * * *

Listwise Deletion of Missing Data

Equation Number 1 Dependent Variable.. TOEFL

Block Number 1. Method: Enter

Variable(s) Entered on Step Number
   1.. ATOT

Multiple R	.34380
R Square	.11820
Adjusted R Square	.09499
Standard Error	42.03925

Analysis of Variance

	DF	Sum of Squares	Mean Square
Regression	1	9001.64089	9001.64089
Residual	38	67157.33411	1767.29827

F = 5.09345   Signif F = .0298

- - - - - - - - - - - - - - - Variables in the Equation - - - - - - - - - - - - - - -

Variable	B	SE B	Beta	T	Sig T
ATOT	5.116167	2.266934	343796	2.257	.0298
(Constant)	338.601774	95.329890		3.552	.0010

End Block Number 1   All requested variables entered.

Chapter 5 Demo. Program - SPSS
DEMO: Simple two-variable regression

The next analysis that R wants to run is a *t* test of the variable TOEFL across the two categories of prior study, yes and no. In SAS, the input code for this would be:

```
proc ttest data=rdat;
   class prior;
   var toefl;
   title2 'DEMO: t-test';
run;
```

The above SAS code is typical SAS command language. In `proc ttest`, it is necessary to tell SAS the name of the grouping variable (the `class` line) and the dependent variable (the `var` line) on separate subcommands, but aside from that, the generic SAS `proc` format should appear quite familiar. The SAS results would appear as follows:

Chapter 5 Demo. Program SAS
DEMO: t-test

TTEST PROCEDURE

Variable: TOEFL

PRIOR	N	Mean	Std Dev	Std Error
n	21	559.33333333	40.82931953	8.90968797
y	19	546.47368421	47.82417847	10.97161900

Variances	T	DF	Prob|T|
Unequal	0.9099	35.6	0.3690
Equal	0.9172	38.0	0.3648

For H0: Variances are equal, $F' = 1.37$ DF $= (18,20)$ ProbF$' = 0.4915$

The layout of t-test results in SAS is a bit odd. We first need to know whether the variances (squared standard deviations) are statistically different across the two groups, `prior='y'` and `prior='n'`. The last line of the above output presents an F-prime test to determine that. The null hypothesis (that the variances are equal) is being tested against the alternative hypothesis that they are different. Assuming that R is working with a standard alpha probability level of .05, she would reject the alternative hypothesis and retain the null hypothesis because the observed probability of the F-prime statistic is 0.4915, which is above .05; the variances are not statistically different. With that determination, we can then look farther up the results and obtain the t statistic. We look at the second, smaller table and see that for the condition of EQUAL variances (because of the F-prime results I have already described), where the observed t statistic is 0.9172 at 38 degrees of freedom, with an observed probability of 0.3648. Assuming, again, that R's alpha level is .05 (well below .3648), she would retain the null hypothesis and reject the alternative hypothesis: There is no difference in TOEFL score across the two conditions of prior study: y and n.

Let's now examine the analogous code in SPSS, which is somewhat different from that in SAS:

```
get file=rdat.
subtitle 'DEMO: t-test'.
t-test groups=prior ('y','n')
    / variables=toefl.
execute.
```

Notice that, in SPSS, we had to specify the grouping variable on the *t*-test command line, and a subcommand specifies the dependent variable(s): TOEFL.

The SPSS output would be:

t-tests for Independent Samples of PRIOR

Variable	Number of Cases	Mean	SD	SE of Mean
TOEFL				
PRIOR y	19	546.4737	47.824	10.972
PRIOR n	21	559.3333	40.829	8.910

Mean Difference = -12.8596

Levene's Test for Equality of Variances: F= .512P= .479

	t-test for Equality of Means				95%
Variances	t-value	df	2-Tail Sig	SE of Diff	CI for Diff
Equal	−.92	38	.365	14.020	(−41.242, 15.523)
Unequal	−.91	35.62	.369	14.134	(−41.534, 15.815)

---Chapter 5 Demo. Program SPSS
DEMO: t-test

SPSS gives a bit more information on its *t*-test output, notably a confidence interval (CI). But you should be able to find the same output: the equality-of-variances test (Levene's test) and the actual *t*-test results.

Next, R is interested in doing some analyses of variance (ANOVAs). She wants to run a between-subjects ANOVA with TOEFL as a dependent variable and PRIOR and NL as independent variables; she also wants to do a mixed design (between or repeated measures mixed with between subjects) in which she takes repeated measures on the 10 attitude variables as her dependent variable. In SAS, a good routine to run ANOVA is proc glm, or general linear model, because it provides much useful flexibility in statistical analysis. (This procedure requires both the run; and quit; commands because it is interactive; see p. 19.) Following is the SAS input code for these two analyses:

```
proc glm data=rdat;
   classes prior nl;
   model toefl=prior nl prior*nl;
   title2 'DEMO: between-subjects ANOVA';
run;
quit;

proc glm data=rdat;
   classes prior nl;
   model att01-att10=prior nl;
   repeated att;
   title2 'DEMO: mixed (between+within) ANOVA';
run;
quit;
```

The above SAS code would yield the following rather lengthy SAS results, for which I interleaf some explanations:

Chapter 5 Demo. Program SAS
DEMO: between-subjects ANOVA

General Linear Models Procedure
Class Level Information

Class	Levels	Values
PRIOR	2	n y
NL	3	Arabic Italian Spanish

Number of observations in data set = 40

Chapter 5 Demo. Program SAS
DEMO: between-subjects ANOVA

General Linear Models Procedure

Dependent Variable: TOEFL

Source	DF	Sum of Squares	Mean Square	F Value	Pr > F
Model	5	16275.6274	3255.1255	1.85	0.1297
Error	34	59883.3476	1761.2749		

Corrected Total 39   76158.9750

R-Square	C.V.	Root MSE	TOEFL Mean
0.213706	7.585981	41.9675	553.225

The first set of results are for the between-subjects design, which is the first `proc glm` in the input code. Immediately above are the SAS `glm` results for the entire model; that is, it treats our requested ANOVA as a linear regressionlike model, and it gives an F-statistic source table. I typically ignore that part of the output in favor of the next segment:

Source	DF	Type I SS	Mean Square	F Value	Pr > F
PRIOR	1	1649.5715	1649.5715	0.94	0.3400
NL	2	11052.7465	5526.3732	3.14	0.0562
PRIOR*NL	2	3573.3094	1786.6547	1.01	0.3733

Source	DF	Type III SS	Mean Square	F Value	Pr > F
PRIOR	1	892.1158	892.1158	0.51	0.4815
NL	2	11587.0430	5793.5215	3.29	0.0494
PRIOR*NL	2	3573.3094	1786.6547	1.01	0.3733

Here, two ANOVA F-statistic source tables are given. The Type III is the appropriate statistic in cases (such as ours) with an unequal n size per cell in the design. The observed F-statistic for the interaction (PRIOR*NL) is 1.01 with an observed probability of 0.37, so there is no significant interaction at the .05 alpha level. Regarding the main effects, there is no effect for PRIOR either, as there should not be because the F-statistic is the square of the t test above. We do have a significant main effect for NL, and that is R's first finding that rejects the null hypothesis. For the dependent variable TOEFL, significant differences are found across the three native languages.

The next SAS output is that for the mixed design. This output is quite long, so I deleted some of it. Again, I intersperse explanation as the output proceeds.

Chapter 5 Demo. Program SAS
DEMO: mixed (between+within) ANOVA

General Linear Models Procedure
Class Level Information

Class	Levels	Values
PRIOR	2	n y
NL	3	Arabic Italian Spanish

Number of observations in data set = 40

Dependent Variable: ATT01

Source	DF	Sum of Squares	Mean Square	F Value	Pr > F
Model	5	2.04880952	0.40976190	0.93	0.4765
Error	34	15.05119048	0.44268207		
Corrected Total	39	17.10000000			

R-Square	C.V.	Root MSE	ATT01 Mean
0.119813	15.29525	0.66534	4.35000

Source	DF	Type I SS	Mean Square	F Value	Pr > F
PRIOR	1	0.55363409	0.55363409	1.25	0.2713
NL	2	0.35097699	0.17548849	0.40	0.6758
PRIOR*NL	2	1.14419845	0.57209922	1.29	0.2878

Source	DF	Type III SS	Mean Square	F Value	Pr > F
PRIOR	1	0.63278661	0.63278661	1.43	0.2401
NL	2	0.38229369	0.19114684	0.43	0.6529
PRIOR*NL	2	1.14419845	0.57209922	1.29	0.2878

:
: [To save space, I deleted eight source tables: ATT02 through ATT09]
:

Dependent Variable: ATT10

Source	DF	Sum of Squares	Mean Square	F Value	Pr > F
Model	5	1.69523810	0.33904762	0.46	0.8034
Error	34	25.07976190	0.73764006		
Corrected Total	39	26.77500000			

	R-Square	C.V.	Root MSE	ATT10 Mean
	0.063314	21.07631	0.85886	4.07500

Source	DF	Type I SS	Mean Square	F Value	Pr > F
PRIOR	1	0.01810777	0.01810777	0.02	0.8764
NL	2	0.42523957	0.21261978	0.29	0.7514
PRIOR*NL	2	1.25189076	0.62594538	0.85	0.4369

Source	DF	Type III SS	Mean Square	F Value	Pr > F
PRIOR	1	0.04609284	0.04609284	0.06	0.8041
NL	2	0.47723012	0.23861506	0.32	0.7258
PRIOR*NL	2	1.25189076	0.62594538	0.85	0.4369

The first interesting bit of output above was a separate ANOVA F-statistic source table, with both Type I and Type II sums of squares, for each of the 10 attitude variables.

General Linear Models Procedure
Repeated Measures Analysis of Variance
Repeated Measures Level Information

Dependent Variable	ATT01	ATT02	ATT03	ATT04	ATT05
Level of ATT	1	2	3	4	5
Dependent Variable	ATT06	ATT07	ATT08	ATT09	ATT10
Level of ATT	6	7	8	9	10

Source	DF	Type III SS	Mean Square	F Value	Pr > F
PRIOR	1	0.205450	0.205450	0.22	0.6435
NL	2	1.175885	0.587943	0.62	0.5418
PRIOR*NL	2	0.957398	0.478699	0.51	0.6062
Error	34	32.037500	0.942279		

Source: ATT

DF	Type III SS	Mean Square	F Value	Pr > F	G - G	Adj Pr > F H - F
9	5.75483044	0.63942560	1.35	0.2107	0.2253	0.2107

Source: ATT*PRIOR

DF	Type III SS	Mean Square	F Value	Pr > F	Adj Pr > F G - G	H - F
9	2.79234661	0.31026073	0.65	0.7495	0.7165	0.7495

Source: ATT*NL

DF	Type III SS	Mean Square	F Value	Pr > F	Adj Pr > F G - G	H - F
18	4.46010396	0.24778355	0.52	0.9467	0.9235	0.9467

Source: ATT*PRIOR*NL

DF	Type III SS	Mean Square	F Value	Pr > F	Adj Pr > F G - G	H - F
18	6.28290078	0.34905004	0.74	0.7724	0.7421	0.7724

Source: Error(ATT)

DF	Type III SS	Mean Square
306	144.99464286	0.47383870

We next obtained the results for the repeated measures and inter-action of repeated measures with the between-subjects factors. The columns labeled Pr > F are the observed probabilities for each effect, first the three-way interaction, ATT*PRIOR*NL; then two two-way interactions, ATT*NL and ATT*PRIOR; and the ATT repeated measures main effect. Because all the observed probabilities are above R's alpha level of .05, the null hypothesis would be retained and she would conclude that not much is going on.

The SPSS input code for the above run is also straightforward, except that we run headlong into a thorny problem in SPSS ANOVA programming. SPSS does not permit independent variables to be character. It is therefore necessary to recode all our categorical variables to temporary numeric variables just for the purpose of the ANOVAs—a rather awkward necessity. Notice below, for example, that the prior variable is temporarily recoded to a variable called p with the value 1=`y` and 2=`n`. This type of recoding must be done in each program block in which ANOVA is run.[5]

```
get file=rdat.
    * Notice the relevance of Principle 3.3 here.
    do if prior='y'.
```

```
      compute p=1.
   else if prior='n'.
      compute p=2.
   end if.
   do if nl='Arabic'.
      compute l=1.
   else if nl='Italian'.
      compute l=2.
   else if nl='Spanish'.
      compute l=3.
   end if.
   subtitle 'DEMO: between-subjects ANOVA'.
   anova variables=toefl by p (1,2) l (1,3).
execute.

get file=rdat.
   * Notice the relevance of Principle 3.3 here.
   do if prior='y'.
      compute p=1.
   else if prior='n'.
      compute p=2.
   end if.
   do if nl='Arabic'.
      compute l=1.
   else if nl='Italian'.
      compute l=2.
   else if nl='Spanish'.
      compute l=3.
   end if.
   subtitle 'DEMO: mixed (between+within) ANOVA'.
   manova att01 to att10 by p (1,2) l (1,3)
      / wsfactors=att(10).
execute.
```

The SPSS code and the SAS code are rather similar when doing ANOVA, although SPSS does require you to specify the lowest and highest value for the independent variables—for example, (1,3). The results are nonsignificant again. See whether you can match up the values from the SAS results with the SPSS output. Notice that SPSS does not give a separate source table for each ATT variable, as SAS does:

Chapter 5 Demo. Program SPSS
DEMO: between-subjects ANOVA

ANALYSIS OF VARIANCE

TOEFL

by P

L

UNIQUE sums of squares
All effects entered simultaneously

Source of Variation	Sum of Squares	DF	Mean Square	F	Sig of F
Main Effects	13118.446	3	4372.815	2.483	.077
P	892.116	1	892.116	.507	.482
L	11587.043	2	5793.521	3.289	.049
2-Way Interactions	3573.309	2	1786.655	1.014	.373
P L	3573.309	2	1786.655	1.014	.373
Explained	16275.627	5	3255.125	1.848	.130
Residual	59883.348	34	1761.275		
Total	76158.975	39	1952.794		

40 cases were processed.
0 cases (.0 pct) were missing.

Chapter 5 Demo. Program SPSS
DEMO: between-subjects ANOVA

- -

The default error term in MANOVA has been changed from
WITHIN CELLS to WITHIN+RESIDUAL. Notice that these are the
same for all full factorial designs.

Chapter 5 Demo. Program SPSS
DEMO: mixed (between+within) ANOVA

******Analysis of Variance******

40 cases accepted.
  0 cases rejected because of out-of-range factor values.
  0 cases rejected because of missing data.
  6 non-empty cells.
  1 design will be processed.

- -

Chapter 5 Demo. Program SPSS
DEMO: mixed (between+within) ANOVA

* * * * * * A n a l y s i s   o f   V a r i a n c e -- design 1 * * * * * *

Tests of Between-Subjects Effects.

Tests of Significance for T1 using UNIQUE sums of squares

Source of Variation	SS	DF	MS	F	Sig of F
WITHIN CELLS	32.04	34	.94		
P	.21	1	.21	.22	.644
L	1.18	2	.59	.62	.542
P BY L	.96	2	.48	.51	.606

- -

Chapter 5 Demo. Program SPSS
DEMO: mixed (between+within) ANOVA

* * * * * * A n a l y s i s   o f   V a r i a n c e -- design 1 * * * * * *

Tests involving 'ATT' Within-Subject Effect.

Mauchly sphericity test, W =	.28521
Chi-square approx. =	38.63456 with 44 D. F.
Significance =	.700

Greenhouse-Geisser Epsilon =	.80985
Huynh-Feldt Epsilon =	1.00000
Lower-bound Epsilon =	.11111

AVERAGED Tests of Significance that follow multivariate tests are
equivalent to univariate or split-plot or mixed-model approach to
repeated measures. Epsilons may be used to adjust d.f. for the
AVERAGED results.

- -

Chapter 5 Demo. Program SPSS
DEMO: mixed (between+within) ANOVA

* * * * * * A n a l y s i s   o f   V a r i a n c e -- design 1 * * * * * *

EFFECT .. P BY L BY ATT
Multivariate Tests of Significance (S = 2, M = 3 , N = 12)

Test Name	Value	Approx. F	Hypoth. DF	Error DF	Sig. of F
Pillais	.37405	.69016	18.00	54.00	.805
Hotellings	.49313	.68490	18.00	50.00	.809
Wilks	.65217	.68837	18.00	52.00	.806
Roys	.28060				

Note.. F statistic for WILKS' Lambda is exact.

- -

Chapter 5 Demo. Program SPSS
DEMO: mixed (between+within) ANOVA

* * * * * * Analysis of Variance -- design 1 * * * * * *

EFFECT .. L BY ATT
Multivariate Tests of Significance (S = 2, M = 3 , N = 12)

Test Name	Value	Approx. F	Hypoth. DF	Error DF	Sig. of F
Pillais	.29357	.51612	18.00	54.00	.939
Hotellings	.34705	.48201	18.00	50.00	.954
Wilks	.72705	.49915	18.00	52.00	.947
Roys	.17711				

Note.. F statistic for WILKS' Lambda is exact.

- -

Chapter 5 Demo. Program SPSS
DEMO: mixed (between+within) ANOVA

* * * * * * Analysis of Variance -- design 1 * * * * * *

EFFECT .. P BY ATT
Multivariate Tests of Significance (S = 1, M = 3 1/2, N = 12)

Test Name	Value	Exact F	Hypoth. DF	Error DF	Sig. of F
Pillais	.17218	.60088	9.00	26.00	.785
Hotellings	.20800	.60088	9.00	26.00	.785
Wilks	.82782	.60088	9.00	26.00	.785
Roys	.17218				

Note.. F statistics are exact.

- -

Chapter 5 Demo. Program SPSS
DEMO: mixed (between+within) ANOVA

****** Analysis of Variance -- design 1 ******

EFFECT .. ATT
Multivariate Tests of Significance (S = 1, M = 3 1/2, N = 12)

Test Name	Value	Exact F	Hypoth. DF	Error DF	Sig. of F
Pillais	.22544	.84081	9.00	26.00	.586
Hotellings	.29105	.84081	9.00	26.00	.586
Wilks	.77456	.84081	9.00	26.00	.586
Roys	.22544				

Note.. F statistics are exact.

- -

Chapter 5 Demo. Program SPSS
DEMO: mixed (between+within) ANOVA

****** Analysis of Variance -- design 1 ******

Tests involving 'ATT' Within-Subject Effect.

AVERAGED Tests of Significance for ATT using UNIQUE sums of squares

Source of Variation	SS	DF	MS	F	Sig of F
WITHIN CELLS	144.99	306	.47		
ATT	5.75	9	.64	1.35	.211
P BY ATT	2.79	9	.31	.65	.750
L BY ATT	4.46	18	.25	.52	.947
P BY L BY ATT	6.28	18	.35	.74	.772

- -

Chapter 5 Demo. Program SPSS
DEMO: mixed (between+within) ANOVA

Unwilling to relinquish her data that easily, R tries some cross-table frequency analysis. She suspects that students from certain native languages tend to have had greater prior study of English than those from others; to check on this, she wants to run a chi-square test. In SAS, this is done in the same procedure that requests simple frequency tables, `proc freq`:

```
proc freq data=rdat;
   tables prior*nl / chisq;
   title2 'DEMO: CHI-SQUARE analysis';
run;
```

And the SAS results would be:

Chapter 5 Demo. Program SAS
DEMO: CHI-SQUARE analysis

TABLE OF PRIOR BY NL

PRIOR   NL
Frequency
Percent
Row Pct
Col Pct

	Arabic	Italian	Spanish	Total
n	7	8	6	21
	17.50	20.00	15.00	52.50
	33.33	38.10	28.57	
	50.00	61.54	46.15	
y	7	5	7	19
	17.50	12.50	17.50	47.50
	36.84	26.32	36.84	
	50.00	38.46	53.85	
Total	14	13	13	40
	35.00	32.50	32.50	100.00

STATISTICS FOR TABLE OF PRIOR BY NL

Statistic	DF	Value	Prob
Chi-Square	2	0.671	0.715
Likelihood Ratio Chi-Square	2	0.676	0.713
Mantel-Haenszel Chi-Square	1	0.033	0.856
Phi Coefficient		0.130	
Contingency Coefficient		0.128	
Cramer's V		0.130	

Sample Size = 40

This table is keyed to the index in its upper left corner. For example, in the following cell, 7 is the observed cross-frequency: Seven Arabic speakers have a value of n on PRIOR. That is 17.50% of the whole table, 33.33% of that row, and 50.00% of that column. The row, column, and overall totals are given in the margins of the table above.

```
Frequency   |
Percent     |
Row Pct     |
Col Pct     |   Arabic
- - - - - - - - + - - - - - - - - + . . .
n           |       7      |
            |     17.50     |
            |     33.33     |
            |     50.00     |
- - - - - - - - + - - - - - - - - + . . .
            :       :
            :       :
```

The observed probability for R's chi-square test is 0.715, well above our alpha of .05, and so again, R has no findings about this relationship in her data; she must retain her null hypothesis.

Following are the chi-square input code and output listing from SPSS. As usual, if this chapter's "Implementation" were a single, contiguous SPSS program, it would be necessary to erase the temporary file we have called rdat:

```
get file=rdat.
    subtitle 'DEMO: CHI-SQUARE analysis'.
    crosstabs tables=prior by nl
       / statistics=chisq.
execute.

* ----------End-of-program housecleaning----------- .

*clear working file.
new file.
```

```
*erase temporary files created by this program.

erase file='rdat'.

* End of program.
```

And the SPSS output would be as follows (see discussion question 5 for some explanation of the message This procedure cannot . . .):

> Warning # 704 in column 30. Text: NL
> This procedure cannot use string variables longer than 8 characters. Only
> the first 8 will be used.

Chapter 5 Demo. Program SPSS
DEMO: CHI-SQUARE analysis

PRIOR by NL

```
              NL
      Count   |
                                                          Row
              | Arabic  |  Italian  |  Spanish  |        Total
PRIOR   - - - - - - - - - - - - - - - - - - - - - - - - -
          n   |   7     |    8      |    6      |          21
              |         |           |           |        52.5
              - - - - - - - - - - - - - - - - - - - - -
          y   |   7     |    5      |    7      |          19
              |         |           |           |        47.5
              - - - - - - - - - - - - - - - - - - - - -
       Column     14         13          13               40
       Total     35.0       32.5        32.5            100.0
```

Chi-Square	Value	DF	Significance
Pearson	.67091	2	.71501
Likelihood Ratio	.67554	2	.71336

Minimum Expected Frequency   6.175

Number of Missing Observations: 0

Chapter 5 Demo. Program SPSS
DEMO: CHI-SQUARE analysis

This has been a rather fast tour of some basic statistics in SAS and SPSS. I am not teaching statistics here; rather, I am indicating how to set up the data for statistical analysis. Study the "Implementation" program with special attention to that goal. But the most important thing to take away from this chapter is a general sense of the nature of data preparation for these statistical tests.

An interesting question arises: Once you analyze data and obtain substantive money run results, has data handling ended? Not exactly. The precise "end" of data handling is itself rather a complex topic, and it merits an entire chapter, to which we next turn.

5.7. DISCUSSION QUESTIONS: CHAPTER 5

1. Select a major researcher in your field of study. Review a selection of his or her published articles going back several years. Do you see any evidence of the "worn path"? Does the researcher tend to favor particular data types and analyses?

2. Are there worn paths in your own data handling and analysis?

3. Design and conduct a study that requires analyses of correlation, *t* tests, ANOVA, or chi-square. Keep a data log. Were the data easy to structure? Why? Why not?

4. It is important to control for response polarity in survey data (Principle 5.4). Do you want to detect any other data features before doing a money run analysis of your survey? Hint: One such feature is the propensity of some respondents to simply check the same category for a long string of questions: This is known as response set. How can you detect it in your data? In short, how can survey data backfire, and what can you do in data handling to prevent such problems?

5. Recall the message in the SPSS chi-square output:

> This procedure cannot use string variables longer than 8 characters. Only
> the first 8 will be used.

When printing a frequency cross-table, both SAS and SPSS face a dilemma. Suppose one of our languages was Portuguese, a word with 10 characters. SPSS is warning us that character variables with values of over 8 characters will be truncated in the column and row headers, such that a column for Portuguese would presumably look like this:

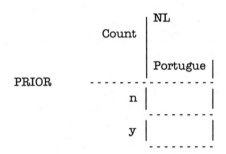

```
                         |  NL
             Count       |
                         |
                         |  Portugue |
   PRIOR       - - - - - - - - - - - - - - - -
                       n |           |
                         | - - - - - - - - - -
                       y |           |
                         | - - - - - - - -
```

SAS, on the other hand, would do this:

```
           PRIOR              Ll

           Frequency |
           Percent   |
           Row Pct   |
           Col Pct   | Portugue |
                     | se       |
           - - - - - - - - + - - - - - - - +
       n                  |          |
                          |          |
                          |          |
           - - - - - - - - + - - - - - - - +
       y                  |          |
                          |          |
                          |          |
           - - - - - - - - + - - - - - - - +
```

That is, SAS splits the word *Portuguese* and wraps it, not necessarily at a linguistic syllable break, though here we are lucky. Furthermore, as you probably noticed when you studied the SAS and SPSS results in this chapter, SAS defaults to provide a row, column, and overall percentage (along with the raw cross-table frequency count) in each cell, whereas by default SPSS gives only the frequencies. These two features of frequency table layout are but samples of the stylistic differences between SAS and SPSS. Such differences appear in the input program code syntax, the results, and as we see in Chapter 6, the execution logs. So, for discussion task 5, I ask you to compare SAS and SPSS. (Clearly, you can do this only if both are available at your setting.) Try some small, sample programs on each and determine which you like better, and why. Why is such an exercise important? Aside from useful practice in examining each software package and learning more about each, comparing the two allows you to make a choice based on your personal preferences. You exert control over the software you select, and that is Principle 2.1 in a new guise. Selecting your software should be a principled activity reflecting your personal preferences and allowing you the greatest likelihood of control.

6. One interesting question to ponder is whether R and EAI are in a worn path and whether they have considered Principle 5.1. Suppose that the literature on attitude and language learning is loaded with ANOVA and that statistic seems to be an arbiter of published findings. Is R right in pursuing that statistic without recourse to other data analyses or data structures? She is pretty well set on ANOVA, and her field of study seems well set on it too. Is that a worn path, and if so, is it desirable? Notice she does try the chi-square because she is "unwilling to relinquish her data that easily." How do you feel about that? This question relates to drawing a sense of balance between Principle 5.1 (the worn path) and Principle 6.1 (the reinvented wheel).

7. Review my interpretation of R's findings above. Consult your favorite statistics book on such topics as ANOVA, correlation, regression, and chi-square. Do you agree with my interpretation? What else can be said about this output?

NOTES

1. I emphasize again that this is not a book on the theory and investigation of second/foreign language acquisition, although the examples here are from that domain. As with all example data in this book, try to generalize to settings relevant to your work. For instance, are you familiar with two presumably opposite teaching methods for some skill like the communicative and audiolingual I use in Chapter 4's "Implementation"?

2. Another method to discovering and possibly leaving your worn path is to consult checklists or decision grids about statistical procedures. These lists and grids are often found in statistical textbooks. They are arranged as a series of questions or points to remember and guide you to selection of the correct statistical test. For example, Hedrick, Bickman, and Rog (1993) offer many such lists (e.g., their treatment of secondary data [p. 73] and the "design matrix" given as Table 4.5).

3. The sample Table 1 also includes reliability coefficients, an important quality of measurement: its consistency. The closer this coefficient gets to 1.00, the greater consistency—less error—there is in the test. It is useful to attend to reliability measures in your data before you use them for substantive analysis; alternatively, reliability can be computed after a test has been administered, and its findings can moderate substantive discussions. Another important quality of measurement is *validity*, or the degree to which measures do assess what they claim to. Some indicators of validity are statistical, but generally, modern scholars of validity treat it as a point for logical establishment. For a general overview of reliability and validity, see Chapters 9 and 10 in Sax (1989) or Chapter 10 in Gronlund (1993). For some provocative discussions of validity, see Messick (1989) or Shepard (1993).

4. Any large correlation matrix can be displayed in a simpler format by rounding the coefficients and indicating significance with an asterisk. For example, suppose you have five variables, V1 through V5, and that only the correlation of V4 and V5 is significant at the alpha level of .05. You could edit your output and display the table like this:

	V1	V2	V3	V4	V5
V1	1.00				
V2	-.21	1.00			
V3	.28	-.13	1.00		
V4	.07	.31	.04	1.00	
V5	.23	-.05	.24	.37*	1.00

NOTE: * $p < .05$

The significance of a correlation is usually reported alongside the coefficient itself in computer output, with or without the n size on which the coefficient is based. In the SAS sample given here, the top number in each cell is the correlation coefficient; the bottom number is its observed significance. In the SPSS output, the top number is the coefficient, then the n size in parentheses, followed by the observed significance. In these sample data, none of the coefficients are significant at the .05

level—a typical probability level in behavioral sciences—but if they were, that could be easily reported with a footnote in a condensed table as shown in this note.

5. In Chapter 3, I discuss the topic of value codes. Following is that chapter's example of some value codes:

```
Native Country Value Codes.

    Albania  = 001
    Austria  = 002
    :
    :
    Germany  = 021
    Ghana    = 022
    :
    :
    Zimbabwe = 103
```

I again advise against this practice because it is far easier to recode a simple typing error if there is a linguistic basis for the mistake—for example, *Zmbabwe* would clearly be a misspelling of *Zimbabwe*, and in debugging you can run frequency tables and quickly detect the error. But how can we tell whether some abstract 099 or 103 is in error without recourse to the original hard copy data?

The SPSS requirement that independent variables be coded as numerics is quite awkward. It is a data entry straightjacket because you are faced with two awkward alternatives: Either (a) you have to use value codes at the time of data entry and hope you do not mistype anything, or (b) you have to go through some pretty serious recoding hassle (a kludge), as I illustrate in the SPSS code here.

SAS does not make this requirement.

The "End" of Data Handling

Overview/Outline

- What is the "End" of Data Handling?
- Organizing your Data Processing
- Saving Output Online
- Report Generation
  (The Output = Data Principle)
- Higher-Order Analysis
  (The Output = Input Principle)
- Implementation
- Discussion Questions: Chapter 6

6.1. WHAT IS THE "END" OF DATA HANDLING?

Let's imagine the following scenario. You work at EAI's world headquarters as a data analyst, and your boss comes to you one day and says: "You know, I understand we teach EFL all over the world. I also understand that we keep records on TOEFL scores for all our students. What is the average range, I mean, what is the average difference between the average maximum TOEFL and minimum TOEFL for each country where we have schools?" After you question your boss for a minute to learn precisely what she or he wants, the boss then says: "Oh, and I need this tomorrow! Thanks!"

You verify that all the above variables are indeed in your database, and that the database does stretch back over 10 years, and then you settle down to produce the report your boss has asked for. In order to do so, you need to have your data and analyses in some sort of organization, so that you can find what you need quickly without much additional reprogramming. I contend that this point is the true "end" of data handling. When you reach this stage, you are finished handling a particular dataset. If you can quickly and easily get a particular piece of information, and rerun a particular program on a given dataset (without again debugging it or manipulating the data), then the data are now no longer being "handled." It has become an operational tool.

By defining the "end" of data handling as I do here, I also help define the end of the mandate for this book. Data handling and data analysis are not distinctly different. As you analyze, you handle data, and as you handle data, you analyze. The process is cyclical.

6.2. ORGANIZING YOUR DATA PROCESSING

The more data you handle, the more you need to organize your work. This organizational need erupts whenever I first start obtaining output, as I approach something like that operational "end" to data processing. As I start to see results of analyses, I realize I want to do something differently. Perhaps I find that I am actually debugging and not analyzing, as explained by Principle 4.2. Perhaps I think of other analyses I want to run, or of other data sets I wish to incorporate in the project, or of certain variables I wish to ignore. Things get out of control: Programs and subset data files proliferate. Temporary files appear, in which I am trying a particular data manipulation or analysis to see if it works, with the hope that I can incorporate it into some later, more finalized program. Unless I exert control over what I am doing, I cannot find what I have done, let alone generate quick reports such as my boss might want. Things can quickly become messy. Most frustrating is to spend hours crafting some elegant solution (or kludge for that matter) to a problem only to come to realize that I figured out exactly the same solution six months ago for some other project. That feels bad!

Recall Principle 2.1 ("Take control of the structure and flow of your data"). Perhaps it is necessary to introduce a "cousin" of that principle, one I still have trouble following (since by personality, I am inherently something of a sloppy packrat):

Principle 6.1: The Reinvented Wheel Principle

In all computer processing, keep an archive of successful procedures, routines, and programs so that you do not have to rediscover and redesign them each time they are needed. Plagiarize yourself (i.e., it is OK to copy your own work). Library yourself (a new verb!).

Principle 6.1 therefore implies that you set up a system to organize and catalog your data and programs. Don't needlessly re-invent the wheel.

Balance this principle against Principle 5.1: the Know Yourself Principle.

Principle 6.1 is truly common sense. It is quite logical not to relearn something you did before. As I learned this principle, I came to evolve my own system of organizing data and program files, so that I could hunt through them to see what I accomplished. I found that in order to "plagiarize" and "library" myself, I needed to first organize myself.[1]

It may seem that an organized archival system is the first step in data handling. If you are able to do so, that's wonderful. However, I have found that I must work with a particular data set or project for some time before I begin to see precisely how I want to organize it.

There are many levels of organization needed for computer analysis of data. First, any data analysis should have a consistent and meaningful system of naming program and data files. This system should evolve naturally from the nature of the project on which you are working. Suppose our now-familiar language school, EAI, is working on a project with data from five countries: Brazil, Japan, Russia, France, and Mexico. Suppose that EAI schools in each of those five countries submit three types of data: background and demographic information, entry/placement test information and achievement/final exam information. Suppose, further, that EAI follows the long-established but frustrating convention of IBM/compatible microcomputers in which a filename can have two parts: eight characters, a dot, and a second name of three characters or fewer. Finally, suppose that the data files coexist on the same computer as the program files, files containing data codebooks (see Chapter 2) and other related information such as memos and project reports. To accommodate all this, EAI might name its data with a convention such as:

brbd.dat   EAI/Brazil background/demographic data, or
jaep.dat   EAI/Japan entry/placement test data, or
ruaf.dat   EAI/Russia achievement/final exam data
(etc.)

The first two characters of the first name specify the country. EAI has, we assume, examined all the countries it serves and has found that they are uniquely identified by the first two characters of the name. The next two characters of the first name tell us if the data are BD (background/demographic), EP (entry/placement exam information), or AF (achievement/final information). In this book, I am assuming that you would temporarily copy data files into your programs before running them, and then after the program is done, delete the data. This is not necessary; you can save data in an external file and have your program call it in for analysis. However, that process is often highly dependent on the particular software you use. I return to this point in discussion question 6 at the end of this chapter.

We could further imagine that EAI has a codebook for each of these three data types, and that this codebook is uniform across all countries with EAI branches, for example:

bd.cbk   codebook for background/demographic data (regardless of country, that is, the file structure is the same for each country)

ep.cbk   codebook for entry/placement data

af.cbk   codebook for achievement/final exam data

As noted above, since the data, codebooks, and programs coexist on the same computer, it is easy to keep track of things by simply looking at the file name.

Second, let's suppose that EAI has programs for each type of data: BD, EP, and AF. If EAI is using SAS, perhaps it has chosen to follow the SAS convention—which is not a requirement— that SAS program files end in .sas. You could conceive, then, of three analysis programs:

bd.sas   program code for background/demographic data

ep.sas   program code for entry/placement data

af.sas   program code for achievement/final data

That seems simple, and as is often the case, simple approaches don't work out. I have never written data programs for a project and had only one program file for a given data set. More likely, there would be separate programs for debugging, initial analysis and final analysis. Possibly, there would be another stage of program names for treating output as data, to which I turn later in this chapter. For example, for analyses of the BD data, the system I have evolved might be something like this:

bd1*.SAS   debugging program series (for BD data; the asterisk is a "wild card" which means that any character or characters may follow up to the eight-character limit before the dot)

bd2*.SAS   early analyses, e.g., descriptive statistics

bd3*.SAS   later, "money run" analyses

bd4*.SAS   output-as-data analyses for report production

Then, if I were looking for some programming that ran a complex statistic, for example, chi-square on frequency counts, I would probably look for a file named bd3a.sas or bd3b.sas. The distinction among each program series ('1' vs. '2' vs. '3' vs. '4') is flexible. Sometimes a '4' series is still programming and output-as-data does not begin until series '5' or, rarely, '6'. On other occasions, I generate reports way down in series '2'. That tends to happen when the initial need is pretty simple and there are not a lot of complex analyses; at the University of Illinois, my stock programs for our ESL placement test are '2' series programs.

I have come to differentiate within a series solely by time; for instance, I would assume that ??3a.sas was written before ??3b.sas. As I work at a particular phase of a project, a program might become large and unwieldy. I then split it or begin a new program. Hence, if for a given sequence I were to find programs up to (for example): bd3g.sas or bd3h.sas, that would indicate that I had tried lots and lots of different things and had produced lots of programs. Generally, after other projects demand my attention—when I am returning to a project to see what I did—I judge the complexity of programming for that project by the number of program files I have and their naming convention. If I worked so much that I reached, say, bd5f.sas or af5g.sas, I'd know that I had lots and lots of programs to choose from.

One other suggestion is to keep filenames short. There are still a lot of programs and computer systems that are restricted to the (basically silly) eight-dot-three filename limit, and if the three-character second name adheres to a convention such as .sas, then you really have only eight characters with which to play. By keeping the program names short, I can have subtypes within a given program series. Sometimes, I return to a project and encounter files like this:

bd3a.sas
bd3b1.sas
bd3b2.sas
bd3b3a.sas
bd3b3b.sas

bd3c.sas
bd3d.sas
(etc.)

Those filenames are like signals. They tell me that in the '3' series
I was doing something pretty complicated. I may have tried it once
and then altered it drastically ('3a' vs. '3b'). After I altered it, I found
I needed to try a couple of different minor approaches to the
alteration ('3b1' vs. '3b2'). And then, based on the alteration, I
discovered what I really wanted to do—run something yet two
more ways ('3b3a' vs. '3b3b'). Precisely what I was doing cannot
be represented by the eight-dot-three filename convention, and
that is why I use large comment boxes at the beginning of my
programs; see the demonstration program in the "Implementation"
section of any chapter of this book for a comment box.

All this is pretty abstract, so let me give you a concrete example.
Some time back, I was assisting a master's degree student to run
some complicated ANOVAs, and something I helped her do re-
minded me of something in another student's project some two
years earlier. The first student's results had been very interesting,
and she needed to do some complex follow-up analyses for situations where she had a significant interaction. To properly follow
up on an interaction, you cannot simply do several one-way
ANOVAs on each main effect. Rather, you should alter the ANOVA
formula to take the presence of the interaction into account for
each main effect; that is, you cannot check if a main effect is
significant without mathematically accommodating the fact that
any main effect significance might be caused by the interaction
itself. The long and short of it is that I remembered that she and I
had had a meeting with a very good consultant who pointed us on
the right track to program that process in SAS. I also recalled that
our need to do this was after she had already analyzed some of her
data—remember, she knew she already had an interaction. So, I
got copies of her program files from my archives (which I had kept
with her permission, of course), and lo and behold, there was a '4'
series, signaling either some pretty high-level analyses or complex
report generation. I called up those files, looked at the comment

box at the top of each, and found one that did the correct procedure and used it as a template for the new student's project. That saved relearning the whole procedure, because once I saw how we did it two years previous, something in my brain went "*click*" and I was able to help the second student with the necessary SAS code.

Scenarios like that are frequent. They are not only limited to searching out solutions for particular analyses, such as follow-up to a significant interaction. A scenario like this can come up when doing data manipulation. I remember that need in some work that continued the Cambridge-TOEFL Comparability Study. Our project team needed to craft a new statistic called the RAP, or Rater Agreement Proportion (Bachman, Davidson, & Milanovic, 1996). I know roughly to which files I'd go back to find it, and I'd guess that the code for that RAP value would appear somewhere in a '1' or possibly '2' series program, because it was basically a data manipulation problem and not an analysis problem.

In both cases—the graduate student and the Cambridge analysis —a simple, consistent filenaming system helps massively in the hunt; I know which files probably contain the code I need.

This entire file-numbering system is my own invention, and it is something I have come to use automatically. As you work with data, you will probably evolve your own system. Alternatively, you could use my system. (Go ahead: I hereby declare it freely released in the public domain.) The point is that you must use some system, because you will probably have to return some day and find what you did before, or you will at some point get a request from your boss such as that above, and you need to return to a program and regenerate its results—quickly. Without a coherent system of file-naming, you will reinvent the wheel, and that is always a waste of time.

Before closing this section, let me give you a couple of other tips implied by Principle 6.1, tips which interact with the topic of filenaming conventions. First, comment your programs extensively. Cody and Smith (1991, p. 15) state that the comment is "one of the most important SAS statements." I agree strongly. Try to use comments liberally throughout the program, and especially, employ something like a comment box at the beginning of the code to tell you what the program is. Whenever you are looking at a program, you can recall what you were doing more easily if you write yourself a note in the form of a comment. Again, see any of the "Implementation" sections in this book for samples of commenting in SAS or SPSS.

Second, use software to search program files. Programs are usually created in or saved to some sort of file compatible with a word processor or computer text management software package. For example, both SAS and SPSS for IBM/compatibles use straight ASCII text as the program file format. I can therefore use any ASCII-compatible word processor to search a program file for a given string to help me remember how to do something. In the above RAP example, what I might do is bring up each program file individually (in that project's '1' or '2' series files) and search for the string array. Alternatively, I might use a more powerful software package that can search my computer for all .sas files for that project and locate that string. Finally, knowing that I comment my programs pretty extensively, and remembering that we named our new statistic RAP, I might search for the string: RAP. There could have been other arrays in the programs, and since array is a SAS command term, I might narrow my search more efficiently if I look for a comment about the RAP statistic which includes the string RAP Array or array computation of RAP or something similar.

6.3. SAVING OUTPUT ONLINE

The boss has asked for a number of reports, and let us assume that your EAI data, codebooks, programs, and related files are organized nicely and commented extensively. With little pain, you are able to locate the precise data and program files which you need to reaccess to get the information. There are two logical possibilities that arise here: Either you have relocated the data and programs, or you have located the data, programs, and the output and program execution logs which you also saved as files. Perhaps you locate a set of files like this:

bd1a.sas
bd1b.sas
bd2a.sas
bd2a1.sas
bd2a2.sas
bd.dat
bd.cbk
bd1a.out
bd1b.out
bd2a.out
bd2a1.out
bd2a2.out
bd1a.log
bd1b.log
bd2a.log
bd2a1.log
bd2a2.log

The .out files are results of their respective .sas files; the .cbk file is a codebook; and the .log files are the SAS execution logs—a copy of the program with SAS messages about execution time, warnings, errors (hopefully none), and so forth; the analogous filenames in SPSS would end in .sps and .lst. There would probably be no separate SPSS log files, because by default, SPSS execution messages are saved as part of the output listing and not in a separate file.

Why on earth would you save execution logs and output files? After all, you can always regenerate bd1a.out and bd1a.log by rerunning the program called bd1a.sas. Two principles are suggested:

Principle 6.2: The Save Output Principle

Save output (and possibly logs) as files because it took an extremely long time to run the program to generate them.

Principle 6.3: The Regenerate Output Principle

Do not save output or logs if it takes a very short time to run the program and regenerate them.

The problem is essentially this: When is it more efficient to rerun a program to regenerate results, and when is it more efficient to save the output as a file and not rerun the original program? The answer to this question, that is, the resolution to Principles 6.2 and 6.3, is itself a principle:

Principle 6.4: The Know Your System Principle

Know your computer system. Know its speed, capabilities, and quirks. Know your preferred software packages; in particular, know how long your software takes to do the tasks you typically need to do.

Suppose the EAI needs a large data analysis job rerun twice an academic term. Perhaps it is a student background information report in which background data are correlated with performance data from classes. Suppose that EAI needs this job run on all its schools worldwide, which, let's imagine, is a very large number: 205 schools in 44 countries teaching some 30,000 students. Each school sends copies of its database to the central EAI world headquarters, and this twice-a-term job is run from there.

Suppose further that the EAI central office prides itself on its computer hardware. Up until this year, they had a system that could hold these data easily, and then some. But the bottleneck was the speed of the computer: It was slow to analyze. The 30,000-student job had to be run overnight, and so the EAI central staff decided to capitalize on what their system had plenty of (storage space) and therefore reduce pressure based on the system's inadequacy (processing time). To do so, the staff saved every job output on tape—a very cheap way to save computer files. That way, if they needed to print another copy of the output or reaccess it and incorporate it in a report (see below), they did not have to rerun the job.

This year, EAI Central has upgraded its system. They still have the same storage capacity, but they have a central processor that is about 100 times as fast. Everybody is remarking—in the offices, lunchroom, parking lot—that "the new computer is really impressive." The 30,000-student, twice-a-term job that used to take overnight is now completed in about 11 minutes.

Should they still save output files? Actually, it does not matter since they still have tape, and tape is a cheap way to store data. But the pressure to save output is gone, because of the upgrade of computer speed. We could throw in some other angle, like a decision to do away with tape storage or a need to use the computer tapes to store something else such as digitized teaching materials, and that would end the debate: They'd regenerate the output whenever it was needed. Regardless, the upgrade of computer processing speed at EAI Central means that they can regenerate some of their programs with little time loss, so they probably will do so. Such decisions are the domain of Principle 6.4.

Hopefully, as you work more and more as a data analyst, you will have the pleasant experience I describe above. At some point, I hope, you will be working on a system that gets replaced, and you will see your turnaround time shrink drastically. The entire history of computer development says that if you do replace your system you will enjoy this speed increase—and it is enjoyable. One function of that increase is that you can redo things more easily, and you will find your own personal balance of Principles 6.2 and 6.3 because of Principle 6.4.

But Principle 6.4 has another implication. It does encourage you to learn the system for purposes of speed, but it also reminds you that every system—every combination of hardware and software— is unique. You will, as you should, develop your own work patterns and preferences. As you do so, you will come to know how long things take. You will come to know where the typical inefficiencies lurk and where the typical quick-and-dirty kludges can succeed. If you come to understand the quirks and niceties of your system, your work will benefit immensely.

In the spirit of Principle 6.4, the "Implementation" section in this chapter has some SAS and SPSS code that keeps track of the overall execution time for a program (timer.sas and timer.sps, below). SAS and SPSS typically report execution time for each procedure, and the code I have added gives you a feeling for the time involved for the whole program. The results of this code appear in execution log statements, so I have also provided execution logs below. I find such time calculations useful to judge the overall effectiveness of my computer system. In addition, I have had experiences where some data (or program) bug caused the program to slow down drastically, and these time checks helped with detection.

Before closing this section, I'd like to provide an argument for saving what may seem to be the least useful result of data handling and processing: the log. The log is a treasure chest of useful information. It confirms the names of the input data set, it confirms the number of variables and cases in the data set, and it is a time record. Even if you do not save logs, learn to find them in your software and read them regularly. They help not only with debugging but also with learning your system—Principle 6.4.

6.4. REPORT GENERATION
(THE OUTPUT = DATA PRINCIPLE)

I am not big on report format. Some of my colleagues spend hours to get a report organized just so. They want the columns just a certain size, the rows aligned in just a certain manner, the values in just a certain print font. In this section, I'd like to deal with the raw source material—the computer program's results—whether my colleagues are using it to produce a fancy report, or whether I am doing a plain-vanilla Davidson-style report.

The raw material in either case is the results of your program. Ideally, you should be able to get the program to save the results in some sort of format that you can then cut-and-paste into a word processor. You can thus embed it in a memo or textual report. You can then tinker with the format to your heart's content (if you are one of my colleagues) or just print it off and go on to something else (if you are like me). Either way, certain aspects and principles of that process mirror closely what we have examined in this book. By analogy, the raw material of the report is itself a form of data, and your word processor is an analysis program. Principle 6.5 draws our attention to this process:

Principle 6.5: The Output = Data Principle

As your analysis ends, your output will probably become part of a report. The output is like data at this point; you are using output of the analysis as data for the report. Know what this implies for your system.

The Implementation below includes some results shown in two methods: First, I have typical SAS output. Then, I give one of the output tables embedded in a report.

6.5. HIGHER-ORDER ANALYSIS (THE OUTPUT=INPUT PRINCIPLE)

Principle 6.6: The Output = Input Principle

As your analysis ends, your output may be incorporated as input to another program. The output is data at this point. Know what this implies for your system.

Principle 6.6 is slightly different than Principle 6.5. Often, the results of a statistical analysis are themselves to become input to another analysis. A simple example is as follows. Suppose the EAI wishes to know the difference between the average minimum and maximum TOEFL score in each EAI country worldwide. We could get a data set with the average minimum and maximum TOEFL for each school, run a by-group analysis, and save the output as a file. We could then edit the file and use it as an input dataset. The output would become input data.

Analysis of output as data is called "higher-order" analysis. It is contrasted with "zero-order" analysis, which is the analysis of the data you actually keyed in and on any manipulations to it.[2] "First-order" analysis is analysis of output. "Second-order" analysis is analysis of the output of first order analysis, and so on. "Higher-order" analysis is any analysis called "first" and above. I contend that principles of good data handling such as described in this book apply equally well to higher-order data as well as to zero-order data.

Note in both Principles 6.5 and 6.6 that I have the phrase "Know what that implies for your system." This sort of like an invocation for Principle 6.4. For some software it is easier to ask the program to do higher-order analysis. Alternatively, it might be easier to get involved directly by cutting and pasting the output file and treating it as input data. This is a judgment call involving the Kludge Principle (3.3) and the simple availability of higher-order analysis in your software.

6.6. IMPLEMENTATION

In this chapter, I have presented several tips for controlling your data processing in a very global manner and handling routine data, which signals the "end" of data handling. At such a stage, you are probably managing large numbers of files: codebooks, data files, execution logs, and programs. Therefore, I wish to present these implementation examples differently. I will present all of each program, so that you become accustomed to seeing a large chunk of contiguous program code. Each sample program below has line numbers in parentheses at the left. These line numbers are not part of the program; rather, I have put them in to help me explain the code later on.

The supposed situation in these samples is that question which the boss posed at the beginning of the chapter. In these programs, I will sort some EAI data by country, compute some means across all EAI countries and by each country, then cut and paste the by-country results as higher-order analysis. The programs do the analyses which the boss requested. There is also a memo to The Boss.

The programs below are arranged as follows, referencing the line numbers at the left:

Lines   3-96:   SAS input program
Lines 100-154:   SAS results
Lines 156-278:   SAS execution log, which echoes the program
Lines 280-303:   A memo to The Boss
Lines 306-436:   SPSS input program
Lines 439-791:   SPSS results with execution log interleaved
                   between command language

```
(  1) -------------- SAS: Input Program --------------
(  2)
(  3) *Start a time check for this program;
(  4) data timechek;
(  5)     start=time();
(  6) run;
(  7)
(  8) *-----------------------------------------------*
(  9) |Name of input program: ch6.sas (SAS)           |
( 10) |              function: demos for Chapter 6:    |
( 11) |                        -output-as-data         |
(      )                        (first order data)
( 12) |                        -timekeeping in the     |
(      )                        execution log
( 13) |                                                |
( 14) |Name(s) of input datasets: in the program, see below. |
( 15) |                                                |
( 16) |-----------------------------------------------  |
( 17) |    Program written by: Fred Davidson            |
( 18) *-----------------------------------------------*;
( 19)
( 20) title1 'Chapter 6 Demo. Program';
( 21)
( 22) data world;
( 23)     input country $ school $ maxtoefl mintoefl nstu;
```

```
( 24)  cards;
( 25)  Brazil    01 647 490 201
( 26)  Brazil    02 640 480 203
( 27)  Brazil    03 637 447 351
( 28)  Brazil    04 640 437 256
( 29)  France    01 620 453 260
( 30)  France    02 623 477 259
( 31)  France    03 613 473 245
( 32)  France    04 617 463 358
( 33)  Germany   01 623 430 245
( 34)  Germany   02 640 470 336
( 35)  Germany   03 647 453 362
( 36)  Germany   04 637 457 344
( 37)  Germany   05 620 493 456
( 38)  Italy     01 630 447 344
( 39)  Italy     02 613 450 255
( 40)  Italy     03 623 453 220
( 41)  ;
( 42)  run;
( 43)
( 44)  *OK to overwrite temp dataset: world;
( 45)  proc sort data=world;
( 46)      by country;
( 47)  run;
( 48)
( 49)  proc means data=world;
( 50)      var maxtoefl mintoefl;
( 51)      title2 'Whole-world means';
( 52)  run;
( 53)
( 54)  proc means data=world;
( 55)      var maxtoefl mintoefl;
( 56)      by country;
( 57)      title2 'Means by country';
( 58)  run;
( 59)
( 60)  data country;
( 61)      input country $ maxtmean mintmean;
( 62)      tmeandif=maxtmean-mintmean;
( 63)  cards;
```

```
( 64) Brazil   641 463
( 65) France   618 466
( 66) Germany 633 460
( 67) Italy    622 450
( 68) ;
( 69) run;
( 70)
( 71) proc print data=country;
( 72)     title2 'Printout of first-order data with
          computed variable: TMEANDIF';
( 73) run;
( 74)
( 75) *-------------------------------------;
( 76) * End of Program get execution time  ;
( 77) *-------------------------------------;
( 78)
( 79) *End the time check for this program --
( 80)   write the time values at the end of the
        execution log;
( 81) data timechek;
( 82)     set timechek;
( 83)     progx ='For this program,';
( 84)     startx='start time =';
( 85)     stopx =' stop time =';
( 86)     stop =time();
( 87)     put                          /
( 88)            progx                  /
( 89)              startx start time.  /
( 90)          @2 stopx stop time.  /;
( 91) run;
( 92)
( 93) proc datasets;
( 94)     delete timechek;
( 95) run;
( 96) quit;


( 97)---------------------- SAS: Output ----------------------
( 98)
( 99)
```

```
(100)                         Chapter 6 Demo. Program
(101)                            Whole-world means
(102)
(103) Variable      N        Mean      Std Dev     Minimum      Maximum
(104) - - - - - - - - - - - - - - - - - - - - - - - - - - - - - - - - - - - - - - - - - - - - - -
(105) MAXTOEFL 16  629.3750000  11.7295922  613.0000000 647.0000000
(106) MINTOEFL 16  460.8125000  18.1997024  430.0000000 493.0000000
(107) - - - - - - - - - - - - - - - - - - - - - - - - - - - - - - - - - - - - - - - - -
(108)
(109)                         Chapter 6 Demo. Program
(110)                            Means by country
(111)
(112) - - - - - - - - - - - - - - - - - COUNTRY=Brazil - - - - - - - - - - - - - - - - - - - -
(113)
(114) Variable      N        Mean      Std Dev     Minimum      Maximum
(115) - - - - - - - - - - - - - - - - - - - - - - - - - - - - - - - - - - - - - - - - - - - -
(116) MAXTOEFL 4  641.000000   4.2426407  637.0000000 647.0000000
(117) MINTOEFL 4  463.500000  25.4885595  437.0000000 490.0000000
(118) - - - - - - - - - - - - - - - - - - - - - - - - - - - - - - - - - - - - - - - - - -
(119)
(120) - - - - - - - - - - - - - - - - - COUNTRY=France - - - - - - - - - - - - - - - - - - -
(121)
(122) Variable      N        Mean      Std Dev     Minimum      Maximum
(123) - - - - - - - - - - - - - - - - - - - - - - - - - - - - - - - - - - - - - - - - - - - -
(124) MAXTOEFL 4  618.2500000   4.2720019  613.000000 623.0000000
(125) MINTOEFL 4  466.5000000  10.7548439  453.000000 477.0000000
(126) - - - - - - - - - - - - - - - - - - - - - - - - - - - - - - - - - - - - - - - - - - -
(127)                         Chapter 6 Demo. Program
(128)                            Means by country
(129)
(130) - - - - - - - - - - - - - - - - - COUNTRY=Germany - - - - - - - - - - - - - - - - - -
(131)
(132) Variable      N        Mean      Std Dev     Minimum      Maximum
(133) - - - - - - - - - - - - - - - - - - - - - - - - - - - - - - - - - - - - - - - - -
(134) MAXTOEFL 5  633.4000000  11.5021737  620.0000000 647.0000000
(135) MINTOEFL 5  460.6000000  23.1581519  430.0000000 493.0000000
(136) - - - - - - - - - - - - - - - - - - - - - - - - - - - - - - - - - - - - - - - - - -
(137)
(138) - - - - - - - - - - - - - - - - - COUNTRY=Italy - - - - - - - - - - - - - - - - - - -
(139)
```

```
(140) Variable    N        Mean     Std Dev    Minimum     Maximum
(141) -----------------------------------------------------------
(142) MAXTOEFL   3   622.0000000 8.5440037 613.0000000 630.0000000
(143) MINTOEFL   3   450.0000000 3.0000000 447.0000000 453.0000000
(144) -----------------------------------------------------------
(145)
(146)                    Chapter 6 Demo. Program
(147) Printout of first-order data with computed variable: TMEANDIF
(148)
(149)       OBS COUNTRY MAXTMEAN MINTMEAN TMEANDIF
(150)
(151)        1   Brazil    641      463     178
(152)        2   France    618      466     152
(153)        3   Germany   633      460     173
(154)        4   Italy     622      450     172
(155)
                ---------------------- SAS: Log ----------------------
(156) 481 *Start a time check for this program;
(157) 482 data timechek;
(158) 483   start=time();
(159) 484 run;
(160)
(161) NOTE: The data set WORK.TIMECHECK has 1 observations
            and 1 variables.
(162) NOTE: The DATA statement used 8.44 seconds.
(163)
(164) 485
(165) 486 * ---------------------------------------------------*
(166) 487 |Name of input program: ch6.sas (SAS)               |
(167) 488 |              function: demos for Chapter 6:       |
(168) 489 |                     -input-as-data               |
                                 (first order data)
(169) 490                       -timekeeping in the
                                 execution log
(170) 491 |                                                  |
(171) 492 | Name(s) of input datasets: in the program, see below.
(172) 493 |                                                  |
(173) 494 |-------------------------------------------------- |
(174) 495 |    Program written by: Fred Davidson            |
(175) 496 * -------------------------------------------------*;
(176) 497
(177) 498   title1 'Chapter 6 Demo. Program';
(178) 499
```

```
(179) 500    data world;
(180) 501        input country $ school $ maxtoefl mintoefl nstu;
(181) 502    cards;
(182)
(183) NOTE: The data set WORK.WORLD has 16 observations and
            5 variables.
(184) NOTE: The DATA statement used 1.27 seconds.
(185)
(186) 519 ;
(187) 520 run;
(188) 521
(189) 522 *OK to overwrite temp dataset: world;
(190) 523 proc sort data=world;
(191) 524 by country;
(192) 525 run;
(193)
(194) NOTE: The data set WORK.WORLD has 16 observations and
            5 variables.
(195) NOTE: The PROCEDURE SORT used 1.59 seconds.
(196)
(197) 526
(198) 527    proc means data=world;
(199) 528        var maxtoefl mintoefl;
(200) 529        title2 'Whole-world means';
(201) 530    run;
(202)
(203) NOTE: The PROCEDURE MEANS used 1.37 seconds.
(204)
(205) 531
(206) 532    proc means data=world;
(207) 533        var maxtoefl mintoefl;
(208) 534        by country;
(209) 535        title2 'Means by country';
(210) 536    run;
(211)
(212) NOTE: The PROCEDURE MEANS used 0.81 seconds.
(213)
(214) 537
(215) 538    data country;
(216) 539        input country $ maxtmean mintmean;
(217) 540        tmeandif=maxtmean-mintmean;
(218) 541    cards;
(219)
```

```
(220) NOTE: The data set WORK.COUNTRY has 4 observations and
            4 variables.
(221) NOTE: The DATA statement used 0.77 seconds.
(222)
(223) 546   ;
(224) 547   run;
(225) 548
(226) 549   proc print data=country;
(227) 550      title2 'Printout of first-order data with computed
                    variable:
(228) TMEANDIF';
(229) 551   run;
(230)
(231) NOTE: The PROCEDURE PRINT used 1.2 seconds.
(232)
(233) 552
(234) 553   *---------------------------------;
(235) 554   * End of Program get execution time  ;
(236) 555   *---------------------------------;
(237) 556
(238) 557   *End the time check for this program --
(239) 558    write the time values at the end of the execution
log;
(240) 559    data timechek;
(241) 560       set timechek;
(242) 561       progx ='For this program,';
(243) 562       startx='start time =';
(244) 563       stopx =' stop time =';
(245) 564       stop =time();
(246) 565       put                          /
(247) 566             progx                  /
(248) 567             startx start time      /
(249) 568          @2 stopx stop time.      /;
(250) 569    run;
(251)
(252) For this program,
(253) start time = 15:56:30
(254)   stop time = 15:56:42
(255)
(256) NOTE: The data set WORK.TIMECHEK has 1 observations
            and 5 variables.
(257) NOTE: The DATA statement used 2.14 seconds.
(258)
(259) 570
```

```
(260) 571   proc datasets;
(261)                   - - - - - Directory - - - - -
(262)
(263)                   Libref:        WORK
(264)                   Engine:        V608
(265)                   Physical Name: C:\SAS\SASWORK
(266)
(267)                   #  Name        Memtype  Indexes
(268)
(269)                   1  COUNTRY     DATA
(270)                   2  TIMECHEK    DATA
(271)                   3  WORLD       DATA
(272) 572   delete timechek;
(273) 573   run;
(274)
(275) NOTE: Deleting WORK.TIMECHEK (memtype=DATA).
(276) 574   quit;
(277)
(278) NOTE: The PROCEDURE DATASETS used 1.91 seconds.
(279)
           -------------- Sample memorandum --------------
```

(280) To: The Boss

(281) From: The Worker

(282) Re: Report on average min-max TOEFL difference
             at EAI schools

(283) Date: 21 JAN 1997

(284)

(285) As per your request, I here provide a table indicating

(286) the difference between the average maximum TOEFL and

(287) minimum TOEFL at all our schools where EFL is taught.

(288) If you have any questions about the table below,

(289) please contact me.

(290)	COUNTRY	MAXTMEAN	MINTMEAN	TMEANDIF
(291)				
(292)	Brazil	641	463	178
(293)	France	618	466	152
(294)	Germany	633	460	173
(295)	Italy	622	450	172
(296)				

(297) Note: 'MINMEAN' = average minimum TOEFL score at

(298)   all our schools for the country
                        shown

```
(299)          'MAXMEAN' = average maximum TOEFL score at
(300)                     all our schools for the country
                          shown
(301)          'TMEANDIF'= difference between MINMEAN and
(302)                     MAXMEAN: this is the information
                          you requested
(303)

(304) ------------- SPSS: Input Program --------------
(305)
(306) *The SPSS execution log will be interleaved in the
      output if the
(307) following SET options are requested here -->.
(308)
(309). set errors=listing
(310)     messages=listing
(311)     printback=listing
(312)     results=listing.
(313)
(314) *Start a time check for this program.
(315) data list fixed
(316)   / startstr 1-35 (a).
(317) begin data.
(318) For this program, the start time is
(319) end data.
(320)     compute start=xdate.time($time).
(321)     save outfile=timechek.
(322) execute.
(323)
(324) *----------------------------------------------*
(325) | Name of input program: ch6.sps (SPSS)        |
(326) |        function: SPSS demos for Chapter 6:    |
(327) |             -output-as-data (first order data)|
(328) |             -timekeeping in the execution log |
(329) |                                              |
(330) |Name(s) of input datasets: in the program, see below.|
(331) |                                              |
(332) | -------------------------------------------- |
(333) |   Program written by: Fred Davidson          |
(334) *----------------------------------------------*.
(335)
```

```
(336) title 'Chapter 6 Demo. Program'.
(337)
(338) data list list
(339)    / country (a7) school (a2) maxtoefl mintoefl nstu.
(340) begin data
(341) Brazil   01 647 490 201
(342) Brazil   02 640 480 203
(343) Brazil   03 637 447 351
(344) Brazil   04 640 437 256
(345) France   01 620 453 260
(346) France   02 623 477 259
(347) France   03 613 473 245
(348) France   04 617 463 358
(349) Germany 01 623 430 245
(350) Germany 02 640 470 336
(351) Germany 03 647 453 362
(352) Germany 04 637 457 344
(353) Germany 05 620 493 456
(354) Italy    01 630 447 344
(355) Italy    02 613 450 255
(356) Italy    03 623 453 220
(357) end data.
(358)    save outfile=world.
(359) execute.
(360)
(361) *OK to overwrite temp dataset: world.
(362) get file=world.
(363)    sort cases by country.
(364)    save outfile=world.
(365) execute.
(366)
(367) get file=world.
(368)    subtitle 'Whole-world means'.
(369)    descriptives variables=maxtoefl mintoefl.
(370) execute.
(371)
(372) get file=world.
(373)    subtitle 'Means by country'.
(374)    report
(375)       / variables=maxtoefl mintoefl
(376)       / break=country
```

```
(377)          / summary=mean
(378)          / summary=stddev
(379)          / summary=min
(380)          / summary=max.
(381) execute.
(382)
(383) data list list
(384)     / country (a7) maxtmean mintmean.
(385) begin data.
(386) Brazil   641 463
(387) France   618 466
(388) Germany 633 460
(389) Italy    622 450
(390) end data.
(391)     compute tmeandif=maxtmean-mintmean.
(392)     save outfile=country.
(393) execute.
(394)
(395) get file=country.
(396)     *In SPSS, titles cannot be longer than
               60 characters.
(397)     subtitle 'Printout of first-order data
                    w/ computed variable: TMEANDIF'.
(398)     list.
(399) execute.
(400)
(401) --------- End-of-program housecleaning --------.
(402)
(403) *clear working file.
(404) new file.
(405)
(406) *erase temporary files created by this program.
(407)
(408) erase file='world'.
(409) erase file='country'.
(410)
(411) *-----------------------------------.
(412) * End of Program get execution time  .
(413) *-----------------------------------.
(414)
(415) get file=timechek.
```

```
(416)     string stopstr (a35).
(417)     compute stopstr=' and the stop time is'.
(418)     compute stop=xdate.time($time).
(419)     print formats startstr (a35) start (time8)
                          stopstr (a35) stop (time8).
(420)     print / startstr start
(421)           / stopstr stop.
(422) execute.
(423)
(424) * Delete timecheck file.
(425)
(426) new file.
(427)
(428) erase file='timechek'.
(429)
(430) * Change the SET options back to system defaults;
           i.e., no log.
(431)
(432) set errors=listing
(433)     messages=none
(434)     printback=none
(435)     results=listing.
(436)
```

(437) - - - - - - - - - - - - - - - - SPSS: Output - - - - - - - - - - - - - - - - -
(438)
(439) ->
(440) -> *Start a time check for this program.
(441)
(442) -> data list fixed
(443) ->   / startstr 1-35 (a).
(444)
(445) This command will read 1 records from the command file
(446)

Variable	Rec	Start	End	Format
(447)				
(448)				
(449) STARTSTR	1	1	35	A35

(450)   -
(451) -> begin data.
(452)
(453) -> For this program, the start time is

```
(454) -> end data.
(455)
(456) Preceding task required 2.03 seconds elapsed.
(457)
(458) ->     compute start=xdate.time($time).
(459)
(460) ->     save outfile=timechek.
(461)
(462) Time stamp on saved file: [date here] 12:26:50
(463) File contains 2 variables, 48 bytes per case before compression
(464) 1 cases were written to c:\spsswin\timechek.
(465)
(466) Preceding task required .99 seconds elapsed.
(467)
(468) -> execute.
(469)
(470) Preceding task required .00 seconds elapsed.
(471)
(472) ->
(473) -> * - - - - - - - - - - - - - - - - - - - - - - - - - - - - - - - - - - - - - - - - - *
(474) -> | Name of input program: ch6.sps (SPSS)                                            |
(475) -> |                function: SPSS demos for Chapter 6:                               |
(476) -> |                              -input-as-data (first order                         |
(477) -> |                               data)                                             |
(477) -> |                              -timekeeping in the                                |
(478) -> |                               execution log                                     |
(479) -> | Name(s) of input datasets: in the program,see below.                            |
(480) -> |                                                                                 |
(481) -> | - - - - - - - - - - - - - - - - - - - - - - - - - - - - - - - - - - - - - - - - |
(482) -> |     Program written by: Fred Davidson                                           |
(483) -> * - - - - - - - - - - - - - - - - - - - - - - - - - - - - - - - - - - - - - - - - *.
(484)
(485) ->
(486) -> title 'Chapter 6 Demo. Program'.
(487)
(488) ->
(489) -> data list list
(490) ->     / country (a7) school (a2) maxtoefl mintoefl nstu.
(491)
(492) -> begin data
```

```
(493) -> Brazil    01 647 490 201
(494) -> Brazil    02 640 480 203
(495) -> Brazil    03 637 447 351
(496) -> Brazil    04 640 437 256
(497) -> France  01 620 453 260
(498)
(499) Chapter 6 Demo. Program
(500) DEMO: CHI-SQUARE analysis
(501)
(502) -> France    02 623 477 259
(503) -> France    03 613 473 245
(504) -> France    04 617 463 358
(505) -> Germany 01 623 430 245
(506) -> Germany 02 640 470 336
(507) -> Germany 03 647 453 362
(508) -> Germany 04 637 457 344
(509) -> Germany 05 620 493 456
(510) -> Italy      01 630 447 344
(511) -> Italy      02 613 450 255
(512) -> Italy      03 623 453 220
(513) -> end data.
(514)
(515) Preceding task required 1.70 seconds elapsed.
(516)
(517) ->     save outfile=world.
(518)
(519) Time stamp on saved file:[date here] 12:26:53
(520) File contains 5 variables, 40 bytes per case before compression
(521) 16 cases were written to c:\spsswin\world.
(522)
(523) Preceding task required .11 seconds elapsed.
(524)
(525) -> execute.
(526)
(527) Preceding task required .00 seconds elapsed.
(528)
(529) ->
(530) ->
(531) -> *OK to overwrite temp dataset: world.
(532)
(533) -> get file=world.
```

(534)
(535) File c:\spsswin\world.
(536)   Created: [date here] 12:26:53 5 variables and 16 cases
(537)
(538) -> sort cases by country.
(539)
(540) The file to be sorted contains 16 cases of 40 bytes each.
(541) At least 12,524 bytes of memory are available to the sort.
(542) 12,524 bytes is the minimum in which the sort will run.
(543) 12,524 bytes would suffice for an in-memory sort.
(544)
(545) The data were already sorted.
(546)
(547) Preceding task required .27 seconds elapsed.
(548)
(549) -> save outfile=world.
(550)
(551) Time stamp on saved file: [date here] 12:26:55
(552) File contains 5 variables, 40 bytes per case before compression
(553) 16 cases were written to c:\spsswin\world.
(554)
(555) Chapter 6 Demo. Program
(556) DEMO: CHI-SQUARE analysis
(557)
(558) Preceding task required 1.16 seconds elapsed.
(559)
(560) -> execute.
(561)
(562) Preceding task required .00 seconds elapsed.
(563)
(564) ->
(565) -> get file=world.
(566)
(567) File c:\spsswin\world.
(568)   Created: [date here] 12:26:55 5 variables and 16 cases
(569)
(570) -> subtitle 'Whole-world means'.
(571)
(572) -> descriptives variables=maxtoefl mintoefl.
(573)
(574) 152 bytes of memory required for the DESCRIPTIVES procedure.

(575) 8 bytes have already been acquired.

(576) 144 bytes remain to be acquired.

(577)

(578) Chapter 6 Demo. Program

(579) Whole-world means

(580)

(581) Number of valid observations (listwise) = 16.00

(582)

(583)   Valid

(584) Variable   Mean Std Dev Minimum Maximum   N Label

(585)

(586) MAXTOEFL 629.38   11.73   613.00   647.00 16

(587) MINTOEFL 460.81   18.20   430.00   493.00 16

(588)

(589) Chapter 6 Demo. Program

(590) Whole-world means

(591)

(592) Preceding task required .22 seconds elapsed.

(593)

(594) -> execute.

(595)

(596) Preceding task required .05 seconds elapsed.

(597)

(598) ->

(599) -> get file=world.

(600)

(601) File c:\spsswin\world.

(602)   Created: [date here] 12:26:55 5 variables and 16 cases

(603)

(604) ->   subtitle 'Means by country'.

(605)

(606) ->   report

(607) ->   / variables=maxtoefl mintoefl

(608) ->   / break=country

(609) ->   / summary=mean

(610) ->   / summary=stddev

(611) ->   / summary=min

(612) ->   / summary=max.

(613)

(614) REPORT problem requires 3464 bytes of memory to store
      specifications

(615) for this task.
(616)
(617) Chapter 6 Demo. Program
(618)
(619)
(620) COUNTRY   MAXTOEFL   MINTOEFL
(621)
(622) Brazil
(623)
(624) Mean   641.00   463.50
(625) StdDev   4.24   25.49
(626) Minimum   637.00   437.00
(627) Maximum   647.00   490.00
(628)
(629) France
(630)
(631) Mean   618.25   466.50
(632) StdDev   4.27   10.75
(633) Minimum   613.00   453.00
(634) Maximum   623.00   477.00
(635)
(636) Germany
(637)
(638) Mean   633.40   460.60
(639) StdDev   11.50   23.16
(640) Minimum   620.00   430.00
(641) Maximum   647.00   493.00
(642)
(643) Italy
(644)
(645) Mean   622.00   450.00
(646) StdDev   8.54   3.00
(647) Minimum   613.00   447.00
(648) Maximum   630.00   453.00
(649)
(650) Chapter 6 Demo. Program
(651) Means by country
(652)
(653) REPORT problem required an additional 1440 bytes of memory.
(654)
(655) Preceding task required 1.32 seconds elapsed.

```
(656)
(657) -> execute.
(658)
(659) Preceding task required .00 seconds elapsed.
(660)
(661) ->
(662) -> data list list
(663) ->      / country (a7) maxtmean mintmean.
(664)
(665) -> begin data.
(666)
(667) - Brazil      641 463
(668) - France      618 466
(669) - Germany  633 460
(670) - Italy       622 450
(671) - end data.
(672)
(673) Preceding task required 1.15 seconds elapsed.
(674)
(675) ->    compute tmeandif=maxtmean-mintmean.
(676)
(677) ->    save outfile=country.
(678)
(679) Time stamp on saved file: [date here] 12:27:01
(680) File contains 4 variables, 32 bytes per case before compression
(681) 4 cases were written to c:\spsswin\country.
(682)
(683) Preceding task required .94 seconds elapsed.
(684)
(685) -> execute.
(686)
(687) Preceding task required .00 seconds elapsed.
(688)
(689) ->
(690) -> get file=country.
(691)
(692) File c:\spsswin\country.
(693)    Created: [date here] 12:27:01 4 variables and 4 cases
(694)
(695) ->      *In SPSS, titles cannot be longer than 60 characters.
(696)
```

(697) ->   subtitle 'Printout of first-order data w/computed
            variable: TMEANDIF'.
(698)
(699) ->   list.
(700)
(701) 368 bytes of memory required for the LIST procedure.
(702) 224 bytes have already been acquired.
(703) 144 bytes remain to be acquired.
(704)
(705) Chapter 6 Demo. Program
(706) Printout of first-order data w/ computed variable: TMEANDIF
(707)
(708) COUNTRY MAXTMEAN MINTMEAN TMEANDIF
(709)
(710) Brazil   641.00   463.00   178.00
(711) France   618.00   466.00   152.00
(712) Germany   633.00   460.00   173.00
(713) Italy   622.00   450.00   172.00
(714)
(715) Number of cases read: 4 Number of cases listed: 4
(716)
(717) Chapter 6 Demo. Program
(718) Printout of first-order data w/ computed variable: TMEANDIF
(719)
(720) Preceding task required .28 seconds elapsed.
(721)
(722) -> execute.
(723)
(724) Preceding task required .05 seconds elapsed.
(725)
(726) ->
(727) -> *- - - - - - - - - End-of-program housecleaning - - - - - - - - - -.
(728)
(729) ->
(730) -> *clear working file.
(731)
(732) -> new file.
(733)
(734) ->
(735) -> *erase temporary files created by this program.
(736)

```
(737) ->
(738) -> erase file='world'.
(739)
(740) -> erase file='country'.
(741)
(742) ->
(743) -> *---------------------------.
(744)
(745) -> * End of Program get execution time  .
(746)
(747) -> *---------------------------.
(748)
(749) ->
(750) -> get file=timechek.
(751)
(752) File c:\spsswin\timechek.
(753)     Created: [date here] 12:26:50 2 variables and 1 cases
(754)
(755) ->    string stopstr (a35).
(756)
(757) ->    compute stopstr= 'and the stop time is'.
(758)
(759) ->    compute stop=xdate.time($time).
(760)
(761) ->    print formats startstr (a35) start (time8) stopstr (a35)
             stop (time8).
(762)
(763) ->    print / startstr start
(764) ->          / stopstr stop.
(765)
(766) -> execute.
(767) For this program, the start time is 12:26:50
(768)                     and the stop time is 12:27:06
(769)
(770) Preceding task required 1.27 seconds elapsed.
(771)
(772) ->
(773) -> * Delete timecheck file.
(774)
(775) ->
(776) -> new file.
```

(777)
(778) ->
(779) -> erase file='timechek'.
(780)
(781) Chapter 6 Demo. Program
(782) Printout of first-order data w/ computed variable: TMEANDIF
(783)
(784) ->
(785) -> * Change the SET options back to system defaults;
          i.e., no log -->.
(786)
(787) ->
(788) -> set errors=listing
(789) ->   messages=none
(790) ->   printback=none
(791) ->   results=listing.

COMMENTS ON THESE
DEMONSTRATION PROGRAMS

The demonstration programs in this chapter show several new
things. (Remember, the line numbers at left are not part of the input
program code.) The most unique aspect of these implementations
is that in addition to input program code and output, you also have
execution logs. In SAS, the default execution log is a separate file,
so there are three SAS files above: the program (3-96), the output
(100-154), and the execution log (156-278). In SPSS, the default
execution log is interleaved in the output. Study the SPSS output
in lines 439-791; lines with the symbol '->' are echoes of the
SPSS input code, and lines without that symbol are SPSS execution messages and the actual SPSS output results. There is also a
memo to The Boss in 280-303, which I discuss below.

As you flip through these implementations, you will note the
kinds of messages that the logs produce. They are quite useful in
many respects, generally subsumed under Principle 6.4. From the
logs, you come to learn how the software handles files and the time
required for certain tasks. I also like to know the overall time
required for the entire program, and so both the SAS and SPSS
implementations above contain extra code to print out the program

start and stop times. Granted, there is a little bit of time used to process the computation of the start and stop times, but that is negligible (and consistent in all programs, allowing you to judge your system). The two program samples below give the generic form of the timing code for both SAS and SPSS:

"timer.sas"

```
*-----------------------------------------------------------*
*Start a time check for this program;

data timechek;
   start=time();
run;


**  INSERT PROGRAM HERE;


*----------------------------------;
* End of Program get execution time ;
*----------------------------------;
*End the time check for this program --
 write the time values at the end of the execution log;
 data timechek;
    set timechek;
    progx ='For this program,';
    startx='start time =';
    stopx =' stop time =';
    stop =time();
    put                            /
            progx                  /
            startx start time. /
        @2 stopx    stop time. /;
run;

proc datasets;
   delete timechek;
run;
quit;
*-----------------------------------------------------------*;
```

"timer.sps"

```
*Start a time check for this program.
data list fixed
    / startstr 1-35 (a).
begin data.
For this program, the start time is
end data.
    compute start=xdate.time($time).
    save outfile=timechek.
execute.


** INSERT PROGRAM HERE.


*---------------------------------------.
* End of Program - get execution time .
*---------------------------------------.

get file=timechek.
    string stopstr (a35).
    compute stopstr='          and the stop time is'.
    compute stop=xdate.time($time).
    print formats startstr (a35) start (time8)
                  stopstr (a35)  stop (time8).
    print / startstr start
          / stopstr stop.
execute.

* Delete timecheck file.

new file.

erase file='timechek'.
```

As with my filenaming conventions, you are free to incorporate these comments into your SAS or SPSS programming. In fact, you are free to incorporate any techniques I present in this book.

I would like to discuss one type of log message in some detail. In the SAS log, you will note messages like this:

```
NOTE: The data set WORK.WORLD has 16 observations and
      5 variables.
NOTE: The data set WORK.COUNTRY has 4 observations and
      4 variables.
```

And in the SPSS output, some of the log messages interleaved in the results look like this:

Time stamp on saved file: [date here] 12:26:53
File contains 5 variables, 40 bytes per case before compression
16 cases were written to c:\spsswin\world.

([date here] represents the date on which the program was run, which I deleted, and c:\spsswin\world is the location of that temporary file on my computer's hard disk.)

These messages echo the names of the various temporary files we have created during the program run, and they are an illustration of another sample of Principle 2.1. We are controlling the flow of our data as well as its structure; we are in charge not only of the arrangement of our data, but of the names of the temporary files, when we bring them into the program, and when we take them out of the program (and erase them, manually, in SPSS). This sort of control is most evident when examining a long contiguous program.

One other SPSS detail is noteworthy. The execute command (e.g., line 365 or 381), which, as I described in Chapter 2, is the end of an SPSS program block, is only necessary when a temporary working file has been defined: either created (e.g., data list) or retrieved (the get command). That is why no "execute" commands are needed for the SPSS erase commands.

At the end of the SAS implementation above is a little memo written to The Boss (280-303); as an exercise, I recommend that you run the SPSS program above and create a similar memo by cutting and pasting from its output. Note that in lines 290-295, I simply copied the table from the SAS output (compare to lines 149-154). The only change is to delete the SAS-generated column called obs, the default internal observation number which SAS records for each case in a data set. I have found, through years of experience (in cutting and pasting SAS output and dealing with people who read my reports) that the OBS column is notoriously hard to explain. The best I seem to come up with, if I do forget to delete it, is something like: "Oh, just ignore that. It is a row number from the software, and I forgot to delete it." If I have to do that in a faculty meeting, in front of my boss and peers, it can be rather embarrassing. I can ask SAS not to print the OBS column (the noobs option available in most SAS procedures), but I myself actually like to have it as a debugging tool. It helps me see if SAS is seeing the same number of observations that I do (see Principle 4.2). Hence, I usually let the computer generate it, and if I do cut and paste the output into a report, I delete it in the report. All else being equal, I don't like to waste time reformatting computer output for transmission to others. It's far easier to train them how to read it, with a few exceptions (like obs).

The memo also contains a Note in which I explain the meaning of each variable. Again, from years of experience, I have found that this kind of rhetorical trick is usually the best. I don't like to spend lots of time formatting it or embedding the information in a lot of prose. The boss is busy and wants an answer—quick, efficient, and concise. It is a "memo-by-request," which is the kind of communication a data analyst should produce in a frenetic organization like the EAI.

The two possible principles above, "don't over edit output" and "keep reports simple," are actually candidates for data-handling principles. Similarly, you might develop preferences for programming style, for example, "put a comment above every program block." Strategies like these illustrate the sole principle in the next chapter—Principle 7.1: "Develop your own principles of data handling." As you work, you will discover that you evolve your own style of programming and your own preferences for output appearance. The latter—the display of results—will be conditioned on what you usually do with them. If you do a lot of cut-and-pasting of output into memos, you will naturally come to design output that is easy to insert into other documents. If you do not, you will probably come to design output that is most readable by yourself and anybody else who has to read it. Regardless, allow your own tastes to emerge as personal preferences—personal principles of data handling.

6.7. DISCUSSION QUESTIONS: CHAPTER 6

Note: Read all of questions 1 through 3 before doing them. Also, review Chapter 4 before doing 1 through 3. How do the people whom you visit (in items 1 and 2 below) execute data debugging?

1. Visit a professional programmer/data analyst; if possible, locate somebody who bears primary responsibility for data handling at a corporation—somebody who deals with critical profit-oriented data on a daily basis. Ask to see his/her system of archival and program libraries. While you are on that visit, also ask about backup procedures. After your visit, return to your teaching/ research setting. How can you take advantage of what you learned on your visit?

   I do not recommend that you combine task 1 above with task (2) below. Get a perspective from some single person who has great responsibility for data integrity (task 1) and compare it with a perspective from group data handling (task 2). In addition, by selecting two different companies, you will see some variation in fairly fundamental issues, for example, how frequently to update off-site backups.

2. Repeat task 1 above, except this time, visit a company or department of a company where data analysis must be archived for use by many people. How does the company ensure that everybody knows and agrees on data-archiving conventions? If data handling at your setting must be shared by many people, what steps can you take to unify your archives? How does the organization which you visit ensure backup security when data sets are handled by many people, and is that feasible in your setting?

3. In 1 and 2 above, explain the concept of data-handling principles to a professional data analyst. Share the principles of this book with that individual, and invite critical analysis of these principles. Also ask that person to describe his or her taste—personal preferences (personal principles) on matters of programming

style and the design of output. Ask him or her to suggest additional principles, a practice I support strongly (see Chapter 7).

4. At your setting, compare the difference in your time if you save output online versus regenerating it. Factor in the time it takes for a person to rerun a program from the archive versus that needed to simply pull up an old output file. Factor in, also, the cost in terms of hard disk storage space. If feasible, compare the hard disk storage space needs to storage on some other media, for instance, tape. (Note: As I write this, in 1995, one truism exists for computer hardware: Space is getting cheaper. You may discover that the cheapest solution is to save output and buy an additional hard disk. It may actually be a savings to add hardware rather than use personnel to redo programs whenever you want results from a previous era.)

5. Do you have any higher-order analysis projects in your setting? If so, what are they, and what are the particular data types that must be saved from lower-order analysis as higher-order input data?

6. In Appendix B, I illustrate how to save data generated by a SAS or SPSS program to an external file. (An external file is a computer file other than the one you are working on, in this case, the program itself.) It is also possible to read data from an external file, which is probably far less cumbersome than copying and recopying data into a program, as I illustrate in the Implementations in this book. When reading data from an external file, the SAS and SPSS data boundary commands are not necessary (the cards; and single semicolon in SAS and the begin data and end data commands in SPSS). Both saving to and reading from external files are highly dependent on the particular version of SAS or SPSS you use, and even more critically, on the operating system of the computer where you work. Yet, as you approach the "end" of data handling, and as your files and data proliferate, you will naturally wish to do so. It is far beyond the scope of this book for me to attempt to list

all the methods for the many operating systems that run SAS and SPSS, hence, I pose this task:

If you use SAS or SPSS, find out precisely how to read from and save to external data files. You will probably need documentation from the software company and/or from local resources, such as a computer center. Better still, consult with somebody else who does that regularly at your setting.

Be sure to get the answers to these questions:

(a) Can I save to and read from files that are over 80 columns in width, which is the typical default? If so, what additional commands are necessary?
(b) How do I fully specify the location (on a computer disk) of the external file?
(c) How much space can I access for external files, and can I access temporary disk space, tape, cartridges, and other temporary media?
(d) Can I get some examples of SAS and SPSS programs that read from and save to external files on this system?

7. Return to question 5 in Chapter 5 and revisit your SAS-SPSS debate. Consider the type of information given in the execution logs in both programs, and the fact that by default, a SAS execution log is a separate file whereas an SPSS execution log is interleaved in the results. Which do you prefer? Why?

8. Recall Cody and Smith's claim (1991, p. 15) that the comment is "one of the most important SAS statements"; I agree strongly with this, but I also believe that commenting and titling is somewhat a matter of personal taste.

Throughout this book, I have presented sample implementation programs that include varying degrees of commenting and titling. For instance, would you comment the Chapter 6 SAS program differently? Consider the following changes to lines 22-73; that is, consider an added comment just before each SAS program block:

```
*Input EAI world data;
data world;
    input country $ school $ maxtoefl mintoefl nstu;
cards;
Brazil    01 647 490 201
Brazil    02 640 480 203
Brazil    03 637 447 351
Brazil    04 640 437 256
France    01 620 453 260
France    02 623 477 259
France    03 613 473 245
France    04 617 463 358
Germany 01 623 430 245
Germany 02 640 470 336
Germany 03 647 453 362
Germany 04 637 457 344
Germany 05 620 493 456
Italy     01 630 447 344
Italy     02 613 450 255
Italy     03 623 453 220
;
run;

* Sort data by country—OK to overwrite temp dataset: WORLD;
proc sort data=world;
    by country;
run;

* compute whole-world statistics;
proc means data=world;
    var maxtoefl mintoefl;
    title2 'Whole-world means';
run;

* compute statistics by country;
proc means data=world;
    var maxtoefl mintoefl;
    by country;
    title2 'Means by country';
run;
```

```
* input (cut-and-paste) higher-order country data from
  the PROC MEANS immediately above. Rerun program;
data country;
    input country $ maxtmean mintmean;
    tmeandif=maxtmean-mintmean;
cards;
Brazil   641 463
France   618 466
Germany  633 460
Italy    622 450
;
run;


* print out higher-order (first-order) country data;
proc print data=country;
    title2 'Printout of first-order data with computed
            variable: TMEANDIF';
run;
```

How much commenting do you prefer? Is the above code easier for you to read and understand? Why or why not? Do those comments seem to help before certain program blocks more so than before others? Why and for which program blocks? Rework some of the SAS and SPSS programs given in this and previous chapters and redo the comments and titles. Try to identify your own tastes—your own principles of commenting and titling. That is another preview of Principle 7.1.

NOTES

1. Self-organization is the primary intent of Principle 6.1, but I should also note that it does compete with Principle 5.1. How can you avoid worn paths if you are constantly archiving yourself and working and reworking procedures with which you are comfortable? I believe this is an issue of balance. We need to be productive—to handle and analyze data in a manner with which we are accustomed. We also need to attend to possible biases in our work—worn paths—in case we are drawing inaccurate conclusions about our data because of ignoring relevant data. Principles 6.1 and 5.1 are in a dynamic tension and suggest that we develop a sense of compromise between them.

2. An interesting question is this: Is a computed variable actually output, and therefore, is analysis of a computed variable actually higher order? (See Chapter 3 on computed variables.) To me, the answer is no. I define higher order analysis to refer to data that are the result of analysis on variable(s) across many cases.

In SAS one can request a mean of a number of variables on a casewise basis:

```
data demo;
    input x y z;
    xbar=mean(of x y z);
cards;
[put data here]
;
run;
```

In the above code, a fourth variable is created on for each case: the mean of x, y, and z. This new variable, xbar, is conceptually similar to the computed variables illustrated in Chapter 3— see, e.g., lines 26 and 27 of the Implementation code there. Is the variable xbar actually first order? I'll still contend that it is not, because it is an alteration of each original data record. It is the creation of a molecule from the atoms, where the molecule is being applied to each case.

On the other hand, we might compute a mean of the variable X across all cases:

```
proc means data=demo;
    var x;
run;
```

The output of the proc means above will give a value that is the average of X across all cases in the dataset. If that value is then input to a later program, I would contend that it is a first-order data value.

I grant that this operational definition is a matter of taste. Increasingly, programs like SAS can do very sophisticated data manipulations on individual cases. For example, SAS has a number of complicated "functions." Alternatively, a SAS programmer can write code to produce complex statistics for each record. The RAP statistic described above was a statistic which I programmed. If SAS does not provide the appropriate functions to obtain the new statistic, there is an entire separate grammar in the SAS language to write a macro—i.e., to get SAS to produce virtually any statistic. What is more, in SAS and similar software, it is possible to run a complex analysis, obtain some statistic for each case, and match-merge it back to the original data set. In research on language test items, where the items themselves identify the records, I have done this numerous times when I treat item means and discrimination indices as entries in an item bank. I obtained those means and discrimination indices by running a statistical proc in SAS.

Perhaps, as time goes by, we will come to see an individual data record as zero order, rather than the entire collection of records in a data set.

Conclusion
Data-Handling Story Problems

The key ideas of this book are best summarized in Appendix A, which is the simple listing of the data-handling principles. The final product of this book should be those principles—in their short and concise form. This is because I cannot predict the precise data you work with, or the computer hardware you prefer, or the software you have available. I contend, however, that I can predict the problems you will encounter, and I have offered—as solutions—those general principles. They should translate into any statistical data-handling situation. Those principles are what you should take away from the book; above all else, they best capture the key dilemmas you will face and the decisions you will have to make as you work with data destined for statistical analysis.

Because the principles are the most important product of the book and because they are best summarized by simply listing them as I have done in Appendix A, I here present a rather different concluding chapter. Instead of summarizing the book and revisiting its main points, I relay a set of thought exercises. I present several data-handling situations, each a story and a problem. Each involves—or more accurately, invokes—at least one principle. As you read through each, try to detect the principle(s) invoked by that story. Try to solve the problem. The answers—at least the answers I think are correct—are given in Appendix C.

As you read these stories, perhaps one or several of them will strike home. Perhaps some facet of a story will seem familiar— vaguely reminiscent of some data problem you have faced, or possibly (hauntingly) right on target. Furthermore, perhaps you can generate your own "data stories," as I suggest in the discussion questions. To that end, I offer my final principle of this book:

Principle 7.1: The Principled Approach

Develop your own principles of data handling.

A *principle* is a statement of general tendency, a claim of generality regardless of a particular data set or software. Your principles should induce from multiple experiences; they should transcend and encompass a variety of needs in your setting. If your new principle evolves from a singular need—from a onetime experience—be careful. Do not overgeneralize the problems of one data-handling event to all data analysis. Step aside, draw together a group of colleagues, and discuss this nature: "Let's look at this data problem that just bothered us. Is it going to happen again? Can it extend to other data sets? Other contexts?" Principles evolve from such discussions.

STORY 1: ZEALOUS DATA

Central States University (CSU), located somewhere in the Midwest, has had an intensive ESL program for 17 years. For that period, student data have been kept in a computer. Although the hardware has been upgraded several times, and on one occasion versions of software were switched, the entire ESL staff has become accustomed to the variable names and possible values. Indeed, the variable names have achieved a nominalized power—one often hears one ESL teacher say to another: "What is so-and-so's COURSE1?" In essence, the staff have internalized the lingo of their data codebook, a codebook that looks like this:

VARIABLE NAME	TYPE	DESCRIPTION	COLUMNS
NAME	Char	Student's name	01-05
COUNTRY	Char	Student's home country	08-12
NL	Char	Student's first language	14-20
SEX	Char	Student's sex	22
PLACTEST	Num	Student's ESL placement test score	24-27
COURSE1	Char	Name of first ESL course taken	29-31
COURSE2	Char	Name of 2nd ESL course taken	33-35
COURSE3	Char	Name of 3rd ESL course taken	37-39
COURSE4	Char	Name of 4th ESL course taken	41-43
TERM1	Char	Academic term in which COURSE1 was taken	45-47
TERM2	Char	Academic term in which COURSE2 was taken	49-51
TERM3	Char	Academic term in which COURSE3 was taken	53-55
TERM4	Char	Academic term in which COURSE4 was taken	57-59
GRADE1	Char	Grade received for COURSE1	61
GRADE2	Char	Grade received for COURSE2	63
GRADE3	Char	Grade received for COURSE3	65
GRADE4	Char	Grade received for COURSE4	67
TOEFTERM	Char	Academic term in which the TOEFL elective was taken	69-71
TGRADE	Char	Grade received for the TOEFL elective	73

The variables COURSE1 to COURSE4 contain values of the form: 101, 102, 103, or 104. The placement test (PLACTEST) indicates in which level a student should begin in the sequence of ESL courses. Some students begin at level 101 (the lowest); others begin at 102, 103, and not infrequently, 104.

The university offers only those four sequenced multiskill ESL courses: ESL 101-104; hence, the maximum number that can theoretically appear on a student record is four. The variables TERM1 to TERM4 contain information such as f91, s92, and u92, for, respectively, fall 1991, spring 1992, and summer 1992 academic terms. The variables GRADE1 to GRADE4 contain typical single-letter grades (e.g., A, B; the university offers no plus/minus grades). The variables are intended to align. For example, if a student takes ESL 102 as COURSE2, then the value in TERM2 indicates when the student took that course, and the value in GRADE2 indicates the grade the student received for that course at that time.

About 10 years ago, CSU staff learned of the big demand for a special elective course in TOEFL preparation. This realization came about because a sizable number of international students began coming to the campus to take ESL courses only, without being accepted to the university. Under CSU statute, ESL is one of several departments offering courses declared "open enrollment," and a student need not be admitted to the university to sign up; the student need only meet that department's entry standards (in this case, the placement test score necessary to get into ESL 101). During the past 10 years, many such nonmatriculated students have desired special preparation in TOEFL in order to apply to CSU or to other colleges. And so a TOEFL preparatory course was added, and the database gained two new fields: TOEFTERM and TGRADE.

Time passed. Recently, a review of the database uncovered something peculiar—something related to accurate entry of the TOEFL prep course information. When a student takes a multiskill ESL course in the same semester as a TOEFL elective, the TOEFL semester is apparently recorded in the variable TOEFTERM and the grade received is recorded in TGRADE. But that was not happening regularly. Some CSU ESL staff were entering the TOEFL class information in the set of variables called COURSE1-COURSE4 and giving the term and grade information in the aligned TERM and GRADE variables. The value TOE seemed, in many records, to appear in COURSE1 or COURSE2. Diligent detective work uncovered a "Database Manual" prepared by a long-departed staff member that declared TOE should be entered in COURSE1-COURSE4 and that made no mention of the TOEFTERM or TGRADE variables. Further diligent detective work, however, uncovered a faction of staff members who routinely ignored that manual and who insisted on entering the TOEFL information where "it damn well belongs," as one of them phrased it.

As a result, the database contained two general types of records for people who did take the TOEFL elective. Those who did not take the TOEFL class were unaffected by what some faculty called "a bug." It became clear that if a student took the TOEFL elective in the same semester as a multiskill ESL course, then the record might have two TERM variables with the same value. One such case was the following student:

```
     NAME:  Jose Milo
       NL:  Spanish
      SEX:  M
PLACTEST:  49
 COURSE1:  101
 COURSE2:  TOE
 COURSE3:  102
 COURSE4:
    TERM1:  f89
    TERM2:  s90
    TERM3:  s90
    TERM4:
   GRADE1:  B
   GRADE2:  A
   GRADE3:  B
   GRADE4:
 TOEFTERM:
   TGRADE:
```

If the keypuncher followed the "Database Manual," however, then a record such as the following was produced:

```
     NAME:  Denise LaTour
  COUNTRY:  France
       NL:  French
      SEX:  F
 PLACTEST:  61
  COURSE1:  102
  COURSE2:  103
  COURSE3:
  COURSE4:
    TERM1:  f93
```

```
TERM2:   s93
TERM3:
TERM4:
GRADE1:  A
GRADE2:  A
GRADE3:
GRADE4:
TOEFTERM:   s93
TGRADE:  A
```

Both Jose and Denise did essentially the same thing: They each took the TOEFL elective in the same term as a multiskill ESL course.

These two students are typical in another respect. It is extremely rare that somebody takes all four CSU ESL multiskill courses. Typically, for matriculated students, a departmental ESL requirement is fulfilled after a semester or two. And nonmatriculated students take the TOEFL prep, get their TOEFL scores up, and go elsewhere or gain admittance to a CSU department on the basis of TOEFL score. The staff never saw this data bug coming because it never had a person who took all four multiskill courses and the TOEFL prep. In fact, the whole problem was identified because of the case of "Mr. Smith," a recent student whom all the faculty came to know quite well:

```
    NAME:   John Smith
 COUNTRY:   Someplace
      NL:   Something
     SEX:   M
PLACTEST:   39
 COURSE1:   101
 COURSE2:   102
 COURSE3:   TOE
 COURSE4:   103
   TERM1:   f94
   TERM2:   s94
   TERM3:   u94
   TERM4:   u94
  GRADE1:   B
  GRADE2:   A
```

```
GRADE3 :   A
GRADE4 :   B
TOEFTERM:   104
TGRADE:   A
```

In effect, the keypuncher saved time by putting in Smith's TOEFL data during the normal COURSE1-COURSE4 stream. But Smith stayed at CSU right through all four courses (which is rare), and he also took the TOEFL elective. He was a zealous glutton for ESL.

At the moment, about 4,000 records are in the database. On review, the administration sees that, in 2,501 records (like Denise), the TOEFL prep information is in its own variables, a count that includes both correctly entered TOEFL data and students from the first years of the system, when the TOEFL class was not offered. In the rest of the database (like Jose), the TOEFL information is given in the COURSE1-COURSE4 sequence. And not until John Smith passed through the system did this become a problem.

After much discussion in two long, arduous afternoon meetings, the CSU ESL staff decided to implement the following solution. They changed the structure of the data and added a large COMMENT field. This COMMENT field uses the capability of the software to "window" into a full-text screen where, effectively, pages and pages of information can be kept on each student. Several faculty members like that anyway because it allows them to save substantive information about students, such as information about student hobbies. Other faculty members are skeptical because, as one said, "Get real. Nobody is going to take the time to key in stuff like hobbies."

After that change, Smith's record looked like this:

```
    NAME:   John Smith
 COUNTRY:   Someplace
      NL:   Something
     SEX:   M
PLACTEST:   39
 COURSE1:   101
 COURSE2:   102
 COURSE3:   TOE
```

```
 COURSE4:  103
   TERM1:  f94
   TERM2:  s94
   TERM3:  s94
   TERM4:  u94
  GRADE1:  B
  GRADE2:  A
  GRADE3:  A
  GRADE4:  B
 TOEFTERM:  104
  TGRADE:  A
 COMMENT:  TOEFL course taken f95.
```

The staff decided not to go back and correct nearly 1,500 records. Sometimes fractious discussion led to the consensus that they just did not want to expend the personnel time to do so. They reasoned that the information they wanted was there and that they could (as one staff member puts it) "solve it in programming" whenever they wanted to print out a data report. Should they have additional students like Smith who take all five possible classes, the staff can use the COMMENT field to record information to clarify precisely what happened.

The above compromise was made final just recently. One new faculty member with extensive background in computer data management watched the extensive debate sparked by Mr. Smith's record. He was amazed that nobody saw another potential problem, one that would be rare but that is theoretically possible. In a fit of egoistic pique, the new faculty member lurked in the main office one night last week after closing, and once everybody was gone, he altered the database structure once more. The new database structure is such that Smith's record now looks like this:

```
     NAME:  John Smith
  COUNTRY:  Someplace
       NL:  Something
      SEX:  M
 PLACTEST:  39
  COURSE1:  101
  COURSE2:  102
```

```
COURSE3 :  TOE
COURSE4 :  103
COURSE5 :
   TERM1 :  f94
   TERM2 :  s94
   TERM3 :  s94
   TERM4 :  u94
   TERM5 :
  GRADE1 :  B
  GRADE2 :  A
  GRADE3 :  A
  GRADE4 :  B
  GRADE5 :
TOEFTERM :  104
  TGRADE :  A
 COMMENT :  TOEFL course taken f95.
```

The zealous faculty member, on finishing the alteration, grinned, made a backup, and crept out of the office.

And that is where things stand at this moment.

STORY 2: DATA INSURANCE

Mr. W was just hired by the Foreign Language Department of A Major University (AMU-FL) to manage all the data analysis. He has long experience with data analysis; in fact, before he returned to graduate school and obtained a master's degree in foreign language education, he had worked for 10 years as a data analyst for a large bank.

Mr. W's job involves half-time teaching and half-time data management. As part of the latter job duties, the AMU-FL staff asked him to survey the data handling of their school and to write a report to the AMU-FL Advisory Committee, a group of senior faculty with whom the AMU-FL department head regularly consults. The committee asked Mr. W to suggest two things in his report: (a) new hardware/software purchases and (b) revised data management and analysis procedures. During his first month at AMU-FL, Mr. W held a series of meetings with teachers and staff members to, as he put it, "Identify and track the existing data paths." He then spent a weekend writing up his recommendations to the advisory committee. Following is his "Executive Summary" for Part B of the report, concerning revised data management and analysis procedures:

Data Management at the AMU-FL Department: Recommendations

1. There is no regular and routine backup procedure. Minor data loss and rekeying are frequent. Major data loss is infrequent, and the two or three times that it occurred (in the past 5 years) were resolved only because a staff member happened to have made a set of backup diskettes. *Recommendation: Institute a routine departmental backup system.*

2. AMU-FL staff spend extensive time on such tasks as sorting, combining, and merging hard copy data, such as information survey forms about prior study or student test answer sheets. The need to handle all this paper is a source of tension at certain high-pressure data-processing times during an academic term—for example, complaints such as, "Data takes over the Conference Room" and "Why do we have to alphabetize the answer sheets? Can't the computer do that?" *Recommendation: Key data in whatever order they arrive and program the computer to do these tasks.*

3. Student records retain information on total language test scores and subscores on subtests. No record is retained of the opscan sheets with original item responses, however, and those data can show whether individual test items are of high quality. Furthermore, data on past items are not analyzed for reuse of test questions or to inform development of new test questions of a similar nature. *Recommendation: Institute routine item-level data capture and item analysis.*

4. Possibly because of the tension noted in (2) above, data analysis often seems "rushed," as one faculty member said. Several staff and faculty relayed worries that decisions about people may be in jeopardy. *Recommendation: Institute routine and complete checking of data entry and online data debugging.*

5. Another source of tension is, as one secretary said, "Our tendency to keep reinventing the wheel." Similar reports are generated each year on similar data structures. *Recommendation:*

Institute careful archiving of data codebooks, analysis programs, and if hard disk space permits and regeneration is too slow, actual output files.

6. Analysis of data during the past 10 years has revealed 52 cases in which student data values were incorrect because a missing value was incorrectly entered as zero. In 17 of these cases, the missing value was on the composite final exam score, which is used to determine advancement within our instructional levels and ultimately exiting from our system. *Recommendation: Institute (a) a rigorous procedure to track and attempt to recover missing data and (b) a new non-analyzable data value to represent missing information.*

What principle(s) are at operation in the above recommendations?

STORY 3: ONCE IN 1,000 YEARS?

As a break from scenarios concerning language education, read the article shown in Figure 7.1. What is the nature of the problem? What should be done? What principles are operating in the evolution of the problem and in its possible solutions? You might enjoy discussing this particular problem with some professional consultants and data handlers; it is just the kind of offbeat dilemma they enjoy, unless they work for an industry that is beset by this problem —people who are going to fork over some of that $100 billion the article mentions!

I present my interpretation of this millennial difficulty in Appendix C.

STORY 4: THE HANCOCK BET

Ms. C. is nearing the end of her doctorate in second/foreign language education. She is comparing usages of language labs. Her project is large and complex, involving data from nine universities in five countries. Each university has sent her 70-item survey to its language education faculty, who responded and returned the information to Ms. C. In all, she has records on 390 language classes taught by 101 faculty members from the nine universities.

For each class, she knows syllabus information, number of students, average amount of prior study of the TL, and other information about the entire class group. She also has extensive answers to questions about each faculty member's use of the respective language lab. And for each university, she has an official description of the lab itself: how it is fitted out, how large it is, how its chairs/booths are arranged, and so forth. (Each university has only one lab; that was a criterion of her project. She did not want to study schools that had several labs; she wanted to focus on variation of use of a single common facility.)

Ms. C has gone through complex procedures to obtain approval for collecting these data. She has communicated with colleagues all over the world—professionals in the language lab industry, faculty who manage labs, and friends who use labs. Because Ms. C has co-managed the lab at her own university for 3 years and because she has already published in the area of language lab design, she is already gaining wide respect as a key figure in research on labs. She has used that budding respect wisely and carefully to obtain these data from the universities; she has been careful not to step on any toes, but she has been persistent. She began by contacting about 20 universities, and after negotiation and fulfillment of various cultural and administrative research regulations, she has wound up with data from just the nine universities.

All the survey forms have arrived back at Ms. C's office. She has checked and rechecked and found no outstanding data. She is ready to key in the data.

One of her dissertation committee members, a veteran at large-scale data management, had this to say way back when she defended her proposal—when this project was but a gleam in Ms. C's eyes: "The real work is in getting the data from the various universities. Once you have it all here on campus, you are looking at a data set that is really not that big: several hundred rows by less than 100 columns. Keying that in will go quickly. I bet you can do it—and check it—in about a weekend."

Ms. C recalls that remark and telephones the professor to discuss key-in. She bets the professor that key-in will take at least

The Paducah Sun

Monday   May 29, 1995   Vol. 117 #149

Chronological coping

Calculations back from year 2000 may be a pain

BY EVAN RAMSTAD
AP BUSINESS WRITER

NEW YORK—As the year 2000 gets closer, many computer users are facing the prospect of a back-to-the-future nightmare.

Many computer programs calculate years from the last two digits, such as 95 for 1995. But when 2000 arrives, the year will be represented by 00. And so the huge number of programs that make calculations based on higher year values, such as 95 minus 45 equals 50, will produce wrong answers.

For example, a computer in 2000 might think a person born in 1970 is 70 years old if its program automatically used the bigger number to begin a calculation, such as 70 minus 00 equals 70. If a pension fund company's computer program did that, a 30-year-old could start getting retirement benefits.

Likewise, a January 2000 monthly mortgage check written on Dec. 31, 1999, might get bounced because a bank computer thinks the check is 99 years old and therefore no good.

Some product executives have been warning about the date trouble for years. But lately, big computer companies have also warned of a possible crisis.

"As gratifying as it is to see some more people doing it, it's not enough," says Michael Lips, president of TransCentury Data Systems, a San Francisco company that helps businesses with date design software. "We are still going to have major problems despite the best of efforts."

The trouble is that just fixing a computer program isn't enough. All the data that work with the program, which sometimes means millions of records or transactions, must be changed to match the program.

In addition, if a company shares data with somone else, such as an oil driller reporting production to a state agency, the two parties must ensure that any changes are compatible with each other's computers.

"In the grand scheme of things that need work, I think this is on the large side," says Ron Rudman, an engineer at Electronic Data Services Corp., the nation's largest computer services company. "The main point is not to become part of the frenzy, stay calm and work on it early."

The Gartner group, a technology research firm in Stamford, Conn., estimates large businesses will spend $100 billion in the next five years to correct their programs. Government agencies may need to spend a similar amount, though Gartner hasn't done a study for them.

"One financial company said it will spend $250 million to solve the problem, Gartner analyst Kevin Schick," says, though he won't identify it.

The two-digit year became standard with the first computers decades ago as a way to preserve data-storage space and maximize processing power, which initially was a fraction of what's available in a $10 calculator today.

USAA, one of the largest insurance and financial services companies, says much of its USAA data have already have been modified to survive the digit reset unscathed. The company says it is also nearly finished converting life insurance and banking software.

"As you change data, that is the life-blood of your company, and so making major modifications like that is always scary," says Jay Holmes, a USAA assistant vice president.

Marc Sokol, vice president of technology at Computer Associates International Inc., one of the largest software companies, says some clients have been updating old programs for five years.

"But there's certainly a class of people out there, there's less and less these days, hoping the problem goes away," he says.

In a survey for the computer services firm Cap Gemini America Inc., just one-third of the 201 large and midsize companies surveyed have assessed the 2000 problem.

Computer engineers have never been forced to make a change of such magnitude with an absolute deadline. By the time people start working on it, there may not be enough experts to help.

"We think it's going to hit the fan in 1997, at which time we think there will be unlimited demand for limited resources," says Bill Goodwin, editor of Tick Tick Tick, a New York City-based newsletter devoted to the issue.

Figure 7.1. A Data-Handling Story From Today's Headlines
SOURCE: Chronological coping: Calculations back from year 2000 may be a pain. (1995, May 24). *The Paducah Sun*, Vol. 117, #149, pp. 1A, 10A. Copyright 1995, The Associated Press. Reprinted with permission. *Paducah Sun* masthead used with permission.

a week. The professor stands by the earlier claim and gambles that it will take only a few days. They agree on a bet, and a pair of tickets to a Herbie Hancock concert at the campus is wagered.

The weekend after that telephone call, Ms. C's husband joins her at their home computer to enter data. They spend Saturday morning devising a data key-in template. They know the analyses will be done in SAS, so they use a word processor to key in data in an orderly fashion, one row per class. Each row must also contain an identifier to indicate its university and must refer to the setup of that university's language lab. They have a template banged out by about lunchtime.

After some sodas and chicken sandwiches, they begin data key-in. Ms. C's husband calls out the data to Ms. C, and she types the data into the computer. The data are entered by dinnertime. They break to have some leftover soup, and they return to the job about 8:00 p.m. They reverse roles, and Ms. C calls out the data while her husband pages through the data file. He finds only three typing errors. Satisfied that they have most of the data in safely, they make two diskette backups. One backup they put in the dining room china cabinet. Ms. C insists on driving in to campus to put the other backup in her desk at the lab. She gets home about 11:30 p.m.

After a slow Sunday morning, they return to the project about 1:00 p.m. They begin by converting the data to a raw text file suitable for uploading to the local mainframe computer, and they upload the data (thereby creating another backup on the mainframe, as Ms. C notes). She digs out her notes on SAS from several intensive short courses and starts writing some simple programs to get frequency tables, printouts, and means and averages. Her programming is done by about 5:00 p.m., and she notes a few additional data bugs. For example, at one university a professor is recorded as teaching 33 different language classes. Knowing this is quite unlikely, she traces back to the hard copy survey form and sees that the professor in fact taught only three classes but that somehow both she and her husband missed that in the entry and checking. Ms. C takes care of these few additional errors that her early SAS programming has identified. She then breaks to watch a favorite program on television, after which she corrals her husband back to the computer, where they go through the data file and compare it with the hard copy surveys one more time. Indeed, they find a few more errors. It is getting late, so she recopies the dining room backup, makes a new text file, and uploads it to the mainframe (as a backup), but she decides not to drive in and replace the backup at her lab.

On Monday morning, Ms. C calls the lab and says she will be in a bit late—about 10:00 a.m. She spends the early morning reviewing her SAS manuals at home. By 9:30 a.m., she is satisfied that her data are ready to be analyzed, as she put it to her husband the night before: "for real." She makes two more diskette backups, replacing the one in the dining room and putting the other in her backpack to take to her office.

Reasoning that she has lost the bet, she goes to the student union during her lunch hour on Tuesday and gets the Hancock tickets.

DISCUSSION QUESTIONS: CHAPTER 7

1. In a group of colleagues, read the data story problems above. Come to a consensus: Are any of these story problems similar to experiences with data in your setting? How?

2. Write some data story problems of your own. See whether they invoke any of the principles of this book, or alternatively, whether they suggest new principles (see my discussion of Principle 7.1, above).

3. Return to your data log, which I suggested at the end of Chapter 1. Suppose administration at your teaching/research institution wanted to formalize data logs—accurate and uniform records of data processing. What information should be routinely recorded in such a log? Should such a formal log regularly cite principles, either those I have written here or others you might develop? When might you want a nonprincipled data log? Hint: Think about the development of a data-processing manual for your office. Sometimes the best way to improve data handling is to provide precise answers to precise questions. Sometimes it is best to stay away from the ethereal domain of principles.

The Principles

This appendix contains all the data-handling principles I have proposed. These principles are the most important messages of this book; because I cannot accurately predict your precise data-handling context or your preferred software, I provide advice and guidance that should work in any setting. Before you study and consult the principles below, however, remember first the two laws of computing which transcend the principles:

Law 1: Back it up.
Law 2: Do it now.

CHAPTER 1: INTRODUCTION: A PRINCIPLED APPROACH

Principle 1.1: The Atomicity Principle

You cannot analyze below the data level that you observe. (You cannot analyze atoms if all you measure are molecules.)

Principle 1.2: The Appropriate Data Principle

You cannot analyze what you do not measure.

Principle 1.3: The Social Consequences Principle

Data about people are about people. Data can have social consequences.

CHAPTER 2: DATA INPUT

Principle 2.1: The Data Control Principle

Take control of the structure and flow of your data.

Principle 2.2: The Data Input Efficiency Principle

Be efficient in getting your data into a computer file, but not at the cost of losing crucial information.

Principle 2.3: The Change Awareness Principle

Data entry is an iterative process. Keep a list of the changes you will have to make (computations), the values you will have to change (recoding), and the problems you will have to solve (debugging), but try to use the computer to do as much computing and debugging as possible.

CHAPTER 3: DATA MANIPULATION

Principle 3.1: The Data Manipulation Principle

Let the computer do as much work as possible. Instruct it to do tasks such as recoding, variable computation, data set catenation, data set subsetting, data merging, and similar tasks that would, frankly, waste your time. Let the computer manipulate your data for you.

Principle 3.2: The Original Data Principle

Always save a computer file copy of the original, unaltered data.

Principle 3.3: The Kludge Principle

Sometimes the best way to manipulate data is not elegant and seems to waste computer resources. A kludge is sometimes justifiable; the ends CAN justify the means.

Principle 3.4: The Default Principle

Know your software's default settings. Know whether those settings meet your needs.

In particular, be aware of the default handling of missing values in your software.

Principle 3.5: The Complex Data Structure Principle

If your software can accommodate complex data structures (e.g., hierarchical relational databases), then you might benefit from using that software feature. Alternatively, you might prefer a kludge (e.g., copying the same information onto each record).

Principle 3.6: The Software's Data Relations Principle

Know whether your software can perform the following four relations and, if so, what commands are necessary to do so: subsetting, catenation, merging, and relational database construction.

Principle 3.7: The Software's Sorting Principle

Know how to perform a sort in your software and whether your software requires a sort before a by-group analysis or before merging.

CHAPTER 4: DATA DEBUGGING

Principle 4.1: The Impossibility/Implausibility Principle

Use the computer to check for impossible and implausible data.

Principle 4.2: Burstein's Data Sensibility Principle

Run your data all the way through to the final computer analysis and ask yourself whether the results make sense. Be prepared to decide that they do not, and hence be prepared to treat the analysis not as final, but as another debugging step.

Principle 4.3: The Extant Error Principle

Data bugs exist.

Principle 4.4: The Manual Check Principle

Nothing can replace another set of eyes to check over a data set. Either check your data entry, input, and manipulation yourself, or get somebody else to help you do it.

Determine the criticality of your data set before expending human resources to check it manually. Highly critical data sets require manual checking regardless, possibly a priori, certainly a posteriori.

Ideally, all data sets require manual checking.

You should debug data by computer (Principle 4.1) before you check it manually so that manual checking is easier.

Principle 4.5: The Error Typology Principle

Debugging includes detection and correction of errors. To ease correction, try to classify each error as you uncover it.

CHAPTER 5: DATA ASPECTS OF STATISTICAL ANALYSIS

Principle 5.1: The Know Yourself Principle

Know yourself. Know your own preferences about data structure. Know your worn path in analysis of data and ask yourself whether you might be interested in other paths, other data types, and other analyses. Balance this principle against Principle 6.1, the Reinvented Wheel Principle.

Principle 5.2: The Correlative Data Principle

Data structure for correlation-based statistics (e.g., correlations and regression) is easy. That does not mean such statistical analyses are always appropriate.

Principle 5.3: The Expected Data Principle

Modify your data to control for expected direction of results (e.g., polarity). But remember Principle 3.2 and always keep a copy of the original unaltered data.

Principle 5.4: The Unit of Observation Principle

The unit of observation is not always the unit of analysis.

Principle 5.5: The Software Unit Principle

Because the unit of observation is not always the unit of analysis (see Principle 5.4), know whether your software requires you to key in data in univariate or multivariate mode. This affects the complexity of data entry.

CHAPTER 6: THE "END" OF DATA HANDLING

Principle 6.1: The Reinvented Wheel Principle

In all computer processing, keep an archive of successful procedures, routines, and programs so that you do not have to rediscover and redesign them each time they are needed. Plagiarize yourself (it is OK to copy your own work). Library yourself (a new verb!).

Principle 6.1 therefore implies that you set up a system to organize and catalog your data and programs. Do not needlessly reinvent the wheel.

Balance this principle against Principle 5.1: The Know Yourself Principle.

Principle 6.2: The Save Output Principle

Save output (and possibly logs) as files if it took an extremely long time to run the program to generate them.

Principle 6.3: The Re-Generate Output Principle

Do not save output or logs if it takes a very short time to run the program and regenerate them.

Principle 6.4: The Know Your System Principle

Know your computer system. Know its speed, capabilities, and quirks. Know your preferred software packages; in particular, know how long your software takes to do the tasks you typically need to do.

Principle 6.5: The Output = Data Principle

As your analysis ends, your output will probably become part of a report. The output is like data at this point; you are using output of the analysis as data for the report. Know what this implies for your system.

Principle 6.6: The Output = Input Principle

As your analysis ends, your output may be incorporated as input to another program. The output is data at this point. Know what this implies for your system.

CHAPTER 7: CONCLUSION: DATA-HANDLING STORY PROBLEMS

Principle 7.1: The Principled Approach

Develop your own principles of data handling.

Tips on Zero-One Test Score Data

In Chapter 4, we saw the 20-item Dataset A and Dataset B. You might want to review the discussion of those two data sets at this point. In this appendix, I provide tips and tricks on handling data sets such as those. My tips include discussion of issues of missing data, as well as other topics related to such data.

Those data sets originated as a four-option multiple-choice character data set, what I call "ABCD Data":

```
                         10   15   20   25
                        ----|----|----|----|
Answer Key, Data Sets A and B: CABACADDACCACACDBABA
```

```
    Data Set A, ABCD data          Data Set B, ABCD data
    ---------------------          ---------------------
    Most students fail             Most students pass
    most items                     most items.
```

```
     5    10   15   20   25          5    10   15   20   25
    ----|----|----|----|----|       ----|----|----|----|----|
0001 BCDDCCCAABCDBDCACDCA       0101 DABACADAACCACACABABA
0002 ABBABBACBABBCDCBDBDA       0102 CABAAADDACCACDCABABA
0003 CABDAA     CAADAC   B      0103 CBBACADDACCBCACDBCBA
0004 BA ABBBCBCCCDDABABCA       0104 CABACADDABCACACCBABA
0005 BABAAABBBBCCDDBACDDB       0105 CABABADDACCACACABABA
0006 BBBAAACBBDBBBDABBDBB       0106 CABACADDACCACACCBCBA
0007 BBBABACAADCBBDDACDCB       0107 DABACADDACCACACABABA
0008 BBAAABACBDCDCACBCDAD       0108 CABACADDACCACACABDBA
0009 CCDACCCCDCACDDAAACBD       0109 DABACADDACCACACCBABA
0010 CABDDBCCCCACCDAACCDC       0110 CABACADAACCACACABABA
0011 AB        BCCDCAA   A      0111 CABAAADDACCACACCBABA
0012 BADAAADCCBCDDADCABDB       0112 DABACADDACCACACABABA
0013 BADAADCCABCBCBCACBDD       0113 BABACADDACCACACABABA
0014 ADBAADCCACCCDDCACBC        0114 DABACADDACCACACCBABA
0015 BBBAACACCCCAABACAACB       0115 CABABADDACCACACABABA
```

As a result of applying the key to each data set, we obtain the scored data sets shown in Chapter 4 and that are often called "zero-one" (0/1) data:

```
        Data Set A                      Data Set B

     5    10   15   20   25          5    10   15   20   25
    ----|----|----|----|----|       ----|----|----|----|----|
0001 00001000101000100001      0101 01111110111111101111
0002 00110000000010100001      0102 11110111111110101111
0003 11100100000001000000      0103 10111111111011111011
0004 01010000011000000001      0104 11111111101111101111
0005 01110100001000000000      0105 11110111111111101111
0006 00110100000000001010      0106 11111111111111101011
0007 00110100101000000000      0107 01111111111111101111
0008 00010000001011100000      0108 11111111111111101011
0009 10011000010000000010      0109 01111111111111101111
0010 11100000010010000000      0110 11111110111111101111
```

```
0011 0110000000010100001      0111 11110111111111101111
0012 0101011000100100000      0112 01111111111111101111
0013 0101000010101010000      0113 01111111111111101111
0014 0011000011100010000      0114 01111111111111101111
0015 0011000011100000100      0115 11110111111111101111
```

To score data, you must apply the key to each response by each student. This implies an iterative operation. Similar to the argument in favor of Principle 3.1, whenever you sense that you want to do the same thing over and over again to the data, you need to write a program loop. *Looping* is a basic necessity in computer handling of data. It takes advantage of the accuracy, speed, and repetitive ease of a computer processor by ensuring that the same thing is done many times.

The particular loop needed here can be written in pseudocode as follows:

```
Generic ABCD data scoring pseudocode:
```

(1) Input the data line of ITEM01 through ITEM20 for each person.

(2) Create an output data set for the scored data. Use different variable names to indicate that the raw and scored data are separate: ITEM01-ITEM20 will represent unscored data, and ITEMX01-ITEMX20 will represent the scored data.
   –Compare the raw data to the key for each item.
   –<u>If it matches the key, insert a value 1 in the corresponding ITEMX variable.</u>
   –Otherwise, insert a 0 in the corresponding ITEMX variable.

(3) Write out the scored data in the same format (same codebook).

As suggested by Principle 3.4, it is also important to know what happens to missing values in ABCD data scoring; notice, for example, that Student 0003 in Data Set A above skipped several items. In the pseudocode as given above, a missing item would be scored wrongly. That could be a problem: Sometimes students miss items because they run out of time, and not because they cannot do the task the item poses; that is, sometimes a missing item score is most definitely not a zero. Perhaps you want to retain the missing value information in the scored data to determine three types of scores: wrong (0), right (1), and missing. The pseudocode would be altered as shown by the underline below:

```
Pseudocode altered to accommodate missing values:
```

(1) Input the data line of ITEM01 through ITEM20 for each person.

(2) Create an output data set for the scored data. Use different variable names to indicate that the raw and scored data are separate: ITEM01-ITEM20 will represent unscored data, and ITEMX01-ITEMX20 will represent the scored data.
    -Compare the raw data to the key for each item.
    -If it matches the key, insert a value 1 in the corresponding ITEMX variable.
    -If it is missing, put a missing value in the corresponding ITEMX variable.
    -Otherwise, insert a 0 in the corresponding ITEMX variable.

(3) Write out the scored data in the same format.

You may have access to software that scores data for you, without writing such a loop in code. That's fine. Just remember Principle 3.4 and be certain that your software can accommodate missing data both as incorrect (the first SAS segment above) and as missing (the second) so that you retain the flexibility to analyze it in both ways.

This is important also because of Principle 1.3. How might errors in data scoring affect actual student decisions? First, obviously, a mistake in the key could create inaccurate data scoring. Second, if you treat missing values as wrong when they are prevalent, you might inadvertently believe that students are of low ability. In fact, missing values do not say that; perhaps even the high-ability students ran out of time. All that missing values can tell you is the student did not answer. A missing value is absent data, and that's all it is. Any assumption that a missing value is an incorrect response must be carefully evaluated.

One final data manipulation is quite common with zero-one data: computing totals and subtotals. The discussion of the Atomicity Principle (1.1) included an example of this. Below are

Data Sets A and B again, this time with a new variable added in columns 27-28, the total score. The *total score* is the sum of all the items the individual student got correct. Usually, when somebody wants to study a test, the total score is ultimately of interest.

```
        Data Set A                          Data Set B
   Most students fail                  Most students pass
   most items.                         most items.
   Total score included.               Total score included.

     5   10   15   20   25              5   10   15   20   25
   ----|----|----|----|----|---       ----|----|----|----|----|---
   0001 00001000101000100001 05       0101 01111110111111101111 17
   0002 00110000000010100001 05       0102 11110111111110101111 17
   0003 11100100000001000000 05       0103 10111111111011111011 17
   0004 01010000011000000001 05       0104 11111111101111101111 18
   0005 01110100001000000000 05       0105 11110111111111101111 18
   0006 00110100000000001010 05       0106 11111111111111101011 18
   0007 00110100101000000000 05       0107 01111111111111101111 18
   0008 00010000001011100000 05       0108 11111111111111101011 18
   0009 10011000010000000010 05       0109 01111111111111101111 18
   0010 11100000010010000000 05       0110 11111110111111101111 18
   0011 01100000000010100001 06       0111 11110111111111101111 18
   0061 01010110001001000000 06       0112 01111111111111101111 18
   0013 01010000101010100000 06       0113 01111111111111101111 18
   0014 00110000111000100000 06       0114 01111111111111101111 18
   0015 00110000011100000100 06       0115 11110111111111101111 18
```

How were these total scores computed? Something similar was performed on each data set: The 1s were summed up. The pseudocode for this operation would be very simple because 0 = wrong and 1 = right and the sum of the 1s is the computed variable called 'total':

```
                total=the sum of the values
                for ITEMX01 through ITEMX20.
```

Now imagine that our 20-item subtest had two subparts: Part A comprised of items 1 to 10, and Part B comprised of items 11 to 20. Perhaps you would like both a subtotal and a total score. You do not need to compute three separate item sums, of course. Your pseudocode would be:

```
totala=the sum of the values for ITEMX01 through
       ITEMX10.
totalb=the sum of the values for ITEMX11 through
       ITEMX20.
total=totala+totalb
```

That is, you can compute two item sums and add them for your total score; three sum variables would be added to the data set, not one. As explained in Chapter 3, you do not need to retain the subscores (or the total, for that matter) and rewrite them to your original input data. A subscore can be a temporary computed variable for a certain processing step.

Below are implementations of the above pseudocode procedures in SAS and SPSS. I use the following assumptions: (a) ABCD data scored into zero-one data using a key, (b) missing values on items retained for item-level zero-one data but counted as wrong in computation of total scores, and (c) both total and subtotals calculated.

```
--------------- SAS: Input Program ---------------

*-----------------------------------------------------*
| Name of input program:appen_c.sas (SAS)             |
|                                                     |
| Function: demonstrate ABCD -->                      |
|           zero/one data scoring                     |
| Name of input ASCII data set(s): internal to program|
| Name of output ASCII data set(s): testx.dat         |
|                                  testx2.dat         |
|                                                     |
|         Program written by: Fred Davidson           |
*-----------------------------------------------------*;

* No titles are needed because this program produces
  no output listing. To check if the program worked
  properly, compare the output data sets (testx.dat
  and testx2.dat) to the input data shown below;

* Caution: this program contains a 'test key' (the
  correct answers), and therefore the program should
  be kept in a secure place;

* Implement pseudocode steps (1) and (2);
data test;
    input id $ 1-4 @6 (item01-item20) ($char1.);
    array item (20) $ item01-item20;
```

```
   array itemx (20) itemx01-itemx20;
   i=1;
   do key='C','A','B','A','C','A','D','D','A','C',
          'C','A','C','A','C','D','B','A','B','A';
      if item(i)=key then itemx(i)=1;
         else if item(i)=' ' then itemx(i)=.;
         else itemx(i)=0;
      i=i+1;
   end;
   totala=sum(of itemx01-itemx10);
   totalb=sum(of itemx11-itemx20);
   total=totala+totalb;
cards;
0001 BCDDCCCAABCDBDCACDCA
0002 ABBABBACBABBCDCBDBDA
0003 CABDAA    CAADAC  B
0004 BA ABBBCBCCCDDABABCA
0005 BABAAABBBBCCDDBACDDB
0006 BBBAAACBBDBBBDABBDBB
0007 BBBABACAADCBBDDACDCB
0008 BBAAABACBDCDCACBCDAD
0009 CCDACCCCDCACDDAAACBD
0010 CABDDBCCCCACCDAACCDC
0011 AB        BCCDCAA  A
0012 BADAAADCCBCDDADCABDB
0013 BADAADCCABCBCBCACBDD
0014 ADBAADCCACCCDDCACBC
0015 BBBAACACCCCAABACAACB
;
run;

* Implement pseudocode step (3);
data output;
   set test;
   * Caution: the precise method to write to an external
     file is dependent on the particular computer you
     are using. Check the manual(s) or seek help from
     a consultant at this stage;
   file 'testx.dat';
   put id $ 1-4 @6 (itemx01-itemx20) (1.);
run;

* Implement pseudocode step (3) with totals;
data output2;
   set test;
```

```
     * Caution: the precise method to write to an external
       file is dependent on the particular computer you
       are using. Check the manual(s) or seek help from
       a consultant at this stage;
     file 'testx2.dat';
     put id $ 1-4
         @6 (item01-item20) (1.)
         totala 27-28
         totalb 30-31
         total  33-34;
run;

* End of program;

---- external 'testx.dat' file as produced by SAS ----

0001 00001000101000100001
0002 00110000000010100001
0003 111001.....001000..0
0004 01.10000011000000001
0005 01110100001000000000
0006 00110100000000001010
0007 00110100101000000000
0008 00010000001011100000
0009 10011000010000000010
0010 11100000010010000000
0011 .11.......0010100..1
0012 01010110001001000000
0013 01010000101010100000
0014 00110000111000010000.
0015 00110000011100000100

--- external 'testx2.dat' file as produced by SAS ----

0001 00001000101000100001  2  3  5
0002 00110000000010100001  2  3  5
0003 111001.....001000..0  4  1  5
0004 01.10000011000000001  3  2  5
0005 01110100001000000000  4  1  5
0006 00110100000000001010  3  2  5
0007 00110100101000000000  4  1  5
0008 00010000001011100000  1  4  5
0009 10011000010000000010  4  1  5
0010 11100000010010000000  4  1  5
0011 .11.......0010100..1  2  3  5
0012 01010110001001000000  4  2  6
0013 01010000101010100000  3  3  6
```

```
0014 0011000011100010000.  4  2  6
0015 0011000011100000100  3  3  6
```

```
---------------- SPSS: Input Program ----------------

*-------------------------------------------------------*
|  Name of input program: appen_c.sps (SPSS)            |
|                                                       |
|       Function:demonstrate ABCD -->                   |
|                 zero/one data scoring                 |
|  Name of input ASCII data set(s): internal to program |
| Name of output ASCII data set(s): testx.dat           |
|                                   testx2.dat           |
|                                                       |
|         Program written by:Fred Davidson              |
*-------------------------------------------------------*.
```

```
* No titles are needed because this program produces
  no output listing. To check if the program worked
  properly, compare the output data sets (testx.dat
  and testx2.dat) to the input data shown below.
* Caution: this program contains a 'test key' (the
  correct answers), and therefore the program should
  be kept in a secure place;
* Implement pseudocode steps (1) and (2);
data list fixed
    / id 1-4 (a)
      item01 to item20 6-25 (a).
begin data
0001 BCDDCCCAABCDBDCACDCA
0002 ABBABBACBABBCDCBDBDA
0003 CABDAA     CAADAC  B
0004 BA ABBBCBCCCDDABABCA
0005 BABAAABBBBCCDDBACDDB
0006 BBBAAACBBDBBBDABBDBB
0007 BBBABACAADCBBDDACDCB
0008 BBAAABACBDCDCACBCDAD
0009 CCDACCCCDCACDDAAACBD
0010 CABDDBCCCCACCDAACCDC
0011 AB        BCCDCAA  A
0012 BADAAADCCBCDDADCABDB
0013 BADAADCCABCBCBCACBDD
0014 ADBAADCCACCCDDCACBC
0015 BBBAACACCCCAABACAACB
end data.
    vector item=item01 to item20.
    vector itemx(20).
    string key (a20).
```

```
compute key='CABACADDACCACACDBABA'.
missing values item01 to item20 (' ').
* Note: missing values for item01-item20 are not
  handled directly in the loop below because the
  SPSS default is to fill an array with system-
  missing values, and so the ordering of this loop
  differs from SAS (though you could do it the same
  way there too).
loop #i=1 to 20.
    do if item(#i)=(substr(key,(#i),1)).
        compute itemx(#i)=1.
    else if item(#i)< > ' '.
        compute itemx(#i)=0.
    end if.
end loop.
compute totala=sum(itemx1 to itemx10).
compute totalb=sum(itemx11 to itemx20).
compute total=totala+totalb.
save outfile=test / drop=key.
execute.

* Implement pseudocode step (3);
get file=test.
    * Caution: the precise method to write to an external
      file is dependent on the particular computer you
      are using. Check the manual(s) or seek help from
      a consultant at this stage.
    write outfile=testx.dat
        / id 1-4 (a)
        itemx1 to itemx20 6-25.
execute.

* Implement pseudocode step (3) with totals;
get file=test.
    * Caution: the precise method to write to an external
      file is dependent on the particular computer you
      are using. Check the manual(s) or seek help from
      a consultant at this stage.
    write outfile=testx2.dat
        / id 1-4 (a)
        itemx1 to itemx20 6-25
        totala 27-28
        totalb 30-31
        total  33-34.
execute.
```

```
*clear working file.
new file.

*erase temporary file(s) created by this program.
*('testx.dat' and 'testx2.dat' are considered permanent
  and are not erased).

erase file='test'.
```

--- external 'testx.dat' file as produced by SPSS ---
```
0001 00001000101000100001
0002 00110000000010100001
0003 111001      001000  0
0004 01  10000011000000001
0005 01110100001000000000
0006 00110100000000001010
0007 00110100101000000000
0008 00010000001011100000
0009 10011000010000000010
0010 11100000010010000000
0011 11          0010100  1
0012 01010110001001000000
0013 01010000101010100000
0014 00110000111000010000
0015 00110000011100000100
```

--- external 'testx2.dat' file as produced by SPSS ---
```
0001 00001000101000100001 2 3 5
0002 00110000000010100001 2 3 5
0003 111001      001000  0 4 1 5
0004 01 10000011000000001 3 2 5
0005 01110100001000000000 4 1 5
0006 00110100000000001010 3 2 5
0007 00110100101000000000 4 1 5
0008 00010000001011100000 1 4 5
0009 10011000010000000010 4 1 5
0010 11100000010010000000 4 1 5
0011 11          0010100 1 2 3 5
0012 01010110001001000000 4 2 6
0013 01010000101010100000 3 3 6
0014 00110000111000010000 4 2 6
0015 00110000011100000100 3 3 6
```

Comments on Chapter 7

STORY 1: ZEALOUS DATA

Principle 2.1 is at play throughout this story. First, notice that the CSU ESL staff have become accustomed to the variable names in their database ("What is so-and-so's COURSE1?"). Although they may not have taken control of the structure of their data, a certain control exists. It is primarily historical; a worn path has evolved over years of use of the database (Principle 5.1). That is both good and bad. On the good side, the staff know what to expect in the database; they know what questions the database can answer. On the bad side (and this is a major concern in this story), it is difficult to make changes when a new data type arises (e.g., John Smith). What is your opinion about the degree of control of these data?

To some extent, Principle 1.3 is also involved. This is a database with social consequences about the students, but it also has social consequences to the users of the database. Notice, for example, the debate among the faculty about whether to change the database structure to handle students who have had all four ESL courses and the TOEFL preparatory class. (Some firm egos are probably involved here.)

Principle 2.2 also comes into play. Notice that one faculty member is quite skeptical that anybody will take the time to enter information about hobbies. The new COMMENT field provides an escape hatch in case another student takes four courses and the TOEFL class. But it also offers an opportunity to capture new data—if people will do so.

Finally, the zealous newcomer sneaks into the database and adds a set of fifth course variables. This is another instance of Principle 2.1; he seems to think even more control is needed. Most likely, he thinks someday a student will take the four ESL courses and the TOEFL class, and will have failed some ESL course at some point, and thus require a fifth entry because the failed course will need to be recorded twice.

If only one person in 4,000 during 10 years has taken four courses and the TOEFL class, how worried are you about what worries our zealous friend?

STORY 2: DATA INSURANCE

This story is pretty straightforward. Each of Mr. W's recommendations is tied directly to some principle or principles in this book. Recommendation 1 is Principle 2.1 in a very important guise. A safe and secure regular backup system can save many headaches later on. Remember the admonition in Section 1.5 in Chapter 1: the two laws of computing—verities so strict that they transcend even the weight of principle:

Law 1: Back it up.
Law 2: Do it now.

For some good examples of careful attention to backup, see Story 4 and my comments on it.

Recommendation 2 is an example of Principle 3.1. Mr. W has noted, wisely, that the staff are frustrated by all the paper they have. We see some of that frustration in the quotes given, and we can imagine other complaints, such as, "We spent all this money on those fancy computers and we still have too much paper!"

Recommendation 3 is an instance of Principle 1.1. Mr. W has noted that the AMU-FL Department is losing data in its system. It is not routinely capturing item information about its tests. But Recommendation 3 goes a bit beyond Principle 1.1. It also implies that AMU-FL should set up an *item bank*—a specialized database in which the records are the test items themselves and in which the entries are the text of the item, performance statistics (e.g., item difficulty as the proportion of people who got the item correct). They will probably also have some text fields, such as curricular agreement information (e.g., which teaching goal is addressed by each item). Item banks are essential to large-scale professional testing companies, but they may be too much work for a single academic department in a university. And so, on the issue of whether to implement an item bank, perhaps Principle 3.3 will resolve the situation. Perhaps the AMU-FL staff will agree to capture item-level data and watch item performance, but perhaps they will not set up an item bank because they lack the personnel time to do so. Perhaps a kludge will emerge: They will compute item statistics but check them against actual test booklets, rather than set up a database containing the text of each question.

Recommendation 4 reflects Principle 1.3, in much the same sense that we saw in Story 1: The people behind data are not only students but also the data handlers. The sense of being rushed is familiar to anybody who has handled large amounts of data in a short, tension-filled time, such as registration week at a school. In addition, Mr. W's fourth recommendation also suggests all the Principles in Chapter 4; my guess is they will set up a criticality metric for data and try to implement some human data checking. Perhaps, if people get used to doing that, the staff will trust the data more and feel less hassled during the intense days of data analysis, whenever they may happen. Trustworthy data make for more comfortable analysis. (That last sentence is almost a meta-principle for the whole of Chapter 4.)

Recommendation 5 is an example of Principles 6.1 through 6.4. Mr. W is suggesting that the AMU-FL Department "archive itself" and create an organized and efficient method to recapture and redo what it has done before. This will help enormously. To do so, the staff must come to know its system intimately; hence, my Principle 6.4 and Mr. W's remark "if hard disk space permits."

Recommendation 6 is a direct example of Principles 2.1 and most particularly 3.4. The AMU-FL staff must come to understand what is happening with missing data in its system. They have data records that are in error because some possible value is being entered when data are actually missing—much like the dBase example in Chapter 3. Remember: A zero does not mean a missing value; it means a zero as Hudson (1993) so aptly illustrates. It is very likely that Mr. W has in mind something like the SAS missing value designator: a dot.

STORY 3: ONCE IN 1,000 YEARS?

One of my favorite episodes of the original *Star Trek* television series has Captain Kirk and the *Enterprise* encountering an Air Force pilot from the 1960s. Through a convoluted time-travel plot, they bring the pilot onto the starship. Discussions ensue, and they face the difficulty of sending the pilot back to Earth. At one point, they discuss using the *Enterprise*'s transporter beam, but it cannot function because of some plot complexity. The pilot—a 20th-century citizen—cogitates a bit on the fact that he cannot be converted to energy and transmitted back to Earth, and he says something like: "You people sure have interesting problems."

That was my first reaction to this peculiar data story when I read it at my grandmother's house in Kentucky. "Those people sure have interesting problems," I reflected. Then, on thinking about it more and noting the estimated $100 billion price tag quoted in the article, I saw that this topic was quite serious. I realized that if left unsolved, this problem could affect many people for years to come—Principle 1.3.

I also found myself thinking of several other data-handling principles. For example, running throughout the story is my sense of Principle 2.1. The various companies now facing this millennial difficulty must not have been in control some 40-odd years ago or so when they set up their computer databases. Couldn't they have anticipated the problem with the year 2000?

But a deeper, subtler demon twists its way into this tale: Principle 3.4. I think the fundamental mistake here is that people at these corporations trusted their system defaults too closely. They did not take human nature into account because software handled year values in a manner that seemed to work just fine. The problem was people, not software.

SAS, SPSS, and most other packages handle dates by counting forward from some arbitrarily early day and year, such as January 1, 1400, or June 21, 1500. Internally, to the software, the value for today might be 10,000; yesterday, 9,999; and tomorrow, 10,001. The software then maintains internal conversion tables or algorithms to allow these simple integer count dates to be represented as something familiar to humans. For instance, if today is January 1, 1997, some of these familiar forms might be:

```
"January 1, 1997"
"January 01, 1997"
"Jan. 01, 1997"
"01 Jan 97"
"Jan 01 97"
"01/01/97" (where the first 01 is the month)
"01/01/97" (where the first 01 is the date)
```

The user can select which form she or he prefers at the time of data input. Internally, the software converts it to the integer count value, but the user is shielded from that conversion. Furthermore, by treating all date forms equally, simple conversion functions are made available to the user to convert from one date form to another (e.g., from "01 JAN 97" to "JAN 01 97").

That is the dilemma. How do you convert from "01 JAN 00" to "JAN 01 2000"? How do you know the precise meaning of the year? For example, in "13 Jan 37," is 37 actually 1837, 1937, or 2037? And as the article suggests, "01 JAN 00" could refer to "JAN 01

2000" or "JAN 01 1900," and incorrect subtractions could ensue. Furthermore, the year 1900 is likely in the insurance business. Its records were computerized several decades ago, and previous data for people who were born in the previous century had to be incorporated. You should also see a bit of the Atomicity Principle (1.1) at work here—because these companies did not record the "century atom," then the "00" molecule might mean 1900, 2000, or any other century date. Who is at fault for not recording the four-digit year? Personnel at these companies could have recorded a full century value—for example, "January 01, 1997" instead of some shortened version (01 JAN 97)—but they did not. I believe it was because their software allowed them not to do so—by default (Principle 3.4).

To fix this "interesting problem," company staff have to do two things. First, they need to change the length of the variables containing these dates, much as we did with the length command in the "Implementation" in Chapter 3. This is because a value like "01 JAN 97" requires two characters less than "JAN 01 1997." That may seem trivial, but if you have a database with millions of records, it can add up to a lot of additional computer disk space. Second, they need to make this change intelligently. They need to evaluate every record and have a foolproof method to convert a two-digit year to a four-digit year. That is probably where most of the $100 billion arises because every record has to be evaluated, possibly manually. Technically, every record in the database has a date bug that needs to be fixed. Bugs really do exist (Principle 4.3).

Perhaps that second problem might be rectified by programming, and extensive manual checking could be avoided. With knowledge of the data—its history and structure—fairly clever algorithms could be designed to deduce the most likely four-digit year for a two-digit year. For example, suppose staff at a life insurance company had computerized about 30 years of records when they switched from paper to computers in 1955. They know that every year in their database is actually 19xx because 1955 minus 30 years is still within the 20th century. Therefore, they can simply write a program to convert all their data. As another example, implausibility cross-checks can be used. Consider the 99-year-old check example from the article: A simple program could print out records for checks that are more than 2 or 3 years old as "implausible data" (Principle 4.1) requiring further human intervention.

In short, programming can solve a lot of this. But programming also costs money. Either way, corporations are going to invest in these changes, and that is why this problem has made the news wires.

I assume this problem will be solved once and for all, and now. First, if corporation and government staffs solve this now, they need not worry about it again. Unless the data are some sort of historical database that needs to go back before that early year, all will be well until the year 10,000 (when another single character width is needed) because all calculations will be done on the correct internal integer.[1]

Things will work well for each upcoming millennium because each date will have been corrected to four-digit-year input and output and all calculations will be accurately derived from the internal integer. The solution now—at the year 2000—will solve things for the years 3000, 4000, and so on, and we data handlers will not pass this problem on to our progeny.

Second, and finally, I believe this problem will be solved because of Principle 1.3. The databases concerned are data about people and the things people care about—such as profits and losses. The motivation to rectify this is great; unless they are fixed, data about people will be wrong, and as the article states, "a 30-year-old could start getting retirement benefits." To the 30-year-old that might seem nice, but to the company paying the benefits— who are people of course—it is not nice. It eats into profits and threatens corporate financial stability. The most interesting data problems are often solved quickly when the financial needs of people are involved.

STORY 4: THE HANCOCK BET

Notice first the sense of cyclical repetition in the entire story. This tale is a cycle of data entry, checking, and fixing. It is an example of Principle 2.3, although Ms. C and her husband do not take that principle in its full advice. They do not keep a data log in which they list what they have done and what they will need to do. As people work with data, they become more and more aware of the data's idiosyncrasies. Ms. C would benefit from a written record, as I suggested in the discussion questions in Chapter 1.

As you have probably guessed, Principle 2.1 is at operation in this story—as it is (and as it should be) in all these story problems in Chapter 7. To some degree, control of data structure and flow is the core of all sound data handling. This becomes most apparent in the Hancock story when Ms. C takes great pains to do careful backups; she is living by the two rules of computing I mentioned above in my comments about the Insurance story. Notice that she makes two backups at the end of each work cycle and that one is always off-site; one backup is not stored at her house. She either stores it at her office on campus or uploads it to the university's mainframe computer. Should, against all our hopes, her house burn down, she would still have a safe and secure copy at another location. Staff at large corporations take this aspect of backup very seriously. They often have several off-site backups, one of which is in a bank vault. Furthermore, they have a cycle of backup such that some backup is made each day, each week, and probably each month. As I suggested in Discussion Question 6 of Chapter 4, visit a professional data analyst or data analysis corporate department and inquire about its backup procedures. These are done for a reason. Staff do not want to live through a disaster they can prevent.

There is one additional precaution Ms. C might take. As she is keying data into her computer at home, she should regularly save it to disk. During data entry, whatever you type is actually in the memory of the computer and not saved onto a hard or floppy disk unless you tell the computer to do so. Suppose Ms. C were entering data and the electricity went out or she happened to kick the power switch on the surge suppressor under her desk. Boom. Everything she typed since the last save to disk would be lost. This can be prevented in two ways: (a) Stop keying and run a command to manually write work to a disk or diskette, or (b) use an auto-save setting in the data entry software to automatically write to a disk at regular intervals. My experience has been that people have disasters because of failure to write data to a disk during key-in more often than by total loss of a computer file. Either catastrophe is an unfortunate and splendid example of failure to attend to Principle 2.1.

You can also see Principles 4.1 through 4.4 at operation in the Hancock story. Ms. C is wisely skeptical about her data (Principle 4.3), so she makes use both of the computer and of her husband to help check (Principles 4.1, 4.2, and 4.4). It would be interesting to interview Ms. C that Monday afternoon and ask, simply: "Do you feel confident? Are the data all correct? Are they safe?"

My final question to Ms. C about her data, and my final question to you about yours, would be: "Are you in control?"

NOTE

1. Even the problem of data from seemingly ancient starting dates (e.g., prior to Jan 01, 1400) can be solved. It would be necessary to treat very early dates as normal nondate integers or to reprogram an earlier date as the starting integer. These solutions are, I believe, feasible in both SAS and SPSS. The key here is to have the correct internal integer value, and then all else will be just fine.

APPENDIX D

Samples of Application Generators in SAS and SPSS

Both SAS and SPSS can perform data manipulation and analysis by using either command language or application generators. I have demonstrated command language in the "Implementation" sections of each chapter. In this appendix, I offer some brief examples of the application generators in each software package so that you can compare command language control with application generators.

An *application generator* is a module or feature of a software package that uses menus, dialogues, and similar screen features to help in your data handling and analysis. As noted in Chapter 1, in SAS, the application generator is in the separate ASSIST module, and in SPSS, the application generator is integrated into the default SPSS screen.

In software packages, the application generator actually forms command language in the background (as I illustrate at the end of this appendix). My preference is to program with command language, although you might prefer the menus, dialogue boxes, and mouse clicks used by application generators.

Following are a series of 15 *screendumps*, or images of the computer screen during application generator sessions in SAS and SPSS. The first 8 are a SAS data manipulation and analysis example; the last 7 are from SPSS. These are carefully selected screendumps, intended to give you a general idea of application generators in each program. They do not show all the screens you would encounter in each software package. In each screendump, I use the data set from the Chapter 4 "Implementation" section, which reported scores on a communicatively oriented language test for two types of teaching methods: audiolingual and communicative. This is the corrected version of the data set, after fixing the bug noted in Chapter 4 (the method labels have been reversed). I call the data file ch4ok.dat in the examples that follow:

```
Data File: CH4OK.DAT:
ANNA Communicative 48
BILL Audiolingual 12
JOSE Audiolingual 20
JUAN Communicative 37
GILL Communicative 39
 SUE Audiolingual 22
DOUG Communicative 37
DAVE Audiolingual 18
LARS Audiolingual 19
HANS Communicative 45
FRED Communicative 44
 TOM Audiolingual 25
 JIM Communicative 40
MIKE Audiolingual 20
```

The examples here were run on an IBM/compatible microcomputer using the Windows 3.1 operating system. In the "Implementation" sections of this book, I have illustrated command language independent of the particular machines on which it is implemented, because the SAS and SPSS command syntax is stable across many computer platforms. To illustrate application generators, however, I must commit to a particular version of each software and to a particular operating system. Hence, the screendumps I show here may not precisely match those available to you. Furthermore, these screens may change as operating systems and software packages evolve to new versions.

In the SAS example (Figures D.1 through D.8), my objective is to sort the data and print out descriptive statistics by using a BY-group based on the variable method. Figure D.1 shows the default SAS ASSIST Primary Menu. From here, I chose DATA MGMT, which led me to the Data Management Menu. Once there, I chose CREATE/IMPORT, which yielded Figure D.2. After selecting the first line (Import data . . .), I arrived at Figure D.3: This is a Define Fields screen, in which a sample line of the data is displayed. As prompted, I indicated the start-stop columns of each variable with a less-than or greater-than sign. Choosing OK from Figure D.3 took me to the screen displayed in Figure D.4, in which I had to tell SAS various characteristics of the variables in my data set. By default, SAS had it about right; the only changes I made were to key in the variable names I wanted. After saving that file (from the Create new data set option in the Locals menu), I went back through the Data Management Menu and selected SORT. This selection led me to the screen displayed in Figure D.5, which I have here displayed after all the dialogues and menus to define the SORT variable.

I then returned to the Primary Menu and chose DATA ANALYSIS, now ready to perform my statistics run. I chose ELEMENTARY for basic statistics. That point in time is illustrated in Figure D.6, which, on choosing Summary statistics . . . , led me to the screen shown in Figure D.7. Here, I selected my variable(s) to analyze (CTCSORE) and, via a series of other menus and dialogue boxes, also my Subset data request—see BY in the upper right

(text continues on page 304)

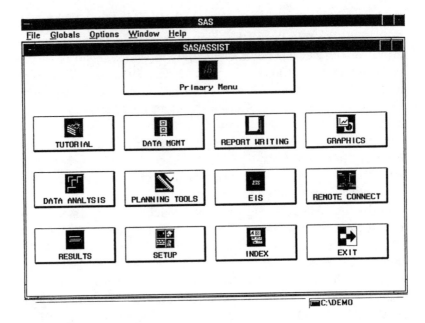

Figure D.1.

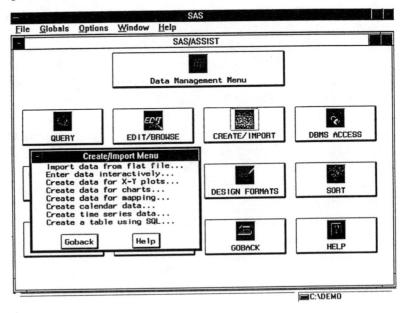

Figure D.2.

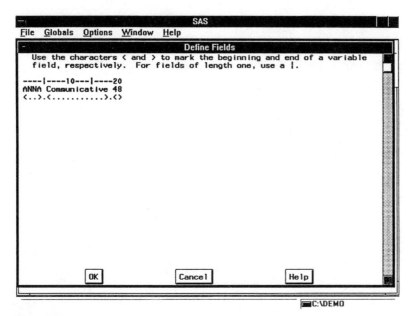

Figure D.3.

SAS - [ASSIST: Import WORK.CH4OUT [E]]

File   Edit   View   Locals   Globals   Options   Window   Help

```
----|----10---|----20---|----30---|----40---|----50---|----60---|----70---|-
ANNA Communicative 48
BILL  Audiolingual 12

In the spaces below, provide information that describes your data.

              Columns
Num   Name    Start End  Other variable attributes

 1    NAME      1    4    Type:  NUM  CHAR     Format:  _____
                          Label:                Informat: _____
                                 _____

 2    METHOD    6    18   Type:  NUM  CHAR     Format:  _____
                          Label:                Informat: _____
                                 _____

 3    CTSCORE   20   21   Type:  NUM  CHAR     Format:  _____
                          Label:                Informat: _____
                                 _____

 4    _____  ___  ___   Type:  NUM  CHAR     Format:  _____
                          Label:                Informat: _____
                                 _____

 5    _____  ___  ___   Type:  NUM  CHAR     Format:  _____
                          Label:                Informat: _____
                                 _____
```

C:\DEMO

Figure D.4.

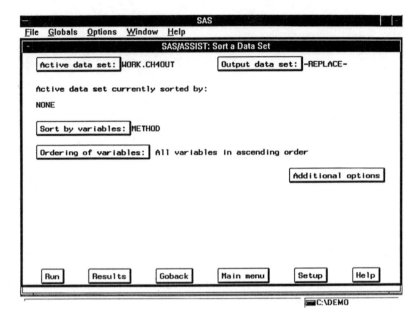

Figure D.5.

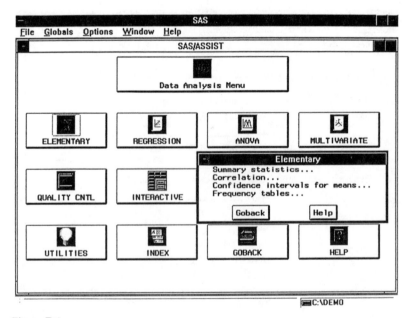

Figure D.6.

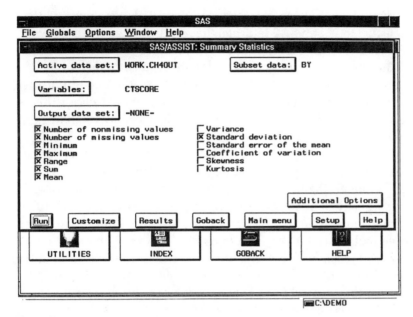

Figure D.7.

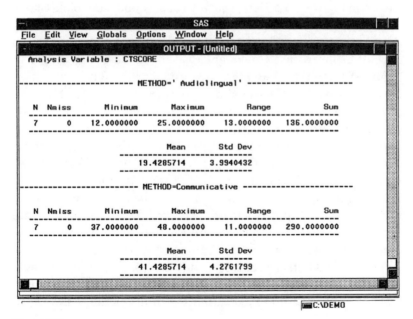

Figure D.8.

corner. I also chose the statistics I wanted, as shown. I then selected Run, and SAS returned the results in the screen shown in Figure D.8, which is the end of the example.

In the SPSS example (Figures D.9 through D.15), my target is to obtain descriptive statistics for students in the communicative method. Rather than print out results for both, I chose this to illustrate an interesting feature of SPSS data display when working with subsetted data.

Figure D.9 is the default opening screen for SPSS. I first defined my data by selecting to read an ASCII (external text) file via the File menu. Figure D.10 shows the process at the point where I had already defined the first two variables (name and method) as string/alphanumeric ((A)), and I had just typed in the third variable and set Data Type to Numeric as is. I chose Add after defining each variable and then OK when done with all three variables, which returned me to the screen shown in Figure D.11. Notice that my data are now displayed in the default Newdata window in a manner much like a spreadsheet. I then chose Select Cases and then If from the Data menu, which led to the screen shown in Figure D.12. Here, I set my subset condition to pull cases only for the condition method = Communicative. Choosing Continue then OK (in the next window) took me back to the Newdata file, which I have enlarged to fit the entire screen in Figure D.13. Notice here the interesting data display item I mentioned above: The deselected data rows (method = Audiolingual) have slashes through their row numbers.

I then performed my analysis in SPSS by choosing the Statistics menu and then Descriptives then Summarize, wshere I clicked my analysis variable (CTSCORE). I then clicked on Options to select the precise statistics I wanted; this point in time is shown in Figure D.14. I then navigated back and executed the run; the SPSS output is shown in Figure D.15. Compare Figure D.15 with Figure D.8, and you will see that SPSS has subset the data to give results only for the communicative group.

Throughout both sets of screen encounters, each software package was generating its command language. In SAS, this command language appears in the execution log in a separate window; in

(text continues on page 308)

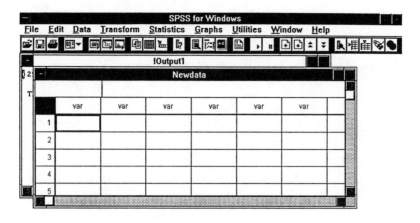

Figure D.9.

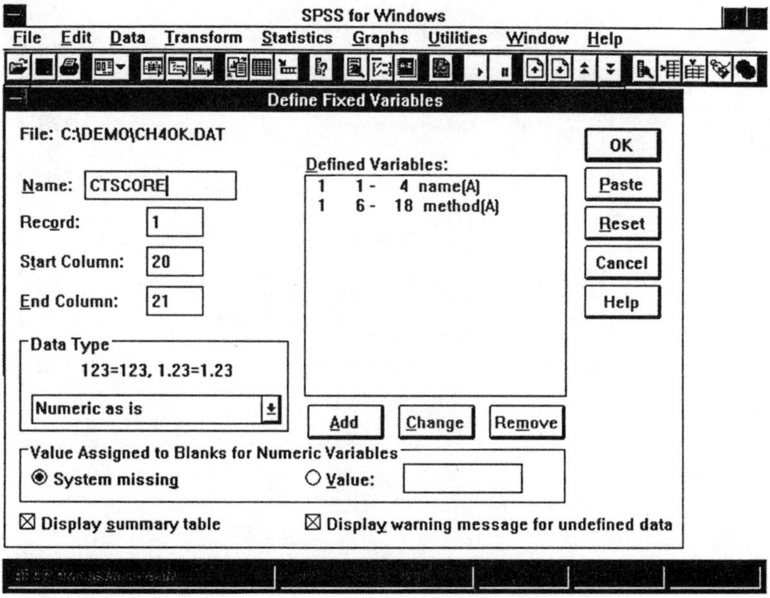

Figure D.10.

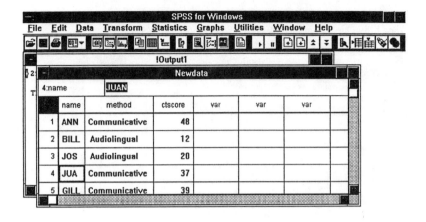

Figure D.11.

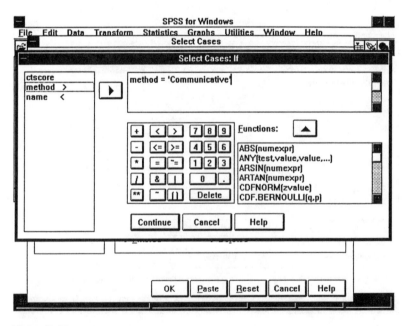

Figure D.12.

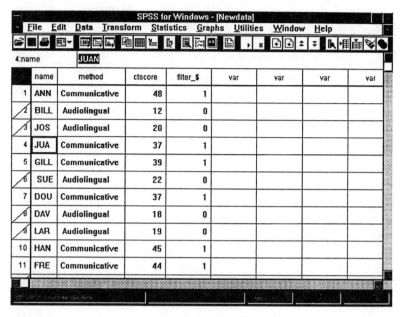

Figure D.13.

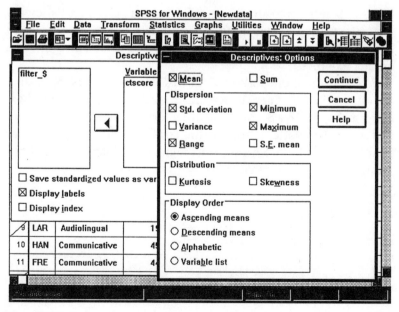

Figure D.14.

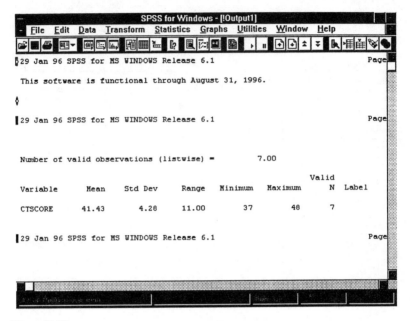

Figure D.15.

SPSS, it is written to an external file called a `journal`. Following are some excerpts from these files to illustrate that each program is actually performing its commands for you as you step through menus like these.

First, I present the portion of the SAS log that shows the sorting operation. Notice that SAS has inserted a lengthy comment box, using an alternative SAS commenting format: enclosure in slashes and asterisks. Notice also that the sorting command is familiar (compare it with the SAS sorting language in Chapter 3); it is just arranged in a manner that is awkward to read:

```
2      /*--------------------------------------------------*
3          Summary:
4              The Proc below sorts SAS data sets.
5          Generated: [data & time]
6          *--------------------------------------------------*/
7      proc sort data = WORK.CH4OUT
8
9          ;
10         by
```

```
11     METHOD
12
13
14   ;
15  run;
```

Below is an excerpt from the SPSS journal. The software has used its Descriptives command and various subcommands to generate the output I want. This syntax is similar to SPSS syntax presented throughout this book:

```
DESCRIPTIVES
 VARIABLES=ctscore
 /FORMAT=LABELS NOINDEX
 /STATISTICS=MEAN STDDEV RANGE MIN MAX
 /SORT=MEAN (A)  .
```

In conclusion, this Appendix has given you a very brief tour of the application generators available in SAS and SPSS under Windows 3.1 on IBM/compatible microcomputers. I hope this short tour has helped you make a principled decision about which is better for your needs: command-line programming or menus and application generators. A third alternative is for you to begin with SAS or SPSS by using application generators, save and print the log (SAS) or journal (SPSS) files, and study them until you learn the command syntax. You could then try the command language of each. This gradual break-in might be best if you ultimately must do large amounts of programming.

References

Bachman, L., Davidson, F., & Milanovic, M. (1996). The use of content analysis in the design and moderation of EFL proficiency tests. *Language Testing, 13*(2).

Bachman, L., Davidson, F., Ryan, K., & Choi, I. (1995). *An investigation into the comparability of two tests of two tests of English as a foreign language: The Cambridge-TOEFL Comparability Study.* Cambridge, UK: Cambridge University Press.

Cody, R. P., & Smith, J. K. (1991). *Applied statistics and the SAS programming language* (3rd ed.). Englewood Cliffs, NJ: Prentice Hall.

Davidson, F. (1988). An exploratory modeling survey of the trait structures of some existing language test datasets. *Dissertation Abstracts International, 49,* 1441. (University Microfilms No. DA8815771)

Davidson, F., & Henning, G. (1985). A self-rating scale of English difficulty: Rasch scalar analysis of items and rating categories. *Language Testing, 2*(1), 164-179.

Educational Testing Service (ETS). (1993). *TOEFL score user's manual.* Princeton, NJ: Author.

Gronlund, N. E. (1993). Validity and reliability. In *How to make achievement tests and assessments.* Boston: Allyn & Bacon.

Hedrick, T. E., Bickman, L., & Rog, D. J. (1993). *Applied research design: A practical guide.* Newbury Park, CA: Sage.

Hudson, T. (1993). *Nothing does not equal zero: Problems with applying developmental sequence findings to assessment and pedagogy.* [followed by] Pienemann, M., Johnston, M., & Meisel, J. The multidimensional model, linguistic relations, and related issues: A reply to Hudson. *Studies in Second Language Acquisition, 15*(4), 461-503.

Hughes, A. (1989). *Testing for language teachers.* New York: Cambridge University Press.

Iversen, G. R., & Norpoth, H. (1987). *Analysis of variance* (2nd ed.) (Sage University Paper #1). Newbury Park, CA: Sage.

Kerlinger, F. (1986). *Foundations of behavioral research* (3rd ed.). New York: Holt, Rinehart & Winston.

Lewis-Beck, M. S. (1980). *Applied regression: An introduction* (Sage University Paper #22). Beverly Hills, CA: Sage.

Lewis-Beck, M. S. (1995). *Data analysis: An introduction* (Sage University Paper #103). Thousand Oaks, CA: Sage.

McLaughlin, B. (1987). *Theories of second-language learning.* London: Edward Arnold.

Messick, S. (1989). Validity. In R. L. Linn (Ed.), *Educational measurement* (3rd ed., pp. 13-103). New York: Macmillan.

Minium, E. W., King, B. M., & Bear, G. (1993). *Statistical reasoning in psychology and education* (3rd ed.). New York: John Wiley.

Oscarson, M. (1989). Self-assessment of language proficiency: Rationale and applications. *Language Testing, 6*(1), 1-13.

Runkel, P. J. (1990). *Casting nets and testing specimens: Two grand methods of psychology.* New York: Praeger.

SAS Institute, Inc. (1990). *SAS/Stat user's guide* (Vol. 2., GLM-VARCOMP, Version 6, 4th ed.). Cary, NC: Author.

SAS Institute, Inc. (1995). Statistical Analysis System (Release 6.10) [Computer software]. Cary, NC: Author.

Sax, G. (1989). *Principles of educational and psychological measurement and evaluation* (3rd ed.). Belmont, CA: Wadsworth.

Schroeder, L. D., Sjoquist, D. L., & Stephan, P. E. (1986). *Understanding regression: An introductory guide* (Sage University Paper #57). Newbury Park, CA: Sage.

Shepard, L. A. (1993). Evaluating test validity. In L. Darling-Hammond (Ed.), *Review of research in education* (Vol. 19, pp. 405-450). Washington, DC: AERA.

SPSS Inc. (1994). Statistical Package for the Social Sciences (Release 6.1) [Computer software]. Chicago: Author.

Index

About the Author

Fred Davidson is a faculty member in the Division of English as an International Language at the University of Illinois at Urbana-Champaign. He holds a Ph.D. in applied linguistics from the University of California at Los Angeles (1988), where he specialized in language testing. His scholarly interests include data structures for research in second/foreign language education, statistical modeling of language ability, criterion-referenced approaches to language testing, and the history of education with particular reference to second and foreign language teaching. He has published in several journals and edited volumes, and he is a coauthor of *An Investigation Into the Comparability of Two Tests of English as a Foreign Language: The Cambridge-TOEFL Comparability Study* (1995). He is active in the International Language Testing Association and also consults frequently with state and local educators who work with language minority students, both in Illinois and in other states.